Editor

Heather Douglas

Managing Editor

Ina Massler Levin, M.A.

Illustrator

Clint McKnight

Cover Artist

Brenda DiAntonis

Art Production Manager

Kevin Barnes

Art Coordinator

Renée Christine Yates

Imaging

Craig Gunnell

Publisher

Mary D. Smith, M.S. Ed.

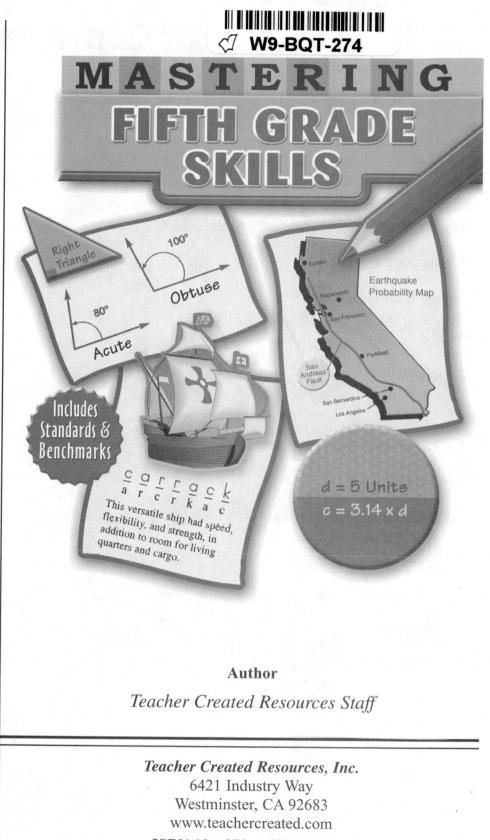

MASTERING FIFTH GRADE SKILLS

Includes Standards & Benchmarks

Author

Teacher Created Resources Staff

Teacher Created Resources, Inc.

6421 Industry Way

Westminster, CA 92683

www.teachercreated.com

ISBN 13: 978-1-4206-3941-4

©2006 Teacher Created Resources, Inc.

Reprinted, 2007

Made in U.S.A.

Table of Contents

Introduction 3

Meeting Standards 4

Grammar

Nouns, Verbs, Adjectives, and Adverbs. . 8

Conventions 20

Spelling and Vocabulary 24

Reading

Prediction 48

Main Idea 50

Cause and Effect 54

Sequence 56

Comprehension. 57

Writing

Poetry 63

Letters. 67

Graphic Organizers. 72

Proofreading 82

Math

Multiplication 83

Division 92

Fractions, Decimals, and Percents . . . 100

Money 112

Measurement and Geometry 123

Tables, Charts, and Graphs 143

Social Studies

Explorers. 157

Native Americans 166

Colonies 161-164, 173

Westward Movement 178

Civil War 187

World War II 190

Civil Rights 193

Science

Weather. 194

Earthquakes and Volcanoes 206

Human Body 212

Ecology 217

Solar System. 220

Matter 224

Energy. 226

Answer Key 231

Introduction

The wealth of knowledge a person gains throughout his or her lifetime is impossible to measure, and it will certainly vary from person to person. However, regardless of the scope of knowledge, the foundation for all learning remains a constant. All that we know and think throughout our lifetimes is based upon fundamentals, and these fundamentals are the basic skills upon which all learning develops. *Mastering Fifth Grade Skills* is a book that reinforces a variety of fifth grade basic skills.

- **Writing**
- **Reading**
- **Social Studies**
- **Grammar**
- **Math**
- **Science**

This book was written with the wide range of student skills and ability levels of fifth grade students in mind. Both teachers and parents can benefit from the variety of pages provided in this book. Parents can use the book to provide an introduction to new material or to reinforce material already familiar to their children. Similarly, teachers can select pages that provide additional practice for concepts taught in the classroom. When tied to what is being covered in class, pages from this book make great homework reinforcement. The worksheets provided in this book are ideal for use at home as well as in the classroom.

Research shows us that skill mastery comes with exposure and drill. To be internalized, concepts must be reviewed until they become second nature. Parents may certainly foster the classroom experience by exposing their children to the necessary skills whenever possible, and teachers will find that these pages perfectly complement their classroom needs. An answer key, beginning on page 231, provides teachers, parents, and children with a quick method of checking responses to completed worksheets.

Basic skills are utilized every day in untold ways. Make the practice of them part of your children's or students' routines. Such work done now will benefit them in countless ways throughout their lives.

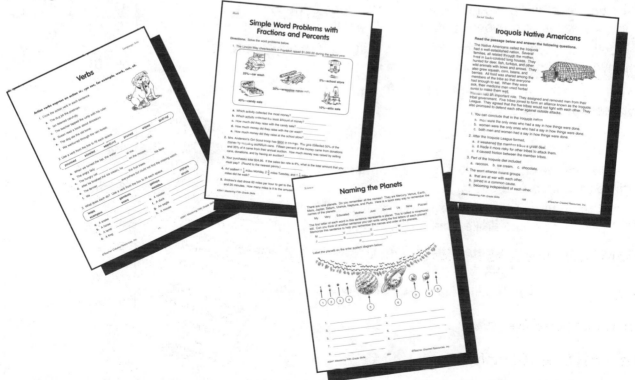

Meeting Standards

Each lesson in *Mastering Fifth Grade Skills* meets one or more of the following standards, which are used with permission from McREL (Copyright 2000, McREL, Mid-continent Research for Education and Learning. Telephone: 303-337-0990. Website: *www.mcrel.org*).

Standard	Page Number
Language Arts:	
Uses the general skills and strategies of the writing process	
• Uses prewriting strategies to plan written work	72–81
• Uses strategies to edit and publish written work	82
• Uses strategies to write for a variety of purposes	67–82
• Uses strategies to write for different audiences	67–71
• Writes narrative accounts, such as poems and stories	63–66
Uses grammatical and mechanical conventions in written compositions	
• Uses nouns in written compositions	8–10
• Uses pronouns in written compositions	18–19
• Uses verbs in written compositions	11–13
• Uses adjectives in written compositions	14–15
• Uses adverbs in written compositions	16–17
• Uses conventions of capitalization in written compositions	20–21
• Uses conventions of punctuation in written compositions	22–23
Uses the general skills and strategies of the reading process	
• Makes, confirms, and revises simple predictions about what will be found in a text	48–49
• Uses phonetic and structural analysis techniques to decode unknown words (e.g., vowel patterns, syllabication, root words, affixes)	32–45
• Understands level-appropriate reading vocabulary (e.g., synonyms, antonyms, homophones, multi-meaning words)	24–31
Uses reading skills and strategies to understand a variety of literary passages and texts	
• Uses reading skills and strategies to understand a variety of literary passages and texts	48–56
• Understands basic concept of plot (e.g., main problem, conflict, resolution, cause-and-effect)	48–56
• Understands the ways in which language is used in literary texts (e.g., personification, simile, metaphor, imagery, rhythm)	46–47
Uses reading skills and strategies to understand and interpret a variety of informational texts	
• Uses reading skills and strategies to understand a variety of informational texts	57–62

Meeting Standards (cont.)

Standard	Page Number
Math:	
Understands and applies basic and advanced properties of the concepts of numbers	
• Understands equivalent forms of basic percents, fractions, and decimals	105, 108, 111
• Understands the relative magnitude and relationships among whole numbers, fractions, decimals, and mixed numbers	100-103, 105–107, 109–110
Uses basic and advanced procedures while performing the processes of computation	
• Adds, subtracts, multiplies, and divides whole numbers and decimals	83–99
• Adds and subtracts simple fractions	104
• Solves real-world problems involving number operations (e.g., computations with dollars and cents)	112–122
Understands and applies basic and advanced properties of the concepts of measurement	
• Understands the basic measures perimeter, area, volume, capacity, mass, angle, and circumference	129–140
Understands and applies basic and advanced properties of the concepts of geometry	
• Knows basic geometric language for describing and naming shapes (e.g., trapezoid, parallelogram, cube, sphere)	128
• Understands basic properties of figures (e.g., two- or three-dimensionality, symmetry, number of faces, type of angle)	126–127, 141
• Understands that shapes can be congruent or similar	142
• Understands characteristics of lines (e.g., parallel, perpendicular, intersecting) and angles (e.g., right acute)	123–125
• Understands and applies basic and advanced concepts of statistics and data analysis	
• Organizes and displays data in simple bar graphs, pie charts, and line graphs	150–151
• Reads and interprets simple bar graphs, pie charts, and line graphs	146–149, 152–156
Understands and applies basic and advanced properties of functions and algebra	
• Knows basic characteristics and features of the rectangular coordinate system (e.g., the horizontal axis is the X axis and the vertical axis is the Y axis)	143–146, 150

Meeting Standards (cont.)

Standard	Page Number
Social Studies:	
Understands the political, social, and cultural redefinitions in Europe from 500-1000 CE	
• Understands the significance of Norse migrations and invasions (e.g., locations of Norse settlements, including routes to North America)	157
Understands how the transoceanic interlinking of all major regions of the world between 1450 and 1600 led to global transformations	
• Understands what contributed to increasing oceanic travel in the 15th and 16th centuries	158
• Understands features of Spanish exploration and conquest	159–160
• Understands the interregional trading system that linked peoples of Africa, Asia, and Europe on the eve of the European overseas voyages	162–164
Understands how the values and institutions of European economic life took root in the colonies and how slavery reshaped European and African life in the Americas	
• Understands economic life in the New England, Chesapeake, and southern colonies	161, 173–175
Understands why the Americas attracted Europeans, why they brought enslaved Africans to their colonies and how Europeans struggled for control of North America and the Caribbean	
• Understands peaceful and conflictory interaction between English settlers and Native Americans in the New England, Mid-Atlantic, and lower South colonies	166–167
Understands the causes of the American Revolution, the ideas and interests involved in shaping the revolutionary movement, and reasons for the American victory	
• Understands the major ideas in the Declaration of Independence, their sources, and how they became unifying ideas of the American democracy	176–177
Understands the United States territorial expansion between 1801-1861, and how it affected relations with external powers and Native Americans	
• Understands the impact of territorial expansion on Native American tribes	165, 168–172
Understands how the industrial revolution, increasing immigration, the rapid expansion of slavery, and the westward movement changed American lives and led to regional tensions	
• Understands elements of early western migration	178–186
Understands the course and character of the Civil War and its effects on the American people	
• Understands the provisions and significance of the Emancipation Proclamation	187–189

Meeting Standards (cont.)

Standard	Page Number
Social Studies: *(cont.)*	
Understands how various reconstruction plans succeeded or failed	
• Understands military, political, and social factors affecting the post Civil War period	188–189
Understands the causes and course of World War II, the character of the war at home and abroad, and its reshaping of the U.S. role in world affairs	
• Understands significant military aspects of World War II	190–192
• Understands the struggle for racial and gender equality and for the extension of civil liberties	
• Understands the development of the civil rights movement	193
Science/Health:	
Understands atmospheric processes and the water cycle	
• Knows that water exists in the air in different forms (e.g., in clouds and fog as tiny droplets; in rain, snow, and hail) and changes from one form to another through various processes (e.g., freezing, condensation, precipitation, evaporation)	194–205
• Knows that the Sun is the principle energy source for phenomena on the Earth's surface	228–230
Understands Earth's composition and structure	
• Knows how features on the Earth's surface are constantly changed by a combination of slow and rapid processes (e.g., weathering, erosion, transport, and deposition of sediment caused by waves, wind, water, and ice; landslides, volcanic eruptions, earthquakes, drought)	206–211
Knows how to maintain and promote personal health	
• Knows the basic structure and functions of the human body systems (e.g., how they are interrelated)	212–216
Understands relationships among organisms and their physical environment	
• Knows the organization of simple food chains and food webs	217
• Knows that changes in the environment can have different effects on different organisms	218–219
Understands the composition and structure of the universe and the earth's place in it	
• Knows that the Earth is one of several planets that orbit the Sun and that the Moon orbits the Earth	220–223
Understands the structure and properties of matter	
• Knows that matter has different states (i.e., solid, liquid, gas) and that each state has distinct physical properties; some common materials such as water can be changed from one state to another by heating or cooling	224–225
Understands the sources and properties of energy	
• Knows that light can be reflected, refracted, or absorbed	226–227

Common Nouns

Nouns that are used to name general things are called common nouns. They name a person, place, or thing.

1. Find the nouns in the grid. Write each one beside its meaning.

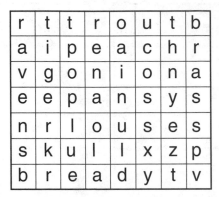

r	t	t	r	o	u	t	b
a	i	p	e	a	c	h	r
v	g	o	n	i	o	n	a
e	e	p	a	n	s	y	s
n	r	l	o	u	s	e	s
s	k	u	l	l	x	z	p
b	r	e	a	d	y	t	v

a. body part _____

b. insect _____

c. fruit _____

d. fish _____

e. bird _____

f. large cat _____

g. metal _____

h. flower _____

i. vegetable _____

j. food _____

2. Color the boxes that contain words that can be used as nouns.

barrel	falcon	bugle	leather	vinegar
happy	silly	orchid	sofa	canal
eel	pitcher	chewing	dirty	tall
old	silk	hamper	ferret	envelope

3. Choose 5 nouns from question 2. Write a sentence using each one.

a. _____

b. _____

c. _____

d. _____

e. _____

Proper Nouns

Proper nouns are the names of particular people, places, or things. They are written with a capital letter at the beginning.

1. Write the proper noun from the box beside the matching common noun below.

| September | Nile | Tuesday | Henry Hudson | Miami | Japan |

a. country _____   **d.** river _____

b. month _____   **e.** day _____

c. explorer _____   **f.** city _____

2. Use the proper nouns in the box to complete the story.

| Vanessa | | Monday | | Long Beach | | April |
| Friday | | Tony | San Francisco | | California | | Seahawk |

3. Write the word from the box that names each group of proper nouns.

On _____ the eighth of _____, two students, a girl named

_____ and a boy named _____, left the seaside city of _____

in _____ to sail a yacht named _____ down the coast to _____.

They arrived safely on _____, much to the relief of their parents.

months	**a.** Chile, Canada, England _____
oceans	**b.** June, August, July _____
planets	**c.** Saturn, Uranus, Neptune _____
countries	**d.** Everest, Kosciusko, Kilimanjaro _____
states	**e.** Pacific, Atlantic, Indian _____
mountains	**f.** Florida, Maine, Oregon _____

Possessive Nouns

An apostrophe is used to show possession (that something belongs to something or someone).

· **For a singular noun add an apostrophe and s at the end of the word.**

 Example:

 the horse's mane

 the child's toys

· **For a plural noun add an apostrophe if the word ends in s**

 (the horses' manes)

 or an apostrophe and s if the word does not end in s

 (the children's toys).

1. **Rewrite the following to show possession.**

 a. the dress of the girl _____

 b. the stripes of the tiger _____

 c. the pencil of the boy _____

 d. the handbags of the lady _____

 e. the leaves of the tree _____

 f. the petals of the flower _____

 g. the antics of the clown _____

 h. the uniform of the police officer _____

2. **Now rewrite the following to show possession.**

 a. the dresses of the girls _____

 b. the ears of the donkeys _____

 c. the books of the men _____

 d. the saddles of the horses _____

 e. the houses of the women _____

 f. the pencils of the boys _____

 g. the nests of the birds _____

 h. the ship of the sailors _____

Verbs

Action verbs express an action we can see, for example, *work, run, sit*.

1. Circle the action verb in each sentence.

   a. The dog bit the postman.

   b. Ian listened carefully.

   c. The teacher tapped the table with his ruler.

   d. Susan read a book about dinosaurs.

   e. The dog ate the old bone.

   f. We wandered through the rain forest.

2. Use a verb from the box to fill each space.

pounced	scowled	searched	pruned	wiped	gushed

   a. When we turned the tap, the water _____ out.

   b. The angry lady _____ at me.

   c. The hungry cat _____ on the mouse.

   d. After he finished the ice cream, he _____ his face.

   e. The farmer _____ the fruit trees.

   f. We _____ everywhere but could not find the missing watch.

3. What does each do? Use a verb from the box to fill each space.

leaps	gambols	gallops	slithers
scampers	soars	waddles	struts

   a. A snake _____ .   **e.** A rooster _____ .

   b. A horse _____ .   **f.** A duck _____ .

   c. A lamb _____ .   **g.** An eagle _____ .

   d. A frog _____ .   **h.** A mouse _____ .

Being and Having Verbs

Being and having verbs tell us about what things are and what they have; for example, *Ben is a bowler.* When forms of the verbs "to be" and "to have" are joined with other main verbs, they become auxiliary or helping verbs; for example, *Gail is riding.* (Together the auxiliary verb and the main verb become a verb phrase. In the example, is riding becomes the verb phrase.)

1. Circle the being or having verb in each sentence.

   a. Max has a bad cold.

   b. Ali is the best speller.

   c. The books are here.

   d. Nick was there a minute ago.

   e. I am the captain of the team.

   f. I have the string.

2. Underline the main verb and circle the auxiliary verb in each sentence.

   a. I am going to the movies tonight.

   b. Mom is painting the house this weekend.

   c. The teacher was helping us.

   d. Tom will run in the race.

   e. Our class has read that book.

   f. I have seen a shooting star.

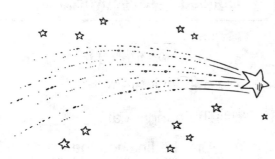

3. Use three of the being and having verbs from number 1 in sentences of your own.

   _____

   _____

   _____

4. Use three of the verb phrases (auxiliary verb plus main verb) from number 2 in sentences of your own.

   _____

   _____

   _____

Helping Verbs

All sentences need a verb. Some verbs are action verbs. They show the action taking place. Other verbs are called helping verbs. Action verbs work together with helping verbs in a sentence.

Helping Verbs									
am	is	has	are	were	was	have	had	can	will

Find the helping and the action verbs in the sentences below.

1. An elephant is raising his trunk.

   helping: _____   action: _____

2. Amy has learned to bake pies.

   helping: _____   action: _____

3. Harold is drawing with a purple crayon.

   helping: _____   action: _____

4. We will drink the water.

   helping: _____   action: _____

5. She has taken the test before.

   helping: _____   action: _____

6. I have seen the bear.

   helping: _____   action: _____

7. We are going to the store.

   helping: _____   action: _____

8. Jenny can ride a bike.

   helping: _____   action: _____

9. I will eat all the cinnamon rolls.

   helping: _____   action: _____

What is an Adjective?

Adjectives are describing words. Adjectives describe a noun. Think of as many ways you can to describe the following items. Write your adjectives in the boxes. The first one has been done for you. When you are finished, share your ideas with the class.

ladybug	pizza	school
small red spotted cute		

birthday party	summer vacation	ice cream

trains	peach	pencil

robot	hamburger	swimming pool

Extension: Write a story about one of the items on this page. Be sure to use all of the adjectives you recorded in your story.

Adjectives

Adjectives are used to describe a noun or pronoun.

1. Choose a word from the box to complete each sentence.

circular	fragile	broad	careful	perilous	childish

   a. A river that is wide is _____ .

   b. Something easily broken is _____ .

   c. If something is round, it is _____ .

   d. An immature person is _____ .

   e. If something is dangerous, it is _____ .

   f. If a person is cautious, he or she is _____ .

2. Choose the most suitable describing adjective from the box.

delicious	rusty	sunny	savage	interesting	woolen	ripe	clever

   a. _____ story   **e.** _____ sweater

   b. _____ student   **f.** _____ weather

   c. _____ knife   **g.** _____ apple

   d. _____ food   **h.** _____ watchdog

3. Rewrite the story, replacing each underlined adjective with one of a similar meaning from the box.

big	minute	scared	thick	strong	high	sour	fat

As we walked through the <u>dense</u> forest, we saw a <u>plump</u> bird eating some <u>bitter</u> fruit that grew on a <u>tall</u> tree. My brother Sam, a <u>sturdy</u> lad, threw a <u>tiny</u> pebble at the bird. The <u>frightened</u> bird flew to the safety of a <u>gigantic</u> bush.

_____

_____

_____

_____

_____

What is an Adverb?

An adverb describes a verb. An adverb tells *when, why, where, how often*, and *how much*. Circle the adjective in each sentence. Then, change the adjective into an adverb. Finally, rewrite the sentence using the adverb instead of the adjective. (Some adverbs are formed by adding **-ly** to adjectives.)

Example: The happy baby smiled.
   Adjective: happy
   Adverb: happily
   Revised Sentence: The baby smiled happily.

1. The quick rabbit scampered under the fence.
   Adjective:
   Adverb:
   Revised Sentence:

2. The happy dogs jumped.
   Adjective:
   Adverb:
   Revised Sentence:

3. The hungry children ate all of the birthday cake.
   Adjective:
   Adverb:
   Revised Sentence:

4. The shy boy raised his hand.
   Adjective:
   Adverb:
   Revised Sentence:

5. The angry man yelled at the store clerk.
   Adjective:
   Adverb:
   Revised Sentence:

6. The nice waitress cleaned up the spill.
   Adjective:
   Adverb:
   Revised Sentence:

7. The calm driver sped away.
   Adjective:
   Adverb:
   Revised Sentence:

16

Adverbs

An adverb is a word that adds meaning to a verb, an adjective, or another adverb.

1. **Select the best adverb to complete each sentence.**

gracefully	neatly	busily	angrily
brightly	tightly	softly	carefully

   a. We should cross a busy street _____.

   b. We tie parcels _____.

   c. Lights can shine _____.

   d. We should write _____ in our books.

   e. The children worked _____.

   f. The lion roared _____.

   g. We should whisper _____.

   h. A swan swims _____.

2. **Beside each adverb write *how*, *when*, or *where* to show what it tells us.**

   a. tomorrow _____
   f. yesterday _____

   b. greedily _____
   g. inside _____

   c. tonight _____
   h. down _____

   d. today _____
   i. sweetly _____

   e. sadly _____
   j. outside _____

3. **Add an adverb of your own to complete each sentence. Make sure your adverb answers the word in parentheses.**

   a. She fell _____. (where)

   b. He whistled _____. (how)

   c. Tom arrived _____. (when)

   d. The window was broken _____. (how)

   e. The kangaroo jumped the fence _____. (how)

   f. I will repay you _____. (when)

What is a Pronoun?

A pronoun is a word that replaces a noun. Replace the underlined nouns in each sentence with the proper pronoun.

Common Pronouns				
she	he	your	her	his
him	you	yours	our	ours
my	it	them	their	they

1. <u>Sally</u> is going to be in first grade next year.

   _____

2. The <u>class</u> is going to go on a field trip.

   _____

3. <u>Jeffrey</u> had better practice if he ever wants to drive again.

   _____

4. I hope <u>Eliza</u> is coming to the play.

   _____

5. The <u>Clarks</u> are the nicest family.

   _____

6. The <u>computer</u> is acting up again.

   _____

7. The <u>boys</u> are speaking to their coach.

   _____

8. The <u>skunk</u> sprayed the tree.

   _____

18

Pronouns

Pronouns are words that take the places of nouns.

1. Rewrite each sentence, replacing the underlined words with a pronoun.

   a. The lady said that <u>the lady</u> was leaving now.

   _____

   b. When the dog stopped barking, it went back to <u>the dog's</u> kennel.

   _____

   c. The teacher told them that <u>the teacher</u> wanted them to work harder.

   _____

   d. The puppies whimpered when <u>the puppies</u> were hungry.

   _____

   e. The queen dismissed <u>the queen's</u> servants.

   _____

   f. Tom's father asked <u>Tom</u> to cut the wood.

   _____

2. Color the boxes that contain a pronoun.

we	paper	us	he
their	they	you	window
rabbit	jealous	my	mine
them	quickly	she	shiny
table	yours	over	silver

Capitalization

Capital letters are used at the beginning of each sentence. They are also used for proper nouns such as names and places.

> **M**y horse is brown and gray.
> **W**e got to go to the store with **D**r. **C**arter.
> **M**y sister is named **D**anielle.
> **T**hey say **D**isneyland is a happy place.
> **M**y mother likes soup at the **O**live **G**arden.

These sentences are missing capital letters. Cross out each letter that should be changed to a capital and write the capital letter above the crossed out letter.

1. when i went to the store, i saw my teacher, mrs. dorner.

2. i am reading a book named *pride and prejudice*.

3. in may, we will be able to go and visit my grandma clark.

4. my brother said, "why does sarah always get to sit in the front?"

5. the andersons, our neighbors, will go to visit paris, france, next year.

6. heidi had a birthday, and we sang "happy birthday to you."

7. on thursday, he will go to see dr. frank, the orthodontist.

8. my sister anne loves to write stories.

Write four sentences of your own. Don't forget the capital letters!

9. _____

10. _____

11. _____

12. _____

More Capitalization

A capital letter is used for:

· **the first letter of a sentence.**

· **the first letter in names—people, places, pets, days, months, countries, states, towns, mountains, rivers.**

· **the pronoun I.**

1. Color the boxes that contain words that should begin with a capital letter.

michelle	swan lake	plate	christmas	beetles
south	uranus	october	canada	mount everest
england	asia	pacific ocean	tables	london
wednesday	summer	easter	kansas city	rialto house
stranger	shamrock hotel	vietnam	murray river	wattle street

2. Complete the sentences.

   a. My given name is _____.

   b. My birthday is in the month of _____.

   c. The street I live on is _____.

   d. The school I attend is _____.

   e. My teacher's name is _____.

   f. I live in the town or city of _____.

   g. The country I would most like to visit is _____.

3. Rewrite the following sentences correctly.

   a. last saturday julie went to chicago

_____

   b. at christmas we are going to italy which is a country in europe

_____

   c. the wedding will take place at st patrick's church in greensboro

_____

Commas

Commas are used to show short pauses in writing. They are used in various ways, including separating nouns, separating adjectives, and after introductory clauses and phrases.

1. Complete each sentence by using words from the box. Don't forget to use commas.

scissors	**roses**	**ash**	**daffodils**	**eucalyptus**
wheat	**skunks**	**pliers**	**hammers**	**penguins**
rice	**zebras**	**sycamore**	**corn**	**hyacinths**

a. _____ are cereals.

b. _____ are flowers.

c. _____ are black and white.

d. _____ are tools.

e. _____ are trees.

2. Each sentence contains a phrase that needs to be set off with commas. The first one has been done for you.

   a. Adelaide, the capital of South Australia, is a beautiful city.

   b. Anders Celsius a Swedish astronomer introduced the Celsius scale in 1742.

   c. The South Pole a featureless spot in a freezing wilderness was first reached by Amundsen.

   d. The toothbrush according to a 17th century encyclopedia was first invented in China in 1498.

   e. Ian one of this class's finest writers has won first prize in the poetry contest.

   f. Interpol the first international crime fighting organization was formed in 1923 in Paris.

Apostrophes

An apostrophe is used:
- **in contractions to indicate where letters have been omitted.**
  I'll (I will)
- **to indicate possession in nouns.**
  a dog's kennel
  the three dogs' kennels

1. Write in full what the following contractions mean.

   a. hasn't _____   e. we'll _____

   b. we've _____   f. can't _____

   c. o'clock _____   g. 'tis _____

   d. didn't _____   h. 'twas _____

2. Write the following as contractions.

   a. I am _____   f. you have _____

   b. I have _____   g. who Is _____

   c. I would _____   h. it is _____

   d. I shall _____   i. he is _____

   e. could not _____   j. were not _____

3. Add apostrophes where they are needed.

   Thats the place well go. Theres bound to be lots of fish. Its a really good spot.

   Were lucky youd seen it before. Theyre going to be jealous when they know

   weve got it. Theyll probably say theyre not coming now.

Synonyms

A synonym is a word that has the same or similar meaning to another word.

1. Circle all the words in the grid. Then write each one beside its synonym.

l	a	r	g	e	t	s
s	l	w	c	r	a	h
o	o	a	l	o	s	a
f	s	i	a	a	t	k
t	e	l	p	m	e	e
s	e	r	i	o	u	s
b	r	a	v	e	r	y

a. howl _____

b. wander _____

c. tender _____

d. tremble _____

e. immense _____

f. misplace _____

g. valor _____

h. applaud _____

i. solemn _____

j. flavor _____

2. Each underlined word can be replaced with a synonym from the box. Find and write the word.

wet	ill	fat	old	odd	gem	sly	get

a. We are trying to <u>obtain</u> some money. _____

b. The <u>crafty</u> fox was captured. _____

c. The clothes are still <u>damp</u>. _____

d. Mary is feeling <u>sick</u>. _____

e. The pig is quite <u>plump</u>. _____

f. This seems quite <u>strange</u>. _____

g. This building is <u>ancient</u>. _____

h. The <u>jewel</u> is very valuable. _____

Synonyms: Almost the Same

Synonyms are especially important when you decide you need a more exact word or a better word to express your meaning when you are writing or reading. At such times, a thesaurus is a helpful reference.

Because a thesaurus entry usually contains several words that are considered synonyms, you need to also use a dictionary to be sure that the word you choose produces the meaning you want. You cannot be sure that every word in the list will work as a substitute for the one you started with.

Use a thesaurus and a dictionary to choose the best synonyms to replace the italicized words in the following sentences. (Remember that one word often leads to another. You may have to go to the next step and look in the dictionary for definitions of one or more unfamiliar words in a definition.)

1. The preacher moved so fast from point to point that Ivan could not easily follow the *lecture*.

    a. sermon   b. harangue   c. speech

2. Between the ages of three and five, Willard had an *imaginary* companion.

    a. real   b. make-believe   c. feign

3. My friend Philomena's grandmother *descended* onto the lawn in a hot-air balloon.

    a. crawled   b. came down   c. climbed

4. Everyone who sees them declares that the Smoky Mountains are a *glorious* sight.

    a. strange   b. bizarre   c. magnificent

5. With the help of an architect, landscaper, and many construction workers, the *enterprising* George Washington Vanderbilt constructed the largest private residence in the United States.

    a. inventive   b. unusual   c. new

6. Presidents Abraham Lincoln and Harry Truman are often described as *humble* men.

    a. humiliated   b. modest   c. subservient

25   *#3941 Mastering Fifth Grade Skills*

Synonyms: Almost the Same (cont.)

7. Socrates was a Greek *philosopher* and teacher.

   a. romantic   b. thinker   c. researcher

8. My mother's voice was rather *shrill* when she told me for the tenth time to do my homework.

   a. harsh   b. inconsiderate   c. noisy

9. A good quarterback should not only have a good throwing arm but should also be *nimble*.

   a. willowy   b. lively   c. agile

10. David did not *quail* as Goliath approached.

    a. chill   b. shrink back   c. recede

11. The *tawny* coat of the young male elk glowed in the Yellowstone sun.

    a. fair   b. blond   c. yellowish-brown

12. As soon as he caught the scent of the fox, the hound let out a *yelp*.

    a. shout   b. snap   c. bark

13. Mr. Chang, our new neighbor, is an *agent* for a life insurance company.

    a. representative   b. ambassador   c. cause

14. The wind was so strong that it broke off a *bough* of our big oak tree.

    a. extremity   b. limb   c. area

15. Many people, in California especially, think it is sensible to be prepared for the *disaster* an earthquake can cause.

    a. tragedy   b. bad luck   c. rage

16. Saying "yes" to the birthday party invitation will *oblige* you to bring a gift.

    a. persuade   b. force   c. obligate

17. After some *reflection*, Luis decided that he would not go to the party after all.

    a. consideration   b. likeness   c. image

Antonyms

An antonym is a word that has the opposite meaning to another word.

1. Circle all the words in the grid. Then write each one beside its antonym.

s	b	u	i	l	d	c
m	c	h	e	a	p	o
i	l	e	a	v	e	w
l	t	i	m	i	d	a
e	s	o	u	t	h	r
l	o	o	s	e	n	d
s	w	a	l	l	o	w
a	w	k	w	a	r	d

a. expensive _____

b. bold _____

c. hero _____

d. north _____

e. demolish _____

f. graceful _____

g. tighten _____

h. return _____

i. frown _____

j. spit _____

2. Select the word from the box that has the opposite meaning to the underlined word in each sentence.

> solid   divide   smash   light   fake   deceitful   entrance   feeble

a. These books are quite <u>heavy</u>. _____

b. Are you going to <u>repair</u> the motor? _____

c. The teacher told us to <u>multiply</u> the numbers. _____

d. He is a very <u>honest</u> boy. _____

e. We left quickly through the open <u>exit</u>. _____

f. After the operation, she felt quite <u>strong</u>. _____

g. These logs are <u>hollow</u>. _____

h. These diamonds are <u>genuine</u>. _____

Antonyms: Almost the Opposite

Learning the antonym of a word can help you better understand the meaning of that word, just as a synonym can.

Just as you may find exactly the right synonym in a thesaurus, you may also find an antonym in a thesaurus entry or in a dictionary. There are dictionaries that list both synonyms and antonyms.

Use a thesaurus and a dictionary to help you choose the sentence that expresses the opposite meaning of the first sentence in each group. (Remember that one word often leads to another. You may have to go to the next step and look in the dictionary for definitions of one or more unfamiliar words in a definition.)

1. José Guerrero *bragged* to everyone in the class about his accomplishments.
    a. José Guerrero was modest.
    b. José Guerrero was confident.
    c. José Guerrero was bluffing.

2. The very gracious Lady Guinevere expressed her *appreciation* to everyone in the room.
    a. Lady Guinevere expressed her challenge.
    b. Lady Guinevere expressed her desperation.
    c. Lady Guinevere expressed her disapproval.

3. After the first three hours of the first day of school, Hiroshi Takahashi was *drowsy*.
    a. Hiroshi Takahashi was frantic.
    b. Hiroshi Takahashi was alert.
    c. Hiroshi Takahashi was grim.

4. Charlotte will always remember the *kindness* of her first-grade teacher, Mrs. Zella Runk.
    a. Charlotte will remember Mrs. Runk's consideration.
    b. Charlotte will remember Mrs. Runk's humor.
    c. Charlotte will remember Mrs. Runk's meanness.

5. The *majesty* of the landscape in Olympic National Park always fills Anastasia with wonder.
    a. The plainness of the landscape fills Anastasia with wonder.
    b. The pleasure of the landscape fills Anastasia with wonder.
    c. The presence of the landscape fills Anastasia with wonder.

6. Donnie decided to *relax* his pace in the bicycle race.
    a. Donnie decided to slow his pace.
    b. Donnie decided to accelerate his pace.
    c. Donnie decided to tinker with his pace.

Antonyms: Almost the Opposite (cont.)

7. Bullies often take advantage of *meek* people.

   a. Bullies often take advantage of timid people.

   b. Bullies often take advantage of sincere people.

   c. Bullies often take advantage of assertive people.

8. The scientist poured a *scant* amount of the poisonous chemical into the bottle.

   a. The scientist poured a large amount.

   b. The scientist poured a small amount.

   c. The scientist poured a moderate amount.

9. The train on the inside tracks seemed to be *stationary*.

   a. The train seemed to be vague.

   b. The train seemed to be peculiar.

   c. The train seemed to be progressing.

10. Everyone at the memorial for the mayor remained *sober* throughout the ceremony.

    a. Everyone at the memorial remained serious.

    b. Everyone at the memorial remained lighthearted.

    c. Everyone at the memorial remained bitter.

11. Some U.S. farmers do not want *imports* of the crops that they grow.

    a. Some farmers do not want trade.

    b. Some farmers do not want exports.

    c. Some farmers do not want increases.

12. Ginnie wanted to *establish* a border around her plants.

    a. Ginnie wanted to destroy a border.

    b. Ginnie wanted to set up a border.

    c. Ginnie wanted to delay a border.

13. Juliet's parents were *stubborn* about her relationship with Romeo.

    a. Juliet's parents were fabulous.

    b. Juliet's parents were flexible.

    c. Juliet's parents were gruff.

14. Jack London wrote a *splendid* book about loyalty.

    a. London wrote an average book.

    b. London wrote a terrifying book.

    c. London wrote a valuable book.

Homonyms

Homonyms are two or more words that have the same sound and often have similar spellings, but they have **different meanings**. These words are problems for many writers, for it is easy to become confused by them.

If certain homonyms are a problem for you, you need to find a way to help you remember what each word means. For example, you can remember that *stationery* is writing paper because the letters *er* are found in both stationery and paper. Try to think of similar ways to distinguish one homonym from another so that you write both words correctly.

Select the correct homonyms to fill in the blanks in the sentences below.

1. Washington, D.C., is the _____ of the United States. (*capital/capitol*)

2. To watch his sister Jane lose the race was more than John could _____. (*bear/bare*)

3. How many times have you _____ the doughnut shop without stopping? (*passed/past*)

4. Mother said, "Go to bed because ___ too late for you to be up on a school night." (*its/it's*)

5. "_____ going to clean up this mess?" my father asked about the spilled milk. (*Who's/Whose*)

6. The drum major _____ the band in the parade. (*lead/led*)

7. Do you think that the world will ever be completely at _____? (*peace/piece*)

8. The Wilson twins learned how to button _____ (*their/there/they're*) shirts when they were only _____ years old. (*to/too/two*)

9. I do not think it is _____ that my brother would not loan me bus _____. (*fair/fare*)

10. My editor does not think it is _____ that the judge will not allow me to _____ a newspaper story about the mysterious _____ that the barbarians were participating in. (*right/rite/write*)

11. Most young doctors learn to show _____ with all of their _____. (*patience/patients*)

12. I hope that our new _____ chef does not _____ us before the big banquet next week. (*desert/dessert*)

Homophones

A homophone is a word that sounds the same as another word but has a different meaning and different spelling.

1. Circle all the words in the grid. Then write each word beside its homophone.

f	l	e	e	m	m	g	w
v	f	h	b	e	a	u	a
a	i	y	a	d	y	e	i
i	n	m	w	a	o	s	s
n	d	n	l	l	r	t	t
t	a	u	g	h	t	x	x

a. fined _____

b. ball _____

c. taut _____

d. flea _____

e. meddle _____

f. waste _____

g. guessed _____

h. him _____

i. vein _____

j. mare _____

2. Circle the correct word in the parentheses.

Two (**buoys boys**) were walking beside a (**creak creek**). They were hoping to (**fined find**) (**sum some**) (**mail male**) (**dear deer**) that had (**been bean**) seen grazing on the (**berry bury**) trees that grew in the vicinity. It was only last (**week weak**) when one had been seen running across the dusty (**road rode**), (**which witch**) runs along the side of the forest.

3. Complete each sentence by using a homophone of the underlined word.

a. The <u>guest</u> won the prize as she _____ the correct answer.

b. On the packet of self-rising <u>flour</u> there is a picture of a red _____.

c. My <u>hair</u> stood on end when the _____ ran between my legs.

d. The <u>poor</u> man began to _____ the cold tea into the cup.

e. I watched her <u>peer</u> at the ship as she stood on the _____.

Word Beginning: "ex"

Use the words in the table below to help you answer the questions on this page and the next.

Word	Syllables	In Context
exercise	ex•er•cise	Daily **exercise** will help you to have a healthy body.
except	ex•cept	I'd go with you, **except** I'm already going somewhere else.
exciting	ex•ci•ting	This is the most **exciting** carnival I've ever seen!
excuse	ex•cuse	You'll need a doctor's **excuse** to sit out of gym class.
expected	ex•pect•ed	My mom **expected** me home an hour ago.
examine	ex•am•ine	After you **examine** this gem, you'll want to have it.
explorer	ex•plor•er	Christopher Columbus is a famous **explorer**.
expand	ex•pand	They're having a baby and need to **expand** their home.
exclaimed	ex•claimed	"What in the world are you doing?" Lisa **exclaimed**.
extremely	ex•treme•ly	It's **extremely** hot in the desert.
exchange	ex•change	She needs to **exchange** the shirt for a larger size.
expert	ex•pert	He's an **expert** on fossils.
excellent	ex•cel•lent	You did an **excellent** job with your class presentation.
exception	ex•cep•tion	It seems like there's an **exception** to every spelling rule.
excitement	ex•cite•ment	The children couldn't hide their **excitement**.

Is the **boldfaced** word spelled wrong? If it is not correct, write it correctly in the middle column. If it is correct, circle **OK**.

1. Let me **examin** that coin more closely.		OK
2. Loren is an **expert** deep sea diver.		OK
3. Marco Polo is a famous **explorer**.		OK
4. The food at their restaurant is **excellent**.		OK
5. Cory **exclaimed**, "Wait! I want to come, too!"		OK
6. What **exscuse** did he give for not showing up?		OK
7. I had **expected** you to come later.		OK
8. Is there ever an **exeption** to the rule?		OK
9. The farmer bought more land to **expand** his orchards.		OK
10. They had an **exciting** day at the race track.		OK
11. It was **extremely** cold here last February.		OK
12. There was a sense of **excitment** in the air.		OK
13. We get to **exersise** during gym class.		OK
14. Please **exchange** papers with a classmate.		OK
15. Your report is perfect **exsept** for this sentence.		OK

Word Beginning: "ex" (cont.)

Word Scramble

Unscramble the words below to form words from the table on the previous page. Put the numbered letters on the lines below to find the answer to the riddle.

Example: etrax   e   x   t   r   a

1. pedeetxc   __ __ __ __ __ __ __ __

2. dapenx   __ __ __ __ __ __
         1

3. texper   __ __ __ __ __
        2

4. cintgixe   __ __ __ __ __ __ __ __

5. clextenle   __ __ __ __ __ __ __ __ __

6. treelymex   __ __ __ __ __ __ __ __ __
                    3

7. cesexu   __ __ __ __ __ __
         4

8. criesexe   __ __ __ __ __ __ __ __
               5

9. declaimxe   __ __ __ __ __ __ __ __ __
               6

10. ecpxet   __ __ __ __ __ __
           7

11. xepetcoin   __ __ __ __ __ __ __ __ __
               8

12. nxagceeh   __ __ __ __ __ __ __ __
         9

13. lporexre   __ __ __ __ __ __ __ __
              10

14. maxinee   __ __ __ __ __ __ __
           11

15. meettcixen   __ __ __ __ __ __ __ __ __ __
      12

Riddle: What increases its value by half when it's flipped upside down?

__ __ __   __ __ __ __ __ __ __ __   __ __ __
7   9   2   11   4   6   2   10   1   3   5   8   12

The Prefix "non"

The prefix *non-* means "not."

Example: *nonsense* means "not sense"

Part I: Write the meaning of each word. You may use a dictionary to help you.

Example: nonviolent _____ not violent _____

1. nonskid _____

2. nonfiction _____

3. nonstop _____

4. nonfat _____

5. nonprofit _____

6. nonstick _____

7. nontoxic _____

8. nonreturnable _____

9. nonverbal _____

10. nonflammable _____

An **antonym** is a word that means the opposite of another. *Hot* and *cold* are antonyms.

nontaxable	**nonsense**	**nonfiction**	**noncredit**
nonsmoker	**nonessential**	**nonstandard**	**nonvoter**
nonresident	**nonviolent**	**nondairy**	**nonexistent**

Part II: Choose the antonym from the box and write it. You may use a thesaurus to help you.

1. existent _____ nonexistent _____

2. sense _____

3. resident _____

4. standard _____

5. essential _____

6. violent _____

7. credit _____

8. smoker _____

9. taxable _____

10. dairy _____

11. fiction _____

12. voter _____

More Practice with the Prefix "non"

The prefix non- means "not."

| nonfat | nonprofit | nontoxic | nonstop | nonverbal | nonfiction |
| nontaxable | nonviolent | nonreturnable | nonskid | nonstick | nonflammable |

Part I: Choose the word from the box that best completes each sentence. Each word is used once.

1. The baby ate a crayon—but don't worry, because crayons are _____.

2. This is a direct, _____ flight to Chicago.

3. Martin Luther King, Jr., used _____ methods to bring about civil-rights changes.

4. The child's pajamas were made of a _____ fabric.

5. This throw rug has a _____ backing, so it won't slide when you step on it.

6. A charity is a _____ organization; it does not try to earn money.

7. Is this_____ yogurt?

8. This frying pan has a special _____ coating that keeps food from sticking to it.

9. We have to read a _____ book about the life of a U.S. president.

10. All clearance item sales are final; the items are _____.

11. In most states, medical care and food items are _____.

12. A nod, a frown, and a wink are _____ signs that need no words to explain.

Part II: Pick two words from the box above. Use each in a sentence.

Example: Kyle likes **nonfat** milk better than whole milk.

1. _____

_____

2. _____

_____

The Prefixes "mid" and "tele"

The prefix *mid-* means "middle." The prefix *tele-* means "distant."

Examples: *midriff* is the middle section of the human body (near the waist)

a *telephoto* lens is a camera lens used to take close-up photos of distant things

Part I: Do the math problem. Match the number to find the answer. Write the word on the line. The first problem has been done for you.

3 = telethon	16 = midsummer	36 = telecommute	12 = midsection
7 = Midwest	48 = television	9 = midweek	72 = telecommunications
56 = telecast	8 = midterm	42 = midst	5 = telemarketing

1. shows events on a screen happening in far-off places (6 x 8) _television (6 x 8 = 48)_

2. the central part of the U.S. (49 ÷ 7) _____

3. the middle part (60 ÷ 5) _____

4. a program broadcast by television (8 x 7) _____

5. about halfway through the summer (4 x 4) _____

6. a long TV show to raise money for a cause (27 ÷ 9) _____

7. around Wednesday (81 ÷ 9) _____

8. selling things by telephone (40 ÷ 8) _____

9. in the middle of (6 x 7) _____

10. sending messages across long distances (8 x 9) _____

11. the middle of a school year (64 ÷ 8) _____

12. work at home, connected to employer by computer (3 x 12) _____

36

The Prefixes "mono," "quad," and "quar"

The prefix *mono-* means "one." The prefixes *quad-* and *quar-* mean "four."

Examples: *monotone* means "in one tone" (unchanging in pitch)
quadrant means "one of four parts" (as in the four quadrants of a city)

| quart | monarch | quadrilateral | monocle |
| quadruplets | monorail | quarter | quartet |

Part I: Write the word from the box beneath its picture:

| 1. monarch | 2. | 3. | 4. |
| 5. | 6. | 7. | 8. |

Part II: Match the word to its meaning. Write the letter on the line next to the word.

_____ 1. monologue

_____ 2. monotonous

_____ 3. quadrant

_____ 4. monotone

_____ 5. quadriceps

a. one of four large muscles at the front of the thigh

b. one of four parts

c. boring

d. one tone

e. a speech given by one person

Part III: Read the sentence. Think about what the bold word means. Then fill in the circle of the letter of the correct answer.

1. If someone said, "The man answered in **monosyllables**," you know the man wouldn't have said the word _____.

   a. up   b. down   c. yes   d. maybe

2. The word **monoxide** refers to a molecule that has _____ oxygen atom.

   a. unlimited   b. one   c. three   d. unknown

3. The police searched the lower west **quadrant** of the park. This means that the police had divided the park into _____ sections.

   a. two   b. three   c. four   d. five

Word Ending: "tive"

Despite the "e" at the end, the word ending "tive" is pronounced with a **short /i/**.
Use the words in the table below to help you answer the questions on this page and the next.

native	na•tive	These plants are **native** to Asia.
active	ac•tive	At 86 she still leads a very **active** life.
negative	neg•a•tive	Don't have a **negative** attitude.
positive	pos•i•tive	It's good to say something **positive** about other people.
effective	ef•fec•tive	The medicine was **effective**, and she recovered quickly.
relatives	rel•a•tives	She went to pick up her **relatives** at the airport.
motive	mo•tive	The police don't know the **motive** for the crime.
adjective	ad•jec•tive	An **adjective** adds details about a noun.
sensitive	sen•si•tive	Don't be harsh; her feelings are **sensitive**.
attractive	at•trac•tive	That furniture is very **attractive**.
detective	de•tec•tive	The **detective** secretly followed the man.
executive	ex•ec•u•tive	The **executive** went to the meeting.
talkative	talk•a•tive	He is so **talkative** that I'm tired of listening to him.
competitive	com•pet•i•tive	They offer a **competitive** salary.
representatives	rep•re•sen•ta•tives	We elect **representatives** to govern our country.

Is the **boldfaced** word spelled wrong? If it is not correct, write it correctly in the middle column. If it is right, circle **OK**.

1. What was his **motive**?		OK
2. Are you **postive** you turned the lights off?		OK
3. The **detective** collected evidence at the scene.		OK
4. The toddler was very **active**.		OK
5. A word describing size, shape, or color is an **ajective**.		OK
6. My **relatives** are coming to visit this Christmas.		OK
7. Does she think that artwork is **atractive**?		OK
8. Keep **negtive** comments to yourself.		OK
9. Team sports are **competitive.**		OK
10. Our company president's office is the **excutive** suite.		OK
11. Is this anti-itch cream **effective**?		OK
12. Most people are **senstive** to criticism.		OK
13. Each state elects two senators as **representatives**.		OK
14. He's not very **talkative**.		OK
15. I'm a **nattive** of Kenya.		OK

Word Ending: "tive" (cont.)

Word Scramble

Unscramble the words below to form words from the table on the previous page. Put the numbered letters on the lines below to find the answer to the riddle.

Example: epacevithyr <u>h</u> <u>y</u> <u>p</u> <u>e</u> <u>r</u> <u>a</u> <u>c</u> <u>t</u> <u>i</u> <u>v</u> <u>e</u>
                                     1   2

1. tomvie   __ __ __ __ __ __
                            3

2. tivesrepsenreta   __ __ __ __ __ __ __ __ __ __ __ __ __ __
                                             4

3. cuteexive   __ __ __ __ __ __ __ __ __
                              5

4. laerstiev   __ __ __ __ __ __ __ __ __
                        6

5. ipetcomtive   __ __ __ __ __ __ __ __ __ __

6. gavetine   __ __ __ __ __ __ __
                        7

7. tracatveit   __ __ __ __ __ __ __ __ __ __
                                    8

8. eectvdiet   __ __ __ __ __ __ __ __ __
                                       9

9. vectfefei   __ __ __ __ __ __ __ __ __
                                         10

10. steinsiev   __ __ __ __ __ __ __ __
                         11

11. jadtecive   __ __ __ __ __ __ __ __ __
                                  12

12. ivecat   __ __ __ __ __ __

13. ivattlake   __ __ __ __ __ __ __ __ __
                           13

14. ispitvoe   __ __ __ __ __ __ __ __
                    14

15. tanive   __ __ __ __ __ __
           15

Riddle: What animals are the most generous?

__ __ __ __ __ __ .   __ __ __ __ __ __ , __ __ __ __
11 13 5 15 13 11   12 1 3 2 6 6   7 9 10 3

__ __ __ __ __ __   __   (__) __ __ __ __
4 15 2 14 15 3   4   11   8 3 15 12

The Suffix "able"

The suffix -able means "able to be."

Examples: *flammable* means "able to go up in flames"

memorable means "able to be remembered"

Part I: Add the suffix -able to these words to form new words.

Example: erase*_____ erasable _____

1. dispose* _____

6. admire* _____

2. notice _____

7. replace _____

3. believe _____

8. manage _____

4. change _____

9. accept _____

5. regret** _____

10. control** _____

* Drop the e before adding the suffix.

** Double the last consonant before adding the suffix.

Part II: Match the word to its meaning. Write the letter on the line next to the word.

_____ 1. immovable

a. able to be controlled

_____ 2. noticeable

b. able to be accepted

_____ 3. erasable

c. able to be admired; to think highly of

_____ 4. controllable

d. not able to be moved

_____ 5. changeable

e. able to be thrown out after use

_____ 6. unforgettable

f. able to be erased

_____ 7. disposable

g. memorable; not able to be forgotten

_____ 8. admirable

h. able to be replaced

_____ 9. acceptable

i. able or likely to change

_____ 10. replaceable

j. obvious; likely to be noticed

Word Ending: "ence"

Use the words in the table below to help you answer the questions on this page and the next.

Word	Syllables	In Context
sentence	sen•tence	You need to change this into a complete **sentence**.
difference	dif•fer•ence	Can you tell the **difference** between frogs and toads?
influence	in•flu•ence	The mayor used her **influence** to get a traffic light put in.
audience	au•di•ence	The **audience** roared with laughter.
reference	ref•er•ence	We had to go to the library to use the **reference** books.
evidence	ev•i•dence	The police need more **evidence** in order to find the thief.
absence	ab•sence	You need a note to explain your **absence** yesterday.
experience	ex•pe•ri•ence	That was a frightening **experience**!
conference	con•fer•ence	My dad is going to have a **conference** with my teacher.
occurrence	oc•cur•rence	If there's another **occurrence** like this, you'll be suspended.
science	sci•ence	In **science** class, we're studying the human body.
patience	pa•tience	The father had **patience** with his whining child.
preference	pref•er•ence	We have red or blue. Do you have a **preference** in color?
intelligence	in•tel•li•gence	Information gathered about enemies is called **intelligence**.
convenience	con•ven•ience	Let's stop at the **convenience** store to get some milk.

Copy the spelling words in the order they appear above. Number them in order from A–Z. You may need to look as far as the third letter. Then write the words in A–Z order.

Word	Number	A–Z Order
1.		
2.		
3.		
4.		
5.		
6.		
7.		
8.		
9.		
10.		
11.		
12.		
13.		
14.		
15.		

Word Ending: "ence" (cont.)

Crossword Puzzle

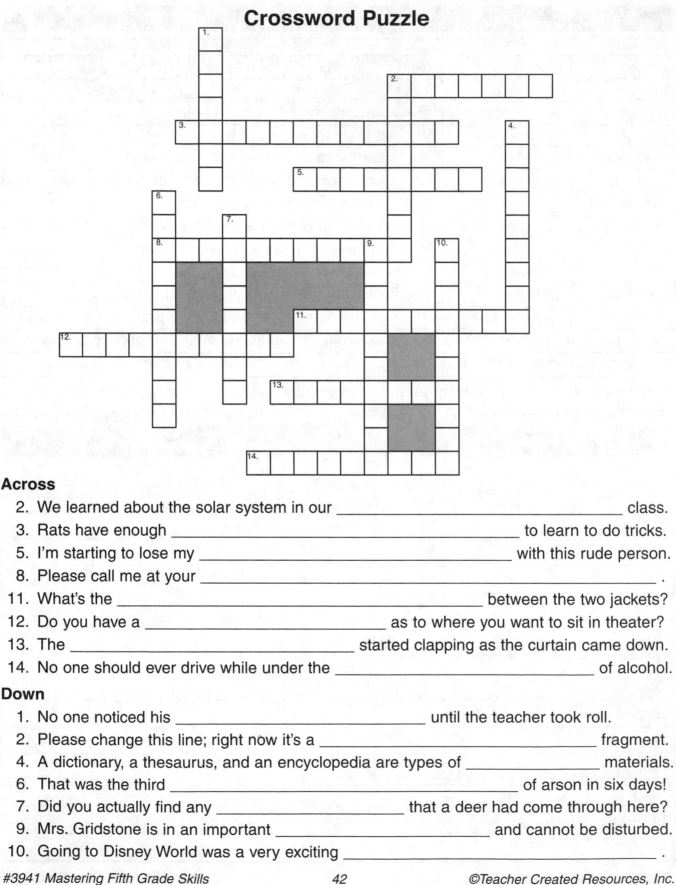

Across

2. We learned about the solar system in our _____ class.

3. Rats have enough _____ to learn to do tricks.

5. I'm starting to lose my _____ with this rude person.

8. Please call me at your _____ .

11. What's the _____ between the two jackets?

12. Do you have a _____ as to where you want to sit in theater?

13. The _____ started clapping as the curtain came down.

14. No one should ever drive while under the _____ of alcohol.

Down

1. No one noticed his _____ until the teacher took roll.

2. Please change this line; right now it's a _____ fragment.

4. A dictionary, a thesaurus, and an encyclopedia are types of _____ materials.

6. That was the third _____ of arson in six days!

7. Did you actually find any _____ that a deer had come through here?

9. Mrs. Gridstone is in an important _____ and cannot be disturbed.

10. Going to Disney World was a very exciting _____ .

Practice with the Suffix "ian"

The suffix *-ian* means "one who."

musician	magician	physician	technician	comedian	vegetarian
librarian	beautician	Canadians	Egyptian	historian	politician

Part II: Choose the word from the box that best completes each sentence. Each word is used once.

1. My _____ ordered some blood tests.

2. The _____ kept the audience laughing for nearly an hour.

3. Madison's mom styles hair; she is a _____.

4. Many _____ can speak both French and English.

5. Zayn enjoys magic and hopes to be a _____ when he grows up.

6. A state governor is an example of a _____.

7. After checking the car thoroughly, the _____ wrote a repair order.

8. Since Janie is a _____, we can't serve her any meat.

9. Elijah is such an expert _____ that he knows how to play six instruments.

10. The town _____ has old maps dating back to 1869.

11. The _____ pyramids took many years to build.

12. Our school _____ suggested we read titles by Emily Rodda.

Part II: Pick two words from the box above. Use each in a sentence.

Example: An Egyptian mummy lay inside the decorated case.

1. _____

_____

2. _____

_____

Practice With the Suffixes "rupt" and "ship"

The suffix -rupt means "to break." The suffix -ship means "having the quality of."

| erupt | disrupted | interrupt | abruptly | bankrupt | corrupt |
| friendship | hardship | leadership | citizenship | scholarship | sportsmanship |

Part I: Choose the word from the box that best completes each sentence. Each word is used once.

1. My _____ with Amber has lasted for six years.

2. The volcano smoked and grumbled as if it were about to _____.

3. Brianna showed _____ by helping others during the flood.

4. Please don't _____ me when I'm speaking.

5. I am a U.S. citizen. In what nation do you hold _____ ?

6. A _____ government does not do what is best for its citizens.

7. Michael showed good _____ by shaking hands with the boy who won the match.

8. The car stopped _____ outside a run-down old house with peeling paint.

9. Morgan received a _____ to a private school.

10. A cell phone's loud ringing _____ the movie.

11. The father lost his job, causing _____ for the Gordon family.

12. If they can't pay their bills, the Gordons may go _____.

Part II: Pick two words from the box above. Use each in a sentence.

Example: _My teacher says that I show **leadership** skills in class._

1. _____

_____

2. _____

_____

The Suffixes "cious" and "tious"

The suffixes *-cious* and *-tious* mean "likely" or "apt to be."

    Examples: *suspicious* means "likely to suspect"

               flirtatious means "apt to flirt"

ferocious	**gracious**	**spacious**	**cautious**
fictitious	**infectious**	**nutritious**	**repetitious**

Part I: Write the word from the box above that is based on the root word given.

1. fiction _____

2. nutrient _____

3. repeat _____

4. space _____

5. caution _____

6. fierce _____

7. infect _____

8. grace _____

Part II: Add the suffix *-cious* or *-tious* to each boot to form a word. Write the new word formed by the pair of boots on the line.

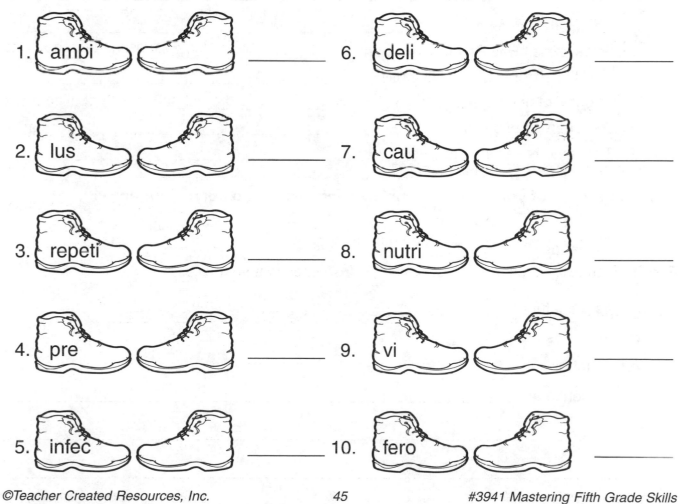

1. ambi _____

2. lus _____

3. repeti _____

4. pre _____

5. infec _____

6. deli _____

7. cau _____

8. nutri _____

9. vi _____

10. fero _____

Similes

A simile is a figure of speech that compares one thing to another. It is a direct comparison introduced by the words **like** or **as**.

1. Use a word from the box to complete each simile.

toast	ice	sugar	mouse	rock	feathers

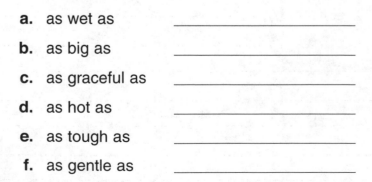

  a. as soft as   _____

  b. as sweet as   _____

  c. as cold as   _____

  d. as hard as a   _____

  e. as warm as   _____

  f. as small as a   _____

2. Use a word from the box to complete each simile.

silk	bee	kitten	coal	eel	snow

  a. The cloth was as black as _____ .

  b. The wet ball was as slippery as an _____ .

  c. My little sister is as playful as a _____ .

  d. The top of this table is as smooth as _____ .

  e. I've been as busy as a _____ lately.

  f. The lamb is as white as _____ .

3. Add a word of your own to complete each simile. Compare your answers with those of a friend.

  a. as wet as   _____

  b. as big as   _____

  c. as graceful as   _____

  d. as hot as   _____

  e. as tough as   _____

  f. as gentle as   _____

           46

Metaphors

A metaphor is more direct than a simile. Instead of saying that one thing is like another, it supposes that one thing is another.

Simile: He is as cunning as a fox.

Metaphor: He is a cunning fox.

1. **Condense each simile and rewrite it as a metaphor.**

    a. All the world is like a stage.

    _____

    b. She was like peaches and cream.

    _____

    c. Fred is like a pig at the table.

    _____

    d. Headlines announcing the crime were like screams.

    _____

    e. Life is like a short summer, and man is like a flower.

    _____

2. **Use each word in two sentences—literally in the first, metaphorically in the second.**

    a. cloud _____

    _____

    b. forest _____

    _____

    c. river _____

    _____

    d. book _____

    _____

    e. galaxy _____

    _____

    f. snail _____

    _____

Prediction

Belize

September 27, 2005

Dear Friend,

While we were in Belize, we went to the Belize City Zoo and it was awesome! It almost felt like you were right in the wildlife with all the animals. My favorite animal that we saw was the tapir. The tapir is the national animal of Belize. A tapir is a hoofed mammal, and it looks a little bit like a mix between a rhinoceros and a hog. It's sort of hard to describe, so you'll just have to look it up and find a picture for yourself.

When we got back to San Ignacio, my dad gave me money to buy an ice cream at the ice cream stand. They had all different kinds of flavors—chocolate chip, coconut, strawberry, and many more. The flavor that sounded interesting to me, though, was corn, so I decided to try it. Guess what it was? Yep, ice cream with corn in it — and I liked it!

We spent the rest of the day in San Ignacio. San Ignacio is a nice town. Most of the streets are dirt, and most of the houses are made of concrete blocks. A lot of the houses do not have hot water faucets, so you have to get used to cold showers. It was really tough at first, but sometimes after a hot day it feels okay. We walked most of the places we went, but when it was too far to walk we took the bus or got a ride from our friend who has a car. It's kind of nice to just enjoy the outdoors and some good company as you walk downtown or to the corner store.

There's one last thing that I want to tell you about in this letter: plantain. Plantain is a lot like bananas. There are quite a few plantain trees in San Ignacio. Our friends like to fix long, thin slices of fried plantain. We like it, too!

Well, it appears that I am almost out of paper, so I will close. I hope that you are getting very interested in Belize! Remember to go look up a picture of a tapir!

Sincerely,

Julia

48

Prediction

Belize (cont.)

Directions: Carefully read "Belize" and then complete the prediction chart below with your predictions about what Julia's next letter will contain. Write your predictions on the left side of the chart. On the right side of the chart, write what caused you to think of those predictions.

Predictions About What Julia Will Write in Her Next Letter	Reasons Why I Made the Predictions
1.	1.
2.	2.
3.	3.
4.	4.
5.	5.

Main Idea

One Man of Peace

Mahatma Gandhi has inspired many important leaders of the world. Gandhi led a life of peaceful resistance to unjust policies. Although he was often attacked and imprisoned for his ideas and acts, Gandhi refused to speak angrily against, or cause harm to, those who hurt him. Many important leaders use Gandhi's life as an example of how to help people and peacefully stand up for human rights.

In 1893 Gandhi went to South Africa and peacefully helped the people win new laws. When Gandhi saw how unfair the people of darker skin—including Indians—were treated in South Africa, Gandhi decided to work for new laws. Gandhi peacefully set about showing that South Africa needed to change. Although Gandhi was a respected, educated man, he stopped wearing his fancy clothes and committed to wearing only a loincloth and shawl—the clothes of peasants in India. People joined Gandhi in his effort to win new laws, and eventually, after much resistance, they were able to win new laws for South Africa.

In 1915 Gandhi returned to India and became a peaceful leader in the movement to free India from British rule. Gandhi also worked to help the many poor people of India. As he did in South Africa, Gandhi taught the people that they must be brave and that they must return love for hate. After much resistance, India won its independence in 1947.

Gandhi's peaceful, powerful way of helping people and leading people to stand up for their rights has influenced many recent leaders. Martin Luther King, Jr. in the United States, Ella Bhatt in India, and Marina Silva in Brazil are only a few of the life-changing leaders who have noted Gandhi as an important influence in their lives. Gandhi's life shows us all that we can accomplish great tasks in peaceful ways.

Main Idea

One Man of Peace (cont.)

Directions: Carefully read "One Man of Peace." Then complete the chart below. Write the main idea of "One Man of Peace" in the oval and then write three supporting details in the triangles below.

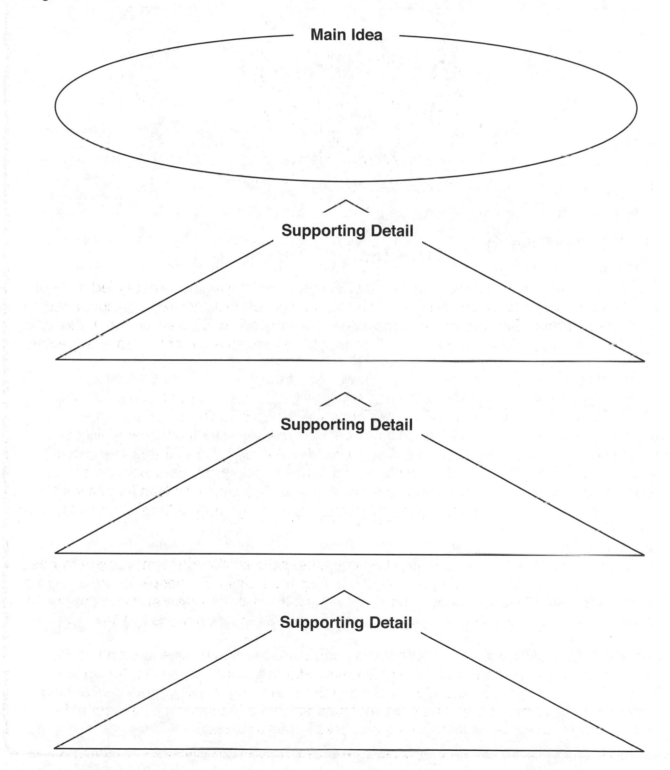

Main Idea

Supporting Detail

Supporting Detail

Supporting Detail

Main Idea

Directions: Read "The Store Manager" below. Then complete the graphic organizer on page 53 with the main idea and supporting details. Write the main idea in the middle oval and the supporting details in the surrounding ovals.

The Store Manager

Mr. Humphreys is an excellent store manager because he has had many experiences of working at stores. When Mr. Humphreys was a young boy, he helped his Uncle Ben by sweeping the floor of his small shoe store. Uncle Ben was the store manager, and he would spend hours telling Mr. Humphreys stories about how to be a successful store manager. Mr. Humphreys was always intrigued by his uncle's stories and decided that he wanted to become a store manager himself one day.

When Mr. Humphreys became a teenager, he began working as a stock boy at the local grocery store. He often worked long hours on weekends, and he learned a lot about how stores are run. He would talk with all of the workers at the grocery store to learn exactly what they had to do as a part of their jobs.

After graduating from school, Mr. Humphreys began working as a clerk at a large department store downtown. Mr. Humphreys was always trying to become just a little bit better at what he did. His boss noticed how hard Mr. Humphreys was working and promoted him to an assistant manager position. Mr. Humphreys was very excited, and he began to work even harder. Several years later, the store needed a new full-time store manager. Mr. Humphreys nervously applied for the position, and he was immediately promoted. Mr. Humphreys was very happy that he had finally fulfilled his dream of becoming a store manager.

Main Idea (cont.)

The Store Manager (cont.)

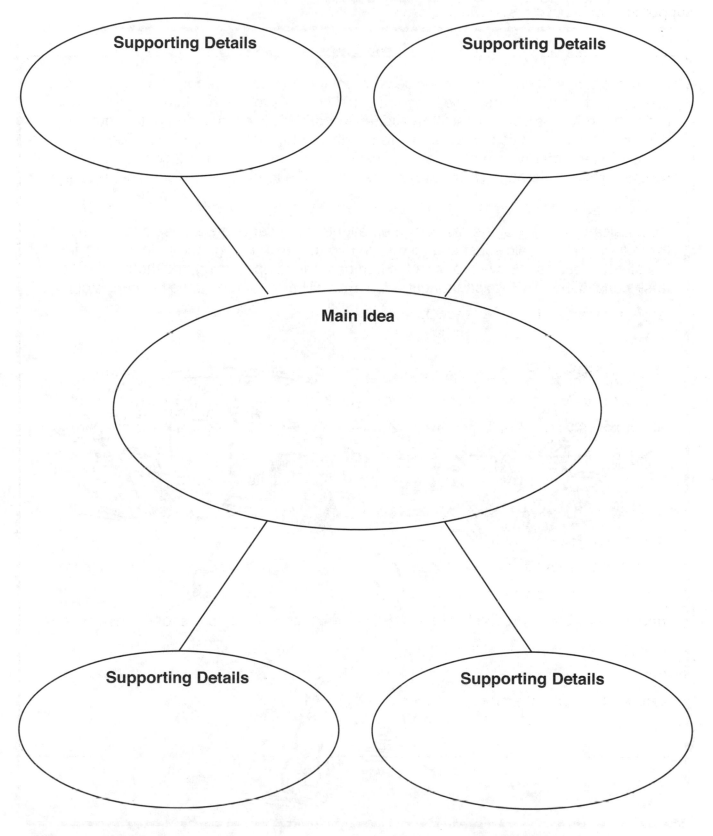

Supporting Details

Supporting Details

Main Idea

Supporting Details

Supporting Details

Cause and Effect

Directions: Read "The Crash" carefully. Follow the directions for each question on page 55 and answer the questions in complete sentences.

The Crash

It was a bright and sunny day when Jessica got into the car. She rolled down the window and turned up the radio. Jessica could not believe that her father was finally letting her drive his car. Jessica had gotten her driver's license a month ago, but her dad was very protective of his car and refused to let her drive it anywhere. Today, however, her father was in an especially happy mood and agreed that she could use his car for the afternoon. Now Jessica was happily headed for her best friend Jacquie's house.

As Jessica pulled out of the driveway, her favorite song came on, and so she turned up the volume of the radio. Just as she pulled onto the road, a dog ran out in the middle of the street. Jessica swerved to miss the dog and ended up running into the neighbors' trash cans. Oh, no! Jessica thought. Now Dad will never let me drive his car!

Cause and Effect

The Crash (cont.)

Directions: Read "The Crash" carefully. Follow the directions for each question and answer the questions in complete sentences.

1. <u>Underline</u> the sentence in "The Crash" that says Jessica's father agreed to let her use his car for the afternoon. Answer the question below:

   What caused Jessica's father to let her drive his car for the afternoon?

   _____

   _____

   _____

2. <u>Underline</u> the sentence in "The Crash" that says Jessica turned up the volume to her radio. Answer the question below:

   What caused Jessica to turn up the volume of her radio? _____

   _____

   _____

3. <u>Underline</u> the sentence in "The Crash" that says Jessica swerved the car and then answer the question below:

   What caused Jessica to swerve? _____

   _____

   _____

4. <u>Underline</u> the part of the story where Jessica thinks that her father will never let her drive his car again. Answer the question below:

   What caused Jessica to think that her father would never let her drive his car again?

   _____

   _____

   _____

5. What caused Jessica to crash? _____

   _____

   _____

6. What are some of the possible effects of Jessica crashing into the neighbors' trash cans?

   _____

   _____

   _____

Sequence

Directions: Read the following story and then number the events in the order in which they occurred.

B-Ball

Eddie has always been into sports. Before playing basketball, he played soccer. His soccer team went to the state championships and won a trophy when he was in the fifth grade. It was a very exciting game, and Eddie scored the winning goal!

Now Eddie plays basketball on the ninth grade basketball team. Next year he will try out for the 10th grade soccer team as well. Then he will be playing team sports practically all year round. When Eddie was five years old, his big sister took him to a college soccer game and that's when he decided that he wanted to play on a sports team.

Today, his sister Jessica comes to his basketball games and claims that she inspired him to be the great athlete that he is. Eddie just laughs when she says that, but he does agree that she had a part in his love for athletics. Jessica frequently tells him that if he works hard he can do anything. Eddie's most recent dream is to go to college on a basketball scholarship and study physics.

_____ Eddie plays on the ninth grade basketball team.

_____ Eddie decides that he wants to play on a sports team.

_____ Eddie's fifth grade soccer team won the state championships.

_____ Eddie hopes to go to college and study physics.

_____ Eddie scored the winning goal on his fifth grade soccer team.

_____ Eddie will try out for the 10th grade soccer team.

56

The Man Who Peacefully Changed America

Directions: Read the passage below and answer the questions.

In January we honor a great leader named Dr. Martin Luther King, Jr with a holiday. He worked to get equal rights for black Americans. He proved that one person can make a real difference.

Until the 1960s, many states had laws separating white people and black people. They couldn't go to the same schools or use the same drinking fountains. Dr. King said that this was wrong, and he made speeches and led marches. He believed in peaceful protest. He won the 1964 Nobel Peace Prize.

Some people attacked him. Racists threw rocks at him in Chicago and bombed his home. This just made King work even harder for justice. In 1968 a man killed him, but King had already won. Major changes had begun in America. The races would no longer be kept apart.

1. **One of the laws Dr. Martin Luther King, Jr. wanted changed was the law that said that black people and white people couldn't . . .**

   a. attend the same schools.
   b. live in the same city.
   c. eat the same kinds of food.

2. **Why did people attack King and bomb his house?**

   a. They didn't like his ideas, and they wanted to scare him into silence.
   b. They believed he'd turn violent after violence was used against him.
   c. They wanted to show their support for his cause.

3. **Before the 1960s you can conclude that blacks and whites. . .**

   a. never saw one another.
   b. could not speak each other's languages.
   c. could not usually marry each other.

4. **Of the following choices, which happened last?**

   a. King was murdered.
   b. King's birthday was made a national holiday.
   c. King led peaceful protests.

Keyboard Master: Mozart

Wolfgang Amadeus Mozart is one of the world's most famous musicians. As an adult, he produced more than 600 works, including symphonies, operas, and other musical pieces. What is most unusual about Mozart is that he amazed the world with his musical brilliance when he was only six years old.

Mozart was born in Austria in 1756. It wasn't long before his father noticed Mozart's talent for music. The small boy would listen to his sister Nannerl's music lessons, then try to play along. Mozart learned an entire piece of music by heart when he was only four years old.

Both Mozart and Nannerl came from a very talented family. Their father, Leopold, was a violinist and composer. Their mother, Anna Maria, came from a family of musicians.

Leopold wanted the world to see what brilliant children Mozart and Nannerl were. When Mozart was six and Nannerl was ten, Leopold took them on a European tour. The family traveled for four years. They went to Austria, Hungary, Germany, France, England, the Netherlands, and Switzerland. Everywhere they went, the children charmed audiences with their musical abilities.

Sometimes Mozart and Nannerl would play duets. Their fingers flew over the keys in a blur. Sometimes Leopold asked Mozart to do musical "tricks." One of Mozart's favorite tricks was to play the harpsichord with a cloth draped over the keys so he couldn't see them. For another trick, Mozart would listen through a door while someone played music he had never heard. Then the boy would enter the room and play the piece perfectly.

After the tour, the family went back home to Austria. But Mozart and Leopold couldn't stay still for long. Soon they went on another tour, then another. By the time Mozart was sixteen, he was one of the best known musicians in Europe. Royalty asked him to compose operas just for them.

As he grew up, people were not quite as amazed at Mozart's talent as they were when he was a child. Mozart made a living by composing music, giving concerts, and teaching, but his music eventually fell out of favor with the people of his time. He died at the age of 35, deeply in debt.

Today, Mozart is recognized as one of the greatest musicians that the world has ever known, and his music and operas are even more popular than when he was alive.

58

Keyboard Master: Mozart (cont.)

Directions: After reading the story, answer the questions. Circle the correct answer.

1. Why did Mozart's father take his children on a European tour?

    a. He wanted to make a living through his children's talents.

    b. He wanted his children to see all of Europe.

    c. He wanted to expand their musical abilities.

    d. He wanted the world to see what brilliant children they were.

2. How old was Mozart when he played his first musical piece by heart?

    a. Six

    b. Sixteen

    c. Four

    d. Ten

3. What does the passage mean by "the children charmed audiences"?

    a. The audiences would be amazed and awed by the children's talents.

    b. The people in the audience would fall asleep.

    c. The children would give small musical charms to the people in the audience.

    d. The children were always polite and well behaved.

4. According to the passage. . .

    a. Mozart died a happy man.

    b. Mozart became more popular as an adult musician.

    c. Mozart's popularity decreased as he got older.

    d. Mozart's operas are less popular now than when he was alive.

5. Which of the following can you conclude from this passage?

    a. Mozart died not knowing that his music would live on.

    b. There has never been a musician as talented as Mozart.

    c. Music changed dramatically after Mozart's death.

    d. Mozart knew he would be remembered as a world famous musician.

6. The web shows some important ideas in the story. Which of these belongs in the empty box?

    a. cloth drape

    b. violinist and composer

    c. musical tricks

    d. deep in debt

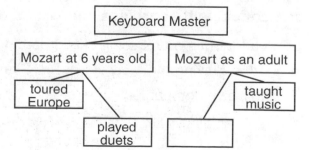

Tony Hawk, Professional Skater

Directions: Read the passage below and answer the questions.

Tony Hawk was born in 1968 in California. He was a difficult child. Then his brother gave him a skateboard at the age of 9. His whole life changed. By the time Hawk was 14, he was a professional skateboarder. Two years later, he was the best in the world.

He entered 103 contests. In 92 of them he took first or second place. He created dozens of tricks. Hawk even did a 900, which everyone said was impossible. (A 900 means that he spun around two-and-a-half times in midair on his skateboard.)

Hawk turned skateboarding into a popular sport. Today he is married and has three sons. He owns a company that sells skateboarding clothes and gear. He also has a popular video game series called Tony Hawk Pro Skater.

1. **From the time he started skateboarding, how many years did it take Hawk to be the top skateboarder worldwide?**

   a. 9 years   b. 5 years   c. 7 years

2. **At the age of 17 Hawk bought an expensive house. How did he afford it?**

   a. He charged people money to teach them how to skateboard.

   b. He had started a company that sold computers.

   c. He won award money at many skateboarding competitions.

3. **Why did skateboarding immediately improve Hawk's life at the age of 9?**

   a. Skateboarding prompted him to open a business and make video games.

   b. Skateboarding gave him something to do that kept him out of trouble.

   c. He liked skateboarding so much that within a year he was a professional.

4. **You can conclude that professional skateboarders must. . .**

   a. spend a lot of time practicing skateboarding tricks.

   b. be good at playing the Tony Hawk Pro Skater video games.

   c. own their own companies.

We All Scream for Ice Cream

Directions: Read the passage below and answer the questions.

Ice cream was first served in 62 BCE. The Roman emperor Nero ate a treat made of snow, fruit, and honey. This happened nearly 1,800 years before the first ice cream plant opened. Jacob Fussell built the first one in 1851.

Making ice cream by hand is hard work, and it doesn't always come out right. People made it at home for a rare treat. Now each person in the U.S. eats about 15 quarts a year. Although people around the world enjoy ice cream, Americans eat the most.

Vanilla is the top-selling flavor. Chocolate comes in second. Neapolitan is third in popularity. It has bands of vanilla, chocolate, and strawberry. The top three flavors have held those slots for many years. Other favorites include butter pecan and cookies and cream.

1. **What did Jacob Fussell do?**

   a. He invented the frozen treat called ice cream.

   b. He started making ice cream in large quantities.

   c. He did a survey to find out the most popular ice cream flavors.

2. **If you have an allergy to nuts, you wouldn't want to try. . .**

   a. butter pecan ice cream.

   b. Neapolitan ice cream.

   c. cookies and cream ice cream.

3. **How did Nero's ice cream differ from today's ice cream?**

   a. His didn't have any milk or cream in it.

   b. His was served cold.

   c. His had chunks of fruit.

4. **Ice cream is most closely related to. . .**

   a. peppermint candy.

   b. frozen juice on a stick.

   c. frozen yogurt.

An Unusual Inmate

Directions: Read the passage below and answer the questions.

In 1924 Pep, a black Labrador retriever, lived in Pennsylvania. Then one day he killed the governor's cat. The governor **ardently** loved his cat. He was so furious that he demanded that Pep go to jail. People thought that he wasn't serious. So the governor put on his judge's robes. He had Pep brought into court. However, there was no jury at Pep's trial. The judge simply pronounced the sentence: "Life imprisonment without the possibility of parole."

Pep went to prison, but he never lived in a cell. Instead he went wherever he pleased within the prison walls. He had a good life because so many of the inmates loved him. He followed them around while they did their assigned chores. Pep was petted and played with until he died in a fellow prisoner's arms in 1930.

1. **Why did Pep have to go to jail?**

    a. His owner didn't want him anymore.

    b. The other inmates needed company.

    c. He had killed the governor's cat.

2. **Why did the judge say Pep could never be paroled?**

    a. The judge wanted Pep to confess to the crime.

    b. The judge didn't want Pep to ever leave the prison.

    c. The judge wanted the jury's support for his decision.

3. **Why did the author choose the title?**

    a. Pep acted strangely for a dog.

    b. Dogs are rarely put in jail.

    c. The other inmates loved Pep very much.

4. **The word *ardently* means. . .**

    a. wrongly.

    b. mildly.

    c. strongly.

Poetry: What's in a Name?

Name poetry is a form of invented poetry. It is a variation of an acrostic poem. To create a name poem, write your name vertically down the side of the page. Now think of a word describing yourself for each letter of your name. An example has been done for the name of Robert.

Rides a bike
Outgoing
Basketball player
Enjoys soccer
Reads and reads and reads
Ten years old

You will notice in the sample that it doesn't matter if the words rhyme, and there is no specific number of words that should be used. To write a name poem, you just write words or phrases that describe the name of the person or thing you are describing.

Try writing a name poem for America   Now write a name poem for yourself or someone you know really well.

A _____   _____

M _____   _____

E _____   _____

R _____   _____

I _____   _____

C _____   _____

A _____   _____

Draw a picture to go with the poem and give it to that person. It might brighten his or her day!

Writing a Haiku

Haiku poetry is a very short, centuries-old form of Japanese poetry that is an intriguing change of pace from the kind of rhythmic, rhyming poetry you may be used to reading.

Haiku is like a photograph. It captures what is happening right in the moment. It paints a picture in your mind. Read the sample haiku:

> *Water flows over,*
> *Cascading waves splashing down,*
> *Trying to get out.*

Haiku is often written about nature or the changing of seasons. Haiku can also be used to express emotion. Haiku uses so few words, the words need to capture the feeling and picture immediately. A haiku should capture the reader's attention immediately.

Traditional Japanese haiku has a total of seventeen syllables divided into three lines:

> five syllables
> seven syllables
> five syllables

Try writing a haiku about a beautiful sunset:

Five syllables: _____

Seven syllables:_____

Five syllables: _____

Now select two new topics and write your own haikus.

Five syllables: _____

Seven syllables:_____

Five syllables: _____

~ ~ ~ ~ ~

Five syllables: _____

Seven syllables:_____

Five syllables: _____

Writing a Limerick

Can you hear the rhythm in this limerick?

There was an old lady named Sue, (A)
da DUM da da DUM da da DUM
who dreamed she was running a zoo. (A)
da DUM da da DUM da da DUM
She awoke from her nap, (B)
da DUM da da DUM
with a dog in her lap, (B)
da da DUM da da DUM
and found out it wasn't quite true. (A)
da DUM da da DUM da da DUM

Write your own limerick on the lines below, following the A/A/B/B/A rhyming pattern, and using the rhythm shown above.

(A) _____

(A) _____

(B) _____

(B) _____

(A) _____

Now write a limerick about an old man named Pat on the lines below, following the A/A/B/B/A pattern, and using the rhythm shown above.

(A) _____

(A) _____

(B) _____

(B) _____

(A) _____

Diamante Poems

A diamante poem is in the shape of a diamond. A diamante poem is a descriptive poem. Write a description of the events listed below. Select one of these events to write a diamante poem.

Event	Descriptive Words
First day of school	_____
Learning to ride a bike	_____
Having a slumber party	_____
Getting a new pet	_____
Family Gathering	_____
Sporting Event	_____

Using these descriptions, write a diamante poem about the life event you selected.

_____

(event being described)

_____ _____

(two words describing touch)

_____ _____ _____

(three words describing the tastes)

_____ _____ _____ _____

(four words describing the sounds)

_____ _____ _____

(three words describing the sights)

_____ _____

(two words describing the smells)

_____

(adjective describing event)

66

Writing A Business Letter

The Six Parts of the Business Letter

I. Heading

The heading usually contains three lines. The first lines are the address of the person who is writing the letter. The last line is the date the letter is written.

II. Inside Address

The inside address is written below the heading. The inside address includes the name of the person to whom the letter is being written (if you know it), the name of the business, and the address of the business. The inside address is usually three or four lines.

III. Salutation

The salutation is the third part of the business letter. The salutation, or greeting of the business letter, is followed by a colon rather than a comma. It is written on the left-hand side of the paper and below the inside address. If you know the name of the person to whom you are writing, be sure to use his or her name in the salutation. If you are unsure who will be receiving your letter, it is acceptable to put "Dear Sir or Madam" in place of the name.

IV. Body

The body follows the salutation of the business letter. Most business letters do not indent for paragraphs. Paragraphs are lined up with the left-hand margin of the paper. Double spacing is used between paragraphs to show the writer has begun a new thought. The writing in the body of the business letter should be clear and concise. Identify your purpose for writing the letter and do not waste time or space by including a lot of unnecessary information.

V. Closing

The closing of the letter may be one word or several words. Only the first word of the closing is capitalized. A comma always follows the closing. In a business letter the closing should be formal. Words such as "Sincerely" or "Cordially" are considered appropriate closings for a business letter. Cute phrases such as "Love ya" or "Catch you later" are not appropriate.

VI. Signature

The signature follows the closing of the business letter. The writer should skip four lines and then type or print his or her name. The signature lines up vertically with the closing. The letter should be signed in the space between the closing and the typed or printed name.

The author of a letter may feel he or she needs to include a phone number, e-mail address, etc. This information can be included in the heading of the letter. If this occurs, the heading becomes four lines in length instead of three lines. There may also be four lines if the writer is from a foreign country and needs to include this information in the heading.

Letters written on business stationery are written in the block style. When the information in the heading is already included on the stationery, all that needs to be added is the date. The rest of the letter will also follow the block format.

Writing A Business Letter (cont.)

The following is an example of a business letter written in block style. Notice the paragraphs are not indented. A line is skipped when a new paragraph begins.

Heading ——→

Inside Address —

Salutation ——→

Body ——

Closing ——→

Signature ——

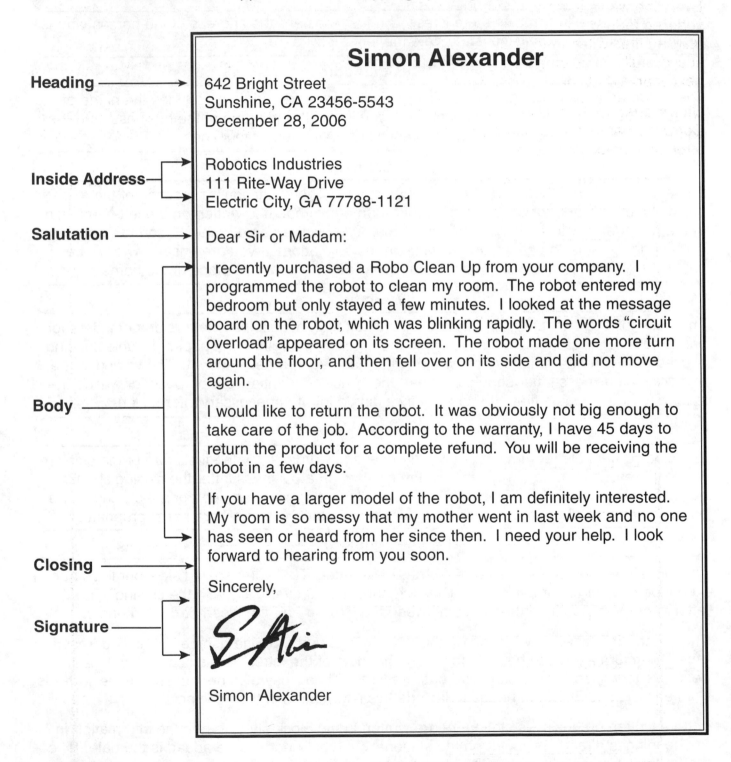

Simon Alexander

642 Bright Street
Sunshine, CA 23456-5543
December 28, 2006

Robotics Industries
111 Rite-Way Drive
Electric City, GA 77788-1121

Dear Sir or Madam:

I recently purchased a Robo Clean Up from your company. I programmed the robot to clean my room. The robot entered my bedroom but only stayed a few minutes. I looked at the message board on the robot, which was blinking rapidly. The words "circuit overload" appeared on its screen. The robot made one more turn around the floor, and then fell over on its side and did not move again.

I would like to return the robot. It was obviously not big enough to take care of the job. According to the warranty, I have 45 days to return the product for a complete refund. You will be receiving the robot in a few days.

If you have a larger model of the robot, I am definitely interested. My room is so messy that my mother went in last week and no one has seen or heard from her since then. I need your help. I look forward to hearing from you soon.

Sincerely,

Simon Alexander

Writing A Business Letter (cont.)

Camp Fun-for-All is accepting applications. Every student that wants to attend the camp must write a business letter to the head director, Mrs. Fisher. The camp is located at 22 Blossom Lane in Nashville, Tennessee 34444-5412.

Everyone wants to go to Camp Fun-for-All. There's no other camp where you get to practice yodeling for two hours each day, knit socks for all of your holiday gift giving, and practice building fires without any matches while standing under a waterfall. Every camper who successfully completes the rigorous activities at Camp Fun-for-All is automatically invited back next year. What could be more fun?

Directions: In the blanks provided, write a business letter to the director of Camp Fun-for-All. Convince her that you should be allowed to attend the summer camp. Some of the letter has already been completed for you.

Mrs. Fisher, Camp Director

-----

22 Blossom Lane

Dear _____ :

Sincerely,

Parts of a Personal Letter

There are five parts of a personal letter. The main parts of a personal letter are the heading, the salutation, the body, the closing, and the signature. Here is a model to guide you when writing your own personal letters.

heading ⟶

908 Diamond Spur
Phoenix, AZ 86501
November 12, 2001

salutation ⟶

Dear Grandma,

I am writing to ask you if you would like to attend Grandparents' Day at my elementary school. It will be held on Tuesday, November 20, at 10:30 A.M.

body ⟶

I would love it if you could come. There are so many reasons why I want you to be my guest. You are funny, you are my friend, I like to be around you, and I think the class will like you, too.

Let me know if you will be able to attend. I will be home most evenings after soccer practice, so you can call me if you like.

closing ⟶ Love,

signature ⟶ *Sandy*

Personal Letter Graphic Organizer

_____

_____

_____

Dear _____ ,

_____

_____

_____

_____

_____

_____

_____

_____

_____

Writing Strategies: Pyramid

Main Idea and Supporting Details: Pyramid

Just as a main idea is supported by facts, the top block of a pyramid is supported by the blocks beneath it. Read the example below and then use the pyramid on the next page to outline your own paragraph.

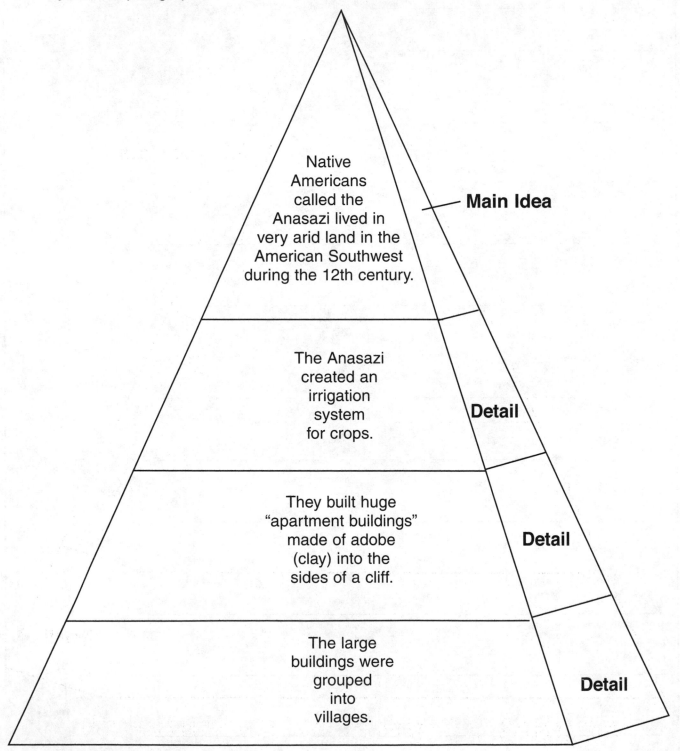

Native Americans called the Anasazi lived in very arid land in the American Southwest during the 12th century. — **Main Idea**

The Anasazi created an irrigation system for crops. **Detail**

They built huge "apartment buildings" made of adobe (clay) into the sides of a cliff. **Detail**

The large buildings were grouped into villages. **Detail**

Writing Strategies: Pyramid (cont.)

Graphic Organizer

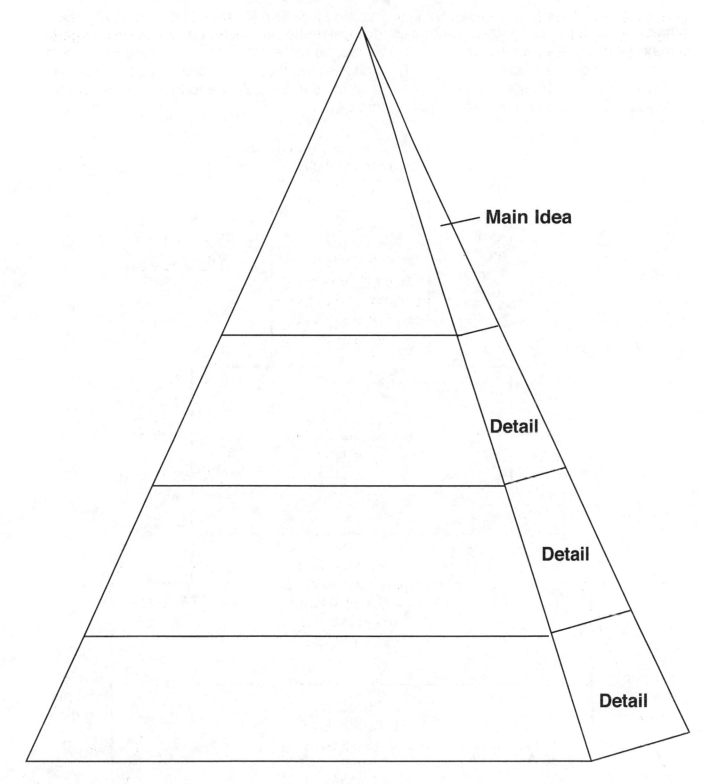

Main Idea

Detail

Detail

Detail

Writing Strategies: Stairstep Organizer

When using the stairstep graphic organizer to outline the order of an event, determine the climax and write it on the top step. Next, choose the three main events leading to the climax and put them on the steps on the left. Then choose the three main events after the climax and write them on the steps on the right. Read the sample below and then use the stairstep organizer on the next page to help you organize your writing.

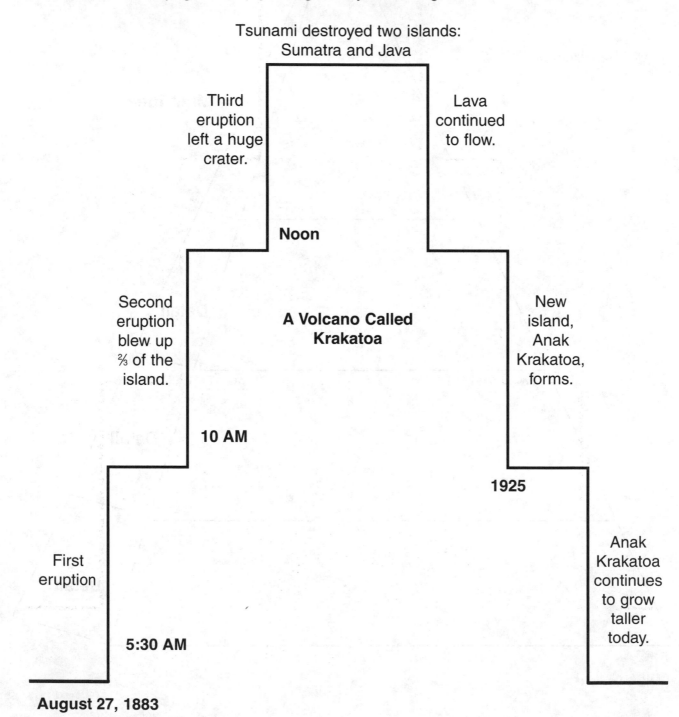

Tsunami destroyed two islands:
Sumatra and Java

Third eruption left a huge crater.

Lava continued to flow.

Noon

Second eruption blew up ⅔ of the island.

A Volcano Called Krakatoa

New island, Anak Krakatoa, forms.

10 AM

1925

First eruption

Anak Krakatoa continues to grow taller today.

5:30 AM

August 27, 1883

Writing Strategies: Stairstep Organizer (cont.)

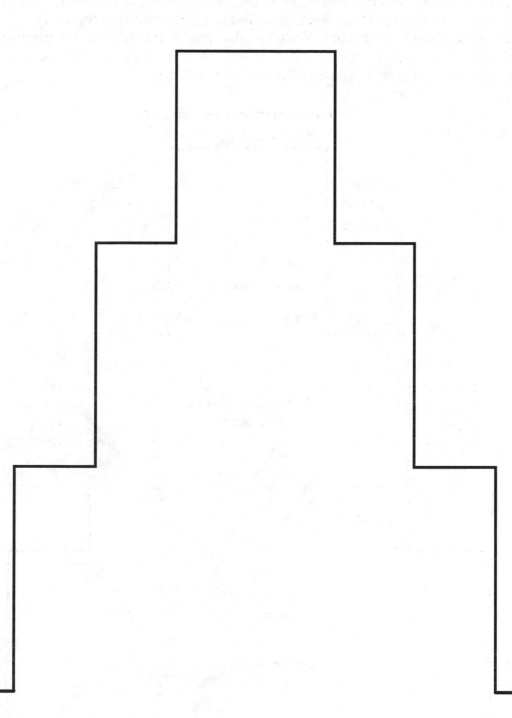

Writing Strategies: Essential Questions

Use the Essential Questions graphic organizer to help you pinpoint the key ideas in your writing. Read the sample below and then use the graphic organizer on the next page to help you organize what information to put in each part of the question for each sentence.

Example: On December 7, 1941, the Japanese bombed Pearl Harbor because they wanted to destroy American ships.

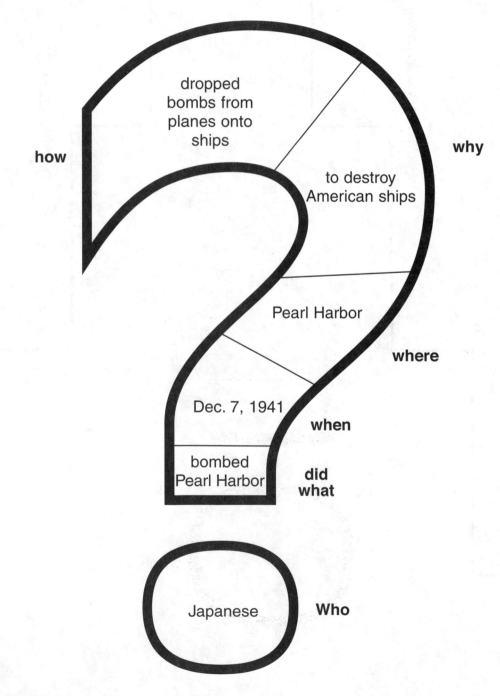

Writing Strategies: Essential Questions (cont.)

Graphic Organizer

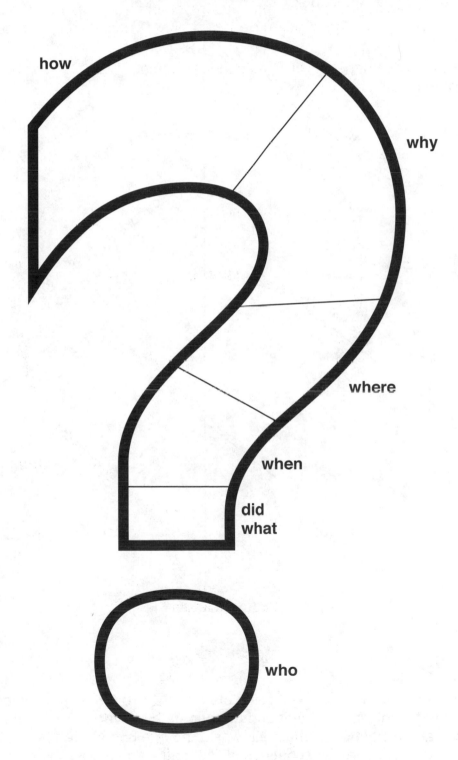

Writing Strategies: Herringbone

A graphic organizer that allows you to quickly display your knowledge of who, what, when, where, why, and how is the herringbone (Tierney, Readence & Dishner, 1990), named for a fish skeleton. A herringbone graphic organizer is provided on the next page. This is how a completed herringbone would look:

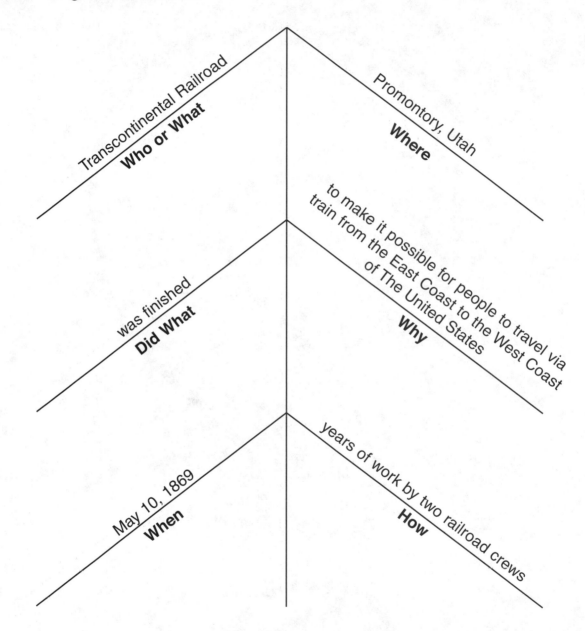

In paragraph form:

The Transcontinental Railroad was completed on May 10, 1869, in Promontory, Utah. Building it had taken years of work and two separate railroad crews. One crew had started laying tracks at the East Coast heading west, and one had started laying tracks at the West Coast heading east. The Transcontinental Railroad made it possible to travel by train across the entire width of America.

Writing Strategies: Herringbone (cont.)

Graphic Organizer

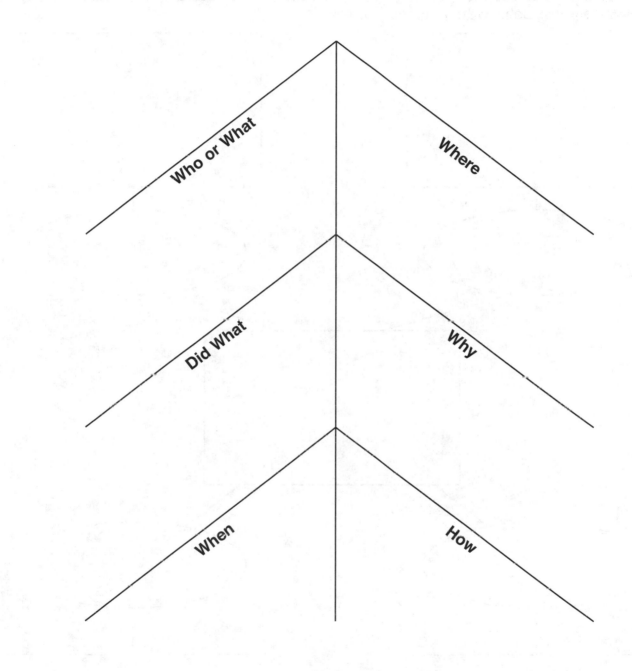

Summary:

Personal Narrative Graphic Organizer

Use this graphic to organize your information about an experience. The inner rectangle contains the name of the experience. The circles contain the events. The outer rectangles record the description and feelings regarding each event. The circles and the outer rectangles can become paragraphs in the personal narrative.

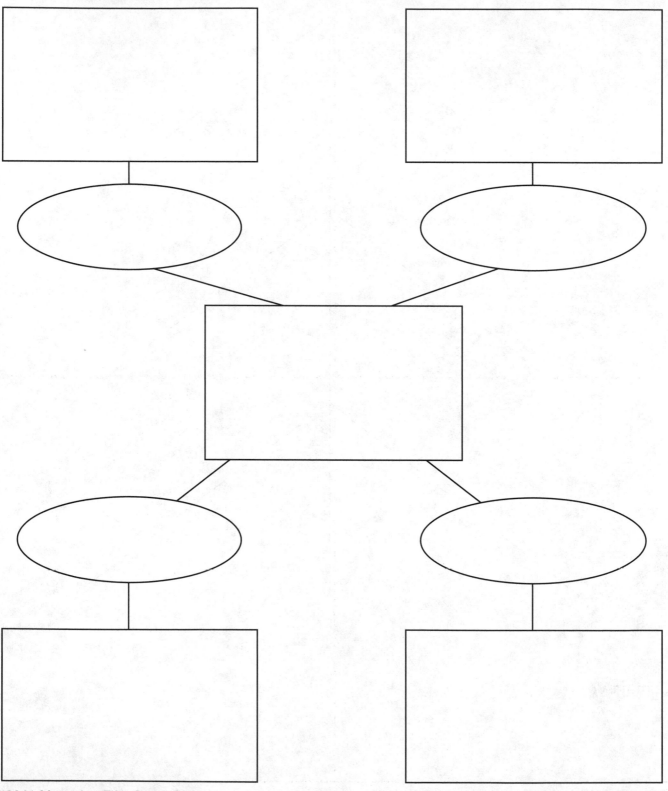

First, Next, Then, Finally...

Use this graphic organizer to help you write sequentially. This can be used with fiction as well as nonfiction writing.

First	Next
Then	**Finally**

Proofreading Marks

Use these proofreading marks to correct your own or others' writing.

Proofreading Marks

Editor's Mark	Meaning	Example
≡	capitalize	they fished in lake tahoe
/	make it lower case	Five Students missed the Bus.
sp.	spelling mistake	The day was clowdy and cold.
⊙	add a period	Tomorrow is a holiday
⸜	delete (remove)	One person knew the the answer.
∧	add a word	Six were in the litter.
⋏	add a comma	He planted peas corn, and squash.
∿	reverse words or letters	An otter swam in the bed kelp
⌄	add an apostrophe	The childs bike was red.
⌄ ⌄	add quotation marks	Why can't I go? she cried.
#	make a space	He ate two redapples.
⌒	close the space	Her favorite game is soft ball.
¶	begin a new paragraph	to know. Next on the list

Using One-Digit Multipliers with Two- and Three-Digit Multiplicands

Step by Step

1. Multiply 5 (ones) times 3 (ones) to equal 15 (1 ten and 5 ones).

2. Write the 5 below the line (in the ones place) and regroup by carrying 1 (ten) above the tens column.

3. Multiply 5 times 9 (tens) to equal 45 (tens).

4. Add the 1 (ten) that was carried over from the ones column to the 45 (tens). Write the 6 below the line (in the tens place) and regroup by carrying the 4 (hundreds) above the hundreds column.

5. Multiply 5 times 1 (hundred) to equal 5 (hundreds).

6. Add the regrouped 4 (hundreds) to the 5 (hundreds) to equal 9 hundreds.

7. The answer is 965.

```
      hundreds  tens  ones
         4     1
         1     9    3
    X               5
         9     6    5
```

Directions: Use the example above as a guide to solving the following problems.

1. 42 x 4	2. 51 x 7	3. 44 x 2	4. 12 x 4	5. 48 x 8
6. 63 x 9	7. 48 x 7	8. 35 x 5	9. 65 x 8	10. 34 x 6
11. 98 x 4	12. 76 x 7	13. 133 x 2	14. 233 x 3	15. 623 x 3

Two Digits Times One Digit

1. $\begin{array}{r} 11 \\ \times\ 4 \\ \hline \end{array}$ 2. $\begin{array}{r} 91 \\ \times\ 3 \\ \hline \end{array}$ 3. $\begin{array}{r} 69 \\ \times\ 4 \\ \hline \end{array}$ 4. $\begin{array}{r} 59 \\ \times\ 5 \\ \hline \end{array}$ 5. $\begin{array}{r} 26 \\ \times\ 4 \\ \hline \end{array}$

6. $\begin{array}{r} 17 \\ \times\ 3 \\ \hline \end{array}$ 7. $\begin{array}{r} 42 \\ \times\ 6 \\ \hline \end{array}$ 8. $\begin{array}{r} 97 \\ \times\ 3 \\ \hline \end{array}$ 9. $\begin{array}{r} 22 \\ \times\ 2 \\ \hline \end{array}$ 10. $\begin{array}{r} 71 \\ \times\ 4 \\ \hline \end{array}$

11. $\begin{array}{r} 12 \\ \times\ 7 \\ \hline \end{array}$ 12. $\begin{array}{r} 26 \\ \times\ 3 \\ \hline \end{array}$ 13. $\begin{array}{r} 25 \\ \times\ 7 \\ \hline \end{array}$ 14. $\begin{array}{r} 85 \\ \times\ 3 \\ \hline \end{array}$ 15. $\begin{array}{r} 58 \\ \times\ 5 \\ \hline \end{array}$

16. $\begin{array}{r} 97 \\ \times\ 4 \\ \hline \end{array}$ 17. $\begin{array}{r} 18 \\ \times\ 9 \\ \hline \end{array}$ 18. $\begin{array}{r} 33 \\ \times\ 1 \\ \hline \end{array}$ 19. $\begin{array}{r} 86 \\ \times\ 3 \\ \hline \end{array}$ 20. $\begin{array}{r} 16 \\ \times\ 6 \\ \hline \end{array}$

21. $\begin{array}{r} 65 \\ \times\ 7 \\ \hline \end{array}$ 22. $\begin{array}{r} 38 \\ \times\ 7 \\ \hline \end{array}$ 23. $\begin{array}{r} 43 \\ \times\ 8 \\ \hline \end{array}$ 24. $\begin{array}{r} 24 \\ \times\ 8 \\ \hline \end{array}$ 25. $\begin{array}{r} 95 \\ \times\ 3 \\ \hline \end{array}$

Multiplying by 10s, 100s, and 1,000s

When multiplying by 10's, 100's, and 1,000's remember the following:

- To multiply a number by 10, just add one zero.

$$\begin{array}{r} 23 \\ \underline{\times\ 10} \\ 230 \end{array}$$

- To multiply a number by 100, add two zeros.

$$\begin{array}{r} 23 \\ \underline{\times\ 100} \\ 2{,}300 \end{array}$$

- To multiply a number by 1,000, add three zeros.

$$\begin{array}{r} 23 \\ \underline{\times\ 1{,}000} \\ 23{,}000 \end{array}$$

Directions: Use the information above to help solve the multiplication problems below.

1. $\begin{array}{r}35\\ \underline{\times\ 10}\end{array}$	**2.** $\begin{array}{r}65\\ \underline{\times\ 10}\end{array}$	**3.** $\begin{array}{r}38\\ \underline{\times\ 10}\end{array}$	**4.** $\begin{array}{r}94\\ \underline{\times\ 10}\end{array}$
5. $\begin{array}{r}99\\ \underline{\times\ 10}\end{array}$	**6.** $\begin{array}{r}77\\ \underline{\times\ 10}\end{array}$	**7.** $\begin{array}{r}52\\ \underline{\times\ 10}\end{array}$	**8.** $\begin{array}{r}42\\ \underline{\times\ 10}\end{array}$
9. $\begin{array}{r}346\\ \underline{\times\ 100}\end{array}$	**10.** $\begin{array}{r}559\\ \underline{\times\ 100}\end{array}$	**11.** $\begin{array}{r}283\\ \underline{\times\ 100}\end{array}$	**12.** $\begin{array}{r}934\\ \underline{\times\ 100}\end{array}$
13. $\begin{array}{r}59\\ \underline{\times\ 100}\end{array}$	**14.** $\begin{array}{r}76\\ \underline{\times\ 100}\end{array}$	**15.** $\begin{array}{r}72\\ \underline{\times\ 1000}\end{array}$	**16.** $\begin{array}{r}86\\ \underline{\times\ 1000}\end{array}$
17. $\begin{array}{r}329\\ \underline{\times\ 1000}\end{array}$	**18.** $\begin{array}{r}348\\ \underline{\times\ 1000}\end{array}$	**19.** $\begin{array}{r}453\\ \underline{\times\ 1000}\end{array}$	**20.** $\begin{array}{r}987\\ \underline{\times\ 1000}\end{array}$

Multiplying with Two-Digit Multipliers

Facts to Know

To multiply 29 x 37, follow this step-by-step approach.

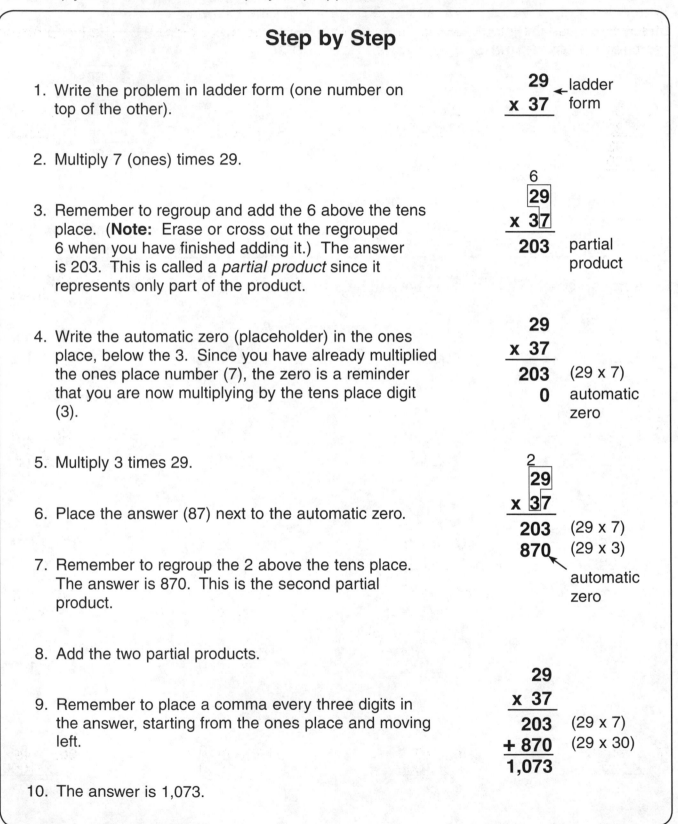

Step by Step

1. Write the problem in ladder form (one number on top of the other).

2. Multiply 7 (ones) times 29.

3. Remember to regroup and add the 6 above the tens place. (**Note:** Erase or cross out the regrouped 6 when you have finished adding it.) The answer is 203. This is called a *partial product* since it represents only part of the product.

4. Write the automatic zero (placeholder) in the ones place, below the 3. Since you have already multiplied the ones place number (7), the zero is a reminder that you are now multiplying by the tens place digit (3).

5. Multiply 3 times 29.

6. Place the answer (87) next to the automatic zero.

7. Remember to regroup the 2 above the tens place. The answer is 870. This is the second partial product.

8. Add the two partial products.

9. Remember to place a comma every three digits in the answer, starting from the ones place and moving left.

10. The answer is 1,073.

Using Two-Digit Multipliers with Two-Digit Multiplicands

Directions: Use the information on page 86 to help you do these problems. The first problem has been started for you.

```
1.    31          2.    24          3.    53          4.    12
    x 33              x 21              x 32              x 14
    ----              ----              ----              ----
      93
  + 930
  ------
```

```
5.    53          6.    63          7.    23          8.    41
    x 23              x 31              x 42              x 23
    ----              ----              ----              ----
```

```
9.    75         10.    45         11.    85         12.    99
    x 44              x 29              x 33              x 27
    ----              ----              ----              ----
```

```
13.    74        14.    27         15.    56         16.    56
     x 34              x 65              x 86              x 37
     ----              ----              ----              ----
```

```
17.    94        18.    87         19.    66         20.    49
     x 26              x 37              x 87              x 52
     ----              ----              ----              ----
```

Math

Multiplication Mystery Puzzle

Directions: Solve the multiplication problems and match the answer to the corresponding letter to solve the mystery.

What did the children discover in the rabbit hutch?

1. ☐
250
x 12

2. ☐
45
x 19

3. ☐
275
x 15

4. ☐
63
x 8

5. ☐
57
x 6

6. ☐
90
x 20

7. ☐
165
x 25

8. ☐
36
x 14

9. ☐
100
x 30

10. ☐
450
x 23

11. ☐
62
x 78

12. ☐
33
x 3

13. ☐
11
x 9

14. ☐
100
x 18

15. ☐
18
x 19

16. ☐
300
x 10

17. ☐
63
x 3

18. ☐
33
x 36

19. ☐
150
x 20

20. ☐
38
x 9

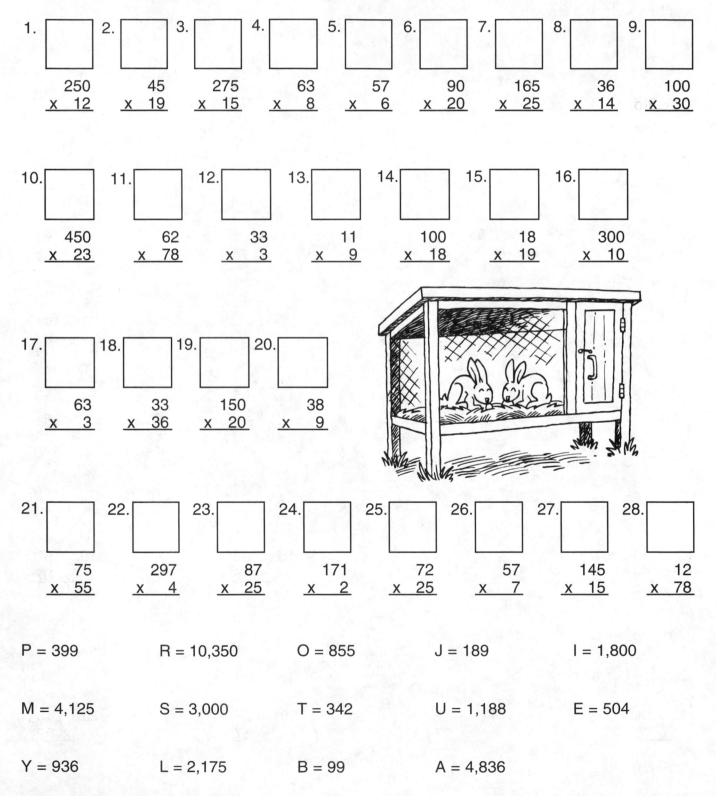

21. ☐
75
x 55

22. ☐
297
x 4

23. ☐
87
x 25

24. ☐
171
x 2

25. ☐
72
x 25

26. ☐
57
x 7

27. ☐
145
x 15

28. ☐
12
x 78

P = 399   R = 10,350   O = 855   J = 189   I = 1,800

M = 4,125   S = 3,000   T = 342   U = 1,188   E = 504

Y = 936   L = 2,175   B = 99   A = 4,836

Easy Mental Multiplication

- To multiply by 2—think double.
- To multiply by 5—multiply by 10 and divide by 2.
- To multiply by 9—multiply by 10 and subtract the multiplicand.
- To multiply by 25—multiply by 100 and divide by 4.
- To multiply by 50—multiply by 100 and divide by 2.

Directions: Use the information in the chart to help solve these problems.

1. 416
   x 2

2. 540
   x 2

3. 350
   x 2

4. 480
   x 2

5. 461
   x 2

6. 230
   x 5

7. 460
   x 5

8. 351
   x 5

9. 840
   x 5

10. 580
    x 5

11. 38
    x 50

12. 67
    x 50

13. 68
    x 50

14. 78
    x 50

15. 44
    x 50

16. 62
    x 25

17. 48
    x 25

18. 92
    x 25

19. 24
    x 25

20. 82
    x 25

21. 21
    x 9

22. 32
    x 9

23. 62
    x 9

24. 43
    x 9

25. 56
    x 9

Checking Multiplication Using Various Techniques

Multiplication can be checked by reversing factors or by division.

$$
\begin{array}{r} 25 \\ \times\ 12 \\ \hline 50 \\ +\ 250 \\ \hline 300 \end{array}
\qquad
\underset{\text{the factors}}{\text{reverse}} \longrightarrow
\qquad
\begin{array}{r} 12 \\ \times\ 25 \\ \hline 60 \\ +\ 240 \\ \hline 300 \end{array}
\qquad
\underset{\text{division}}{\text{use}} \longrightarrow
\qquad
12\overline{)300}
$$

$$
\begin{array}{r}
25 \\
12\overline{)300} \\
24\ \downarrow \\
\hline
60 \\
60 \\
\hline
0
\end{array}
$$

Directions: Use the information in the example above to check these problems by reversing the factors.

1. $\begin{array}{r} 20 \\ \times\ 30 \\ \hline \end{array}$ $\begin{array}{r} 30 \\ \times\ 20 \\ \hline \end{array}$
2. $\begin{array}{r} 90 \\ \times\ 60 \\ \hline \end{array}$ $\begin{array}{r} 60 \\ \times\ 90 \\ \hline \end{array}$
3. $\begin{array}{r} 25 \\ \times\ 31 \\ \hline \end{array}$ $\begin{array}{r} 31 \\ \times\ 25 \\ \hline \end{array}$

4. $\begin{array}{r} 35 \\ \times\ 44 \\ \hline \end{array}$ $\begin{array}{r} 44 \\ \times\ 35 \\ \hline \end{array}$
5. $\begin{array}{r} 48 \\ \times\ 69 \\ \hline \end{array}$ $\begin{array}{r} 69 \\ \times\ 48 \\ \hline \end{array}$
6. $\begin{array}{r} 87 \\ \times\ 32 \\ \hline \end{array}$ $\begin{array}{r} 32 \\ \times\ 87 \\ \hline \end{array}$

Directions: Use the information in the example above to check these problems by using division.

7. $\begin{array}{r} 50 \\ \times\ 90 \\ \hline \end{array}$ $50\overline{)}$
8. $\begin{array}{r} 25 \\ \times\ 15 \\ \hline \end{array}$ $25\overline{)}$
9. $\begin{array}{r} 34 \\ \times\ 22 \\ \hline \end{array}$ $34\overline{)}$

10. $\begin{array}{r} 23 \\ \times\ 41 \\ \hline \end{array}$ $23\overline{)}$
11. $\begin{array}{r} 21 \\ \times\ 48 \\ \hline \end{array}$ $21\overline{)}$
12. $\begin{array}{r} 39 \\ \times\ 41 \\ \hline \end{array}$ $39\overline{)}$

90

Multiplication Workout

Directions: Work out the multiplication problems to find out the name of the founder of the Red Cross.

1. 610
   x 6

2. 523
   x 4

3. 202
   x 3

4. 500
   x 7

5. 943
   x 3

6. 815
   x 2

7. 724
   x 4

8. 718
   x 5

9. 202
   x 7

10. 635
    x 3

11. 955
    x 2

Circle the correct answer:

1.   3150—B
       3006—D
       3660—C

2.   2092—L
       2641—D
       2091—A

3.   636—E
       606—A
       646—I

4.   3501—N
       365—T
       3500—R

5.   2829—A
       2824—B
       2823—C

6.   1638—M
       1630—B
       1646—T

7.   2894—R
       2896—A
       2866—E

8.   3780—W
       3590—R
       3750—X

9.   1614—S
       1444—L
       1414—T

10.   1905—O
       1901—U
       2005—T

11.   1905—P
       1920—M
       1910—N

Answer:

___ ___ ___ ___ ___
 1   2   3   4   5

___ ___ ___ ___ ___ ___
 6   7   8   9 10 11

Using the Multiplication Chart for Division

The multiplication chart shown here can be used to find any basic multiplication or division fact until you have learned them all.

One of the best ways to learn the facts is to practice using the chart.

Rows	Columns											
	1	**2**	**3**	**4**	**5**	**6**	**7**	**8**	**9**	**10**	**11**	**12**
1	1	2	3	4	5	6	7	8	9	10	11	12
2	2	4	6	8	10	12	14	16	18	20	22	24
3	3	6	9	12	15	18	21	24	27	30	33	36
4	4	8	12	16	20	24	28	32	36	40	44	48
5	5	10	15	20	25	30	35	40	45	50	55	60
6	6	12	18	24	30	36	42	48	54	60	66	72
7	7	14	21	28	35	42	49	56	63	70	77	84
8	8	16	24	32	40	48	56	64	72	80	88	96
9	9	18	27	36	45	54	63	72	81	90	99	108
10	10	20	30	40	50	60	70	80	90	100	110	120
11	11	22	33	44	55	66	77	88	99	110	121	132
12	12	24	36	48	60	72	84	96	108	120	132	144

Read across for the rows.

Read up or down for the columns.

Note: To find how many times 9 divides into 54, run one finger across the 9 row until you come to 54, then run a finger up the column with 54, then you come to the top number which is 6. The answer is that 9 divides into 54 exactly 6 times.

Directions:
Use the rows on the multiplication chart to help you find the missing numbers. (Go backwards.)

1. (84, 77, 70, 63, 56, 49, _____, _____, _____, _____, _____, _____)
2. (48, 44, 40, 36, 32, _____, _____, _____, _____, _____, _____, _____)
3. (24, 22, _____, 18, _____, 14, _____, _____, _____, _____, _____, _____)
4. (36, 33, 30, 27, _____, 21, _____, _____, _____, _____, _____, _____)
5. (144, 132, 120, 108, _____, 84, _____, _____, _____, _____, _____, _____)
6. (120, 110, _____, 90, 80, _____, 60, _____, 40, _____, _____, _____)
7. (72, 66, 60, _____, 48, _____, _____, _____, _____, _____, _____, _____)
8. Which row has a zero in every number? _____

92

Division Facts/Mixed Practice

Directions: Do these problems. Use your multiplication/division chart if you are unsure of your division facts.

1. $9\overline{)27}$ 2. $5\overline{)45}$ 3. $12\overline{)60}$ 4. $8\overline{)40}$

5. $12\overline{)48}$ 6. $12\overline{)144}$ 7. $9\overline{)54}$ 8. $4\overline{)12}$

9. $3\overline{)36}$ 10. $9\overline{)63}$ 11. $7\overline{)70}$ 12. $8\overline{)48}$

13. $2\overline{)18}$ 14. $12\overline{)84}$ 15. $6\overline{)66}$ 16. $11\overline{)132}$

17. $7\overline{)28}$ 18. $8\overline{)72}$ 19. $12\overline{)108}$ 20. $5\overline{)35}$

21. $6\overline{)24}$ 22. $12\overline{)96}$ 23. $9\overline{)45}$ 24. $7\overline{)84}$

25. $9\overline{)81}$ 26. $7\overline{)49}$ 27. $8\overline{)56}$ 28. $12\overline{)36}$

Three-digit Dividends/No Remainders

Directions: Do these problems. Use your multiplication/division chart if you are unsure of your division facts. The first two are done for you.

1.
$$
\begin{array}{r}
41 \\
4\overline{)164} \\
-16 \\
\hline
4 \\
-4 \\
\hline
0
\end{array}
$$

2.
$$
\begin{array}{r}
35 \\
5\overline{)175} \\
-15 \\
\hline
25 \\
-25 \\
\hline
0
\end{array}
$$

3. $6\overline{)282}$

4. $8\overline{)336}$

5. $7\overline{)637}$

6. $7\overline{)504}$

7. $6\overline{)486}$

8. $3\overline{)165}$

9. $8\overline{)648}$

10. $9\overline{)189}$

11. $7\overline{)651}$

12. $9\overline{)396}$

13. $7\overline{)553}$

14. $9\overline{)441}$

15. $5\overline{)295}$

16. $3\overline{)324}$

17. $4\overline{)196}$

18. $5\overline{)785}$

19. $7\overline{)483}$

20. $9\overline{)891}$

21. $7\overline{)441}$

22. $6\overline{)294}$

23. $8\overline{)776}$

24. $3\overline{)195}$

94

Three-digit Dividends/With Remainders

Directions: Do these problems. Use your multiplication/division chart if you are unsure of your division facts. The first two are done for you.

1.
$$
\begin{array}{r}
206\ \text{R1} \\
4\overline{)825} \\
-8 \\
\hline
25 \\
-24 \\
\hline
1
\end{array}
$$

2.
$$
\begin{array}{r}
49\ \text{R2} \\
5\overline{)247} \\
-20 \\
\hline
47 \\
-45 \\
\hline
2
\end{array}
$$

3. $6\overline{)259}$

4. $6\overline{)719}$

5. $5\overline{)827}$

6. $9\overline{)662}$

7. $8\overline{)205}$

8. $7\overline{)367}$

9. $9\overline{)179}$

10. $4\overline{)913}$

11. $3\overline{)806}$

12. $9\overline{)827}$

13. $5\overline{)814}$

14. $9\overline{)719}$

15. $7\overline{)929}$

16. $2\overline{)951}$

17. $6\overline{)617}$

18. $7\overline{)634}$

Dividing with 25

Helpful Hint: When dividing by 25, think quarters.

Example: 25$\overline{)78}$

Think: How many quarters could you have in 78 cents?

Answer: 3 quarters and 3 cents left over.

$$\begin{array}{r} 3\text{ R3} \\ 25\overline{)78} \\ -75 \\ \hline 3 \end{array}$$

Directions: Do these problems. Use your multiplication/division chart if you are unsure of your division facts. The first one is done for you.

1. $\begin{array}{r} 7\text{ R20} \\ 25\overline{)195} \\ -175 \\ \hline 20 \end{array}$

2. 25$\overline{)149}$

3. 25$\overline{)214}$

4. 25$\overline{)246}$

5. 25$\overline{)527}$

6. 25$\overline{)384}$

7. 25$\overline{)459}$

8. 25$\overline{)669}$

9. 25$\overline{)288}$

10. 25$\overline{)786}$

11. 25$\overline{)655}$

12. 25$\overline{)923}$

13. 25$\overline{)4829}$

14. 25$\overline{)5665}$

15. 25$\overline{)7788}$

16. 25$\overline{)9729}$

No Leftovers

Divisibility by 2, 5, and 25

Remember the following rules:

- Any even number can be divided evenly by 2 with no remainder.
- Any number ending in 5 or 0 can be divided evenly by 5.
- Any number ending in 25, 50, 75, or 00 can be divided evenly by 25.

Directions: Do these problems. Use your multiplication/division chart if you are unsure of your division facts. The first one is done for you.

1.
$$\begin{array}{r} 161 \\ 2\overline{)322} \\ -2 \\ \hline 12 \\ -12 \\ \hline 02 \end{array}$$

2. $2\overline{)886}$

3. $2\overline{)968}$

4. $2\overline{)1,200}$

5. $2\overline{)8,884}$

6. $2\overline{)10,636}$

7. $5\overline{)85}$

8. $5\overline{)560}$

9. $5\overline{)965}$

10. $5\overline{)1,000}$

11. $5\overline{)2,125}$

12. $5\overline{)6,570}$

13. $5\overline{)9,855}$

14. $5\overline{)10,760}$

15. $5\overline{)20,400}$

16. $25\overline{)125}$

17. $25\overline{)775}$

18. $25\overline{)950}$

19. $25\overline{)1,000}$

20. $25\overline{)4,950}$

21. $25\overline{)10,525}$

Division Mix-Up

The top boxes contain division problems, and the bottom ones contain the answers. Work each problem and find its answer in the bottom boxes. Then, write the word from the problem box into the correct answer box. Your result will be a funny saying!

Problems

926 ÷ 4 **a**	473 ÷ 6 **optometrist**	416 ÷ 9 **made**	493 ÷ 7 **and**
1,729 ÷ 8 **of**	3,414 ÷ 5 **herself**	4,121 ÷ 3 **into**	3,210 ÷ 4 **fell**
2,057 ÷ 3 **lens grinder**	3,002 ÷ 6 **The**	2,751 ÷ 8 **spectacle**	5,605 ÷ 7 **the**

Answers

500 (r2)	78 (r5)	802 (r2)	1373 (r2)
800 (r5)	685 (r2)	70 (r3)	46 (r2)
231 (r2)	343 (r7)	216 (r1)	682 (r4)

I've Been Framed!

Each number in the large grids below is written within a smaller different shape or frame. Using this as a guide, write the correct number in each shape below and solve each problem.

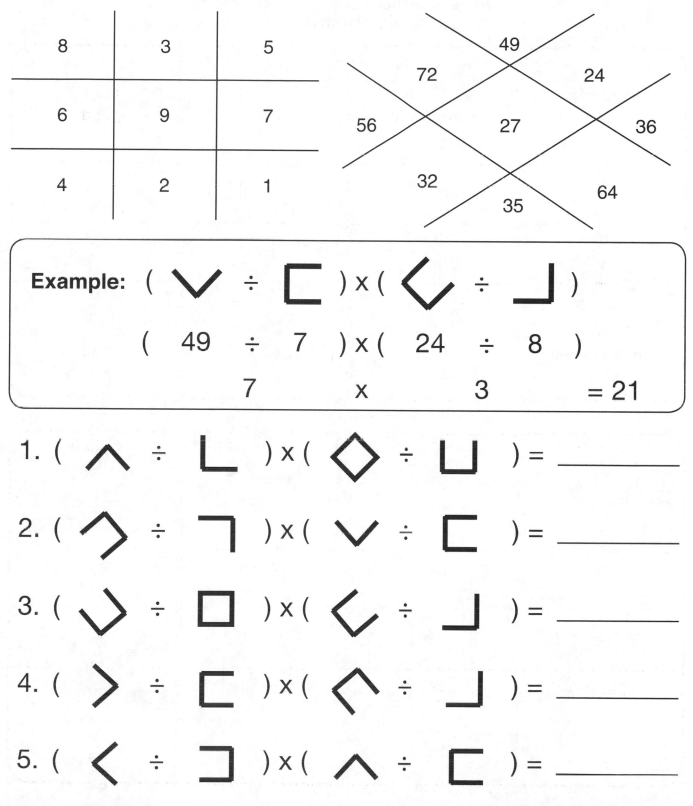

8	3	5
6	9	7
4	2	1

49   72   24   56   27   36   32   35   64

Example: (∨ ÷ ⊏) x (⟨ ÷ ⌟)

(49 ÷ 7) x (24 ÷ 8)

7   x   3   = 21

1. (∧ ÷ ∟) x (◇ ÷ ⊔) = _____

2. (⟩ ÷ ⌐) x (∨ ÷ ⊏) = _____

3. (⟍ ÷ ▢) x (⟨ ÷ ⌟) = _____

4. (⟩ ÷ ⊏) x (⟨ ÷ ⌟) = _____

5. (⟨ ÷ ⌟) x (∧ ÷ ⊏) = _____

Fractions: Numerators and Denominators

A **fraction** is a number that names part of a whole thing. The **numerator** is the number on the top and tells how many parts are being referred to. The **denominator** is the bottom number and shows how many equal parts there are in all. Write what fraction of each shape is shaded. The first one is done for you.

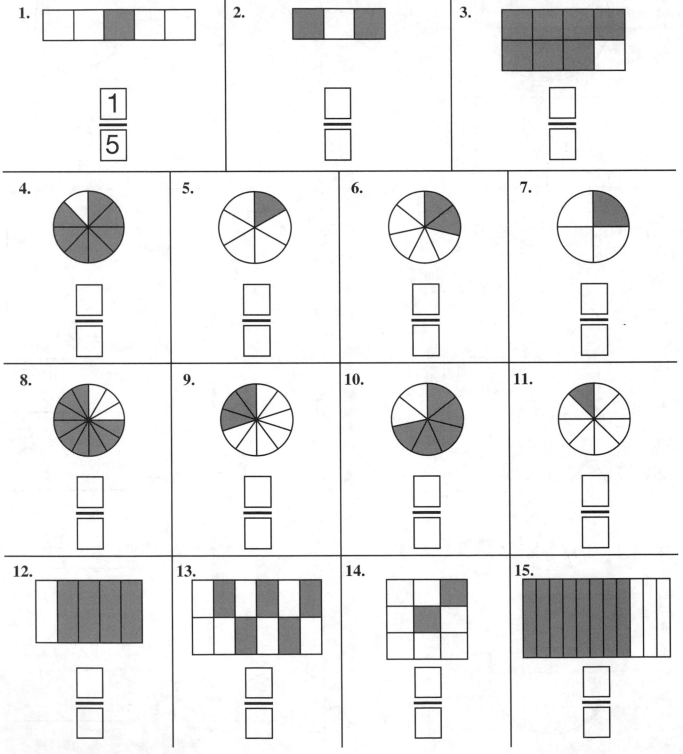

Circle Fractions

Directions: Write the fraction for the unmarked section in each circle below. Reduce each fraction to its simplest form.

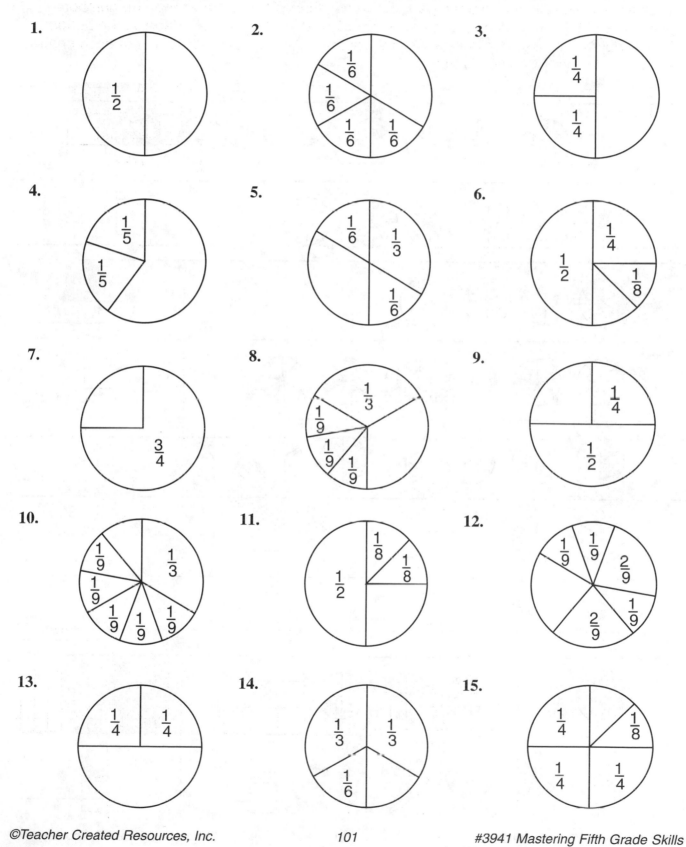

Mixed Fractions

Directions: A mixed fraction contains both a whole number and a fraction. Write the mixed fraction for the shaded areas below. Reduce each fraction to its simplest form. The first one has been done for you.

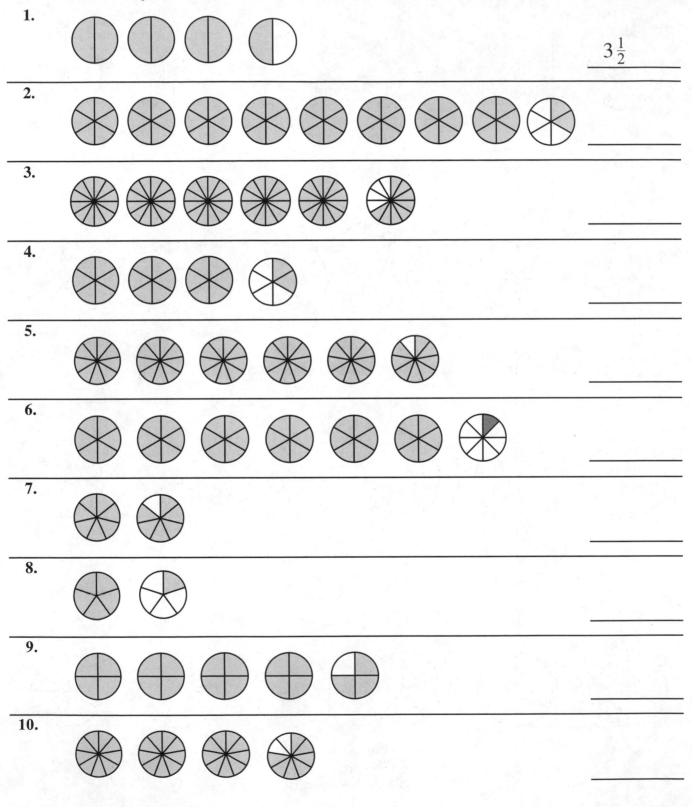

1. $3\frac{1}{2}$

2.

3.

4.

5.

6.

7.

8.

9.

10.

Comparing Fractions

Directions: Shade each circle to show the fraction. Then write a **>, <**, or **=** to make each equation correct. The first one has been done for you.

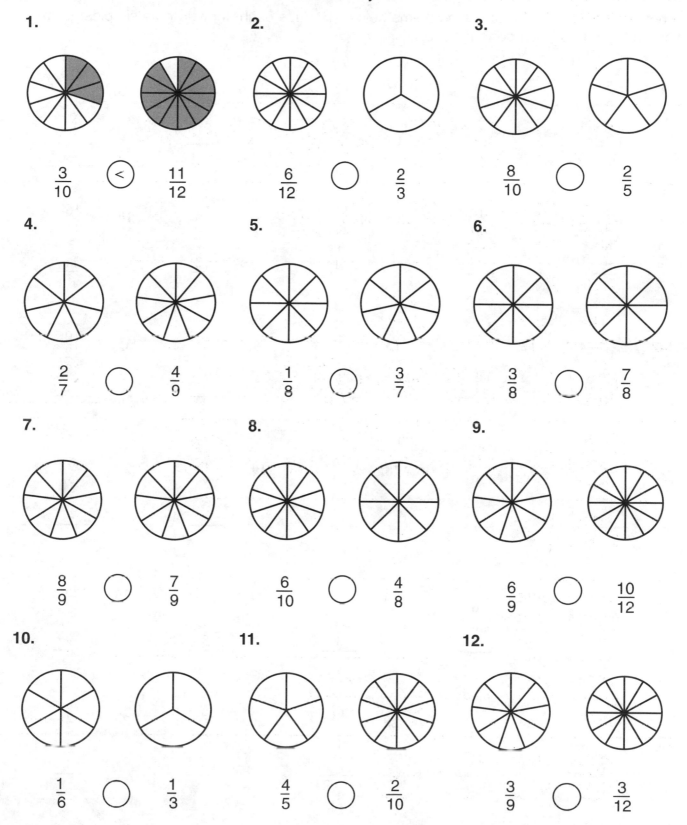

1.

$$\frac{3}{10} \quad < \quad \frac{11}{12}$$

2.

$$\frac{6}{12} \quad \bigcirc \quad \frac{2}{3}$$

3.

$$\frac{8}{10} \quad \bigcirc \quad \frac{2}{5}$$

4.

$$\frac{2}{7} \quad \bigcirc \quad \frac{4}{9}$$

5.

$$\frac{1}{8} \quad \bigcirc \quad \frac{3}{7}$$

6.

$$\frac{3}{8} \quad \bigcirc \quad \frac{7}{8}$$

7.

$$\frac{8}{9} \quad \bigcirc \quad \frac{7}{9}$$

8.

$$\frac{6}{10} \quad \bigcirc \quad \frac{4}{8}$$

9.

$$\frac{6}{9} \quad \bigcirc \quad \frac{10}{12}$$

10.

$$\frac{1}{6} \quad \bigcirc \quad \frac{1}{3}$$

11.

$$\frac{4}{5} \quad \bigcirc \quad \frac{2}{10}$$

12.

$$\frac{3}{9} \quad \bigcirc \quad \frac{3}{12}$$

Adding and Subtracting Improper Fractions

Directions: Solve each of the problems below. Reduce each answer to its simplest form. The first one has been done for you.

1. $\dfrac{5}{6}$
$+\dfrac{8}{6}$
$\dfrac{13}{6} = 2\dfrac{1}{6}$

2. $\dfrac{6}{3}$
$-\dfrac{2}{3}$

3. $\dfrac{15}{12}$
$+\dfrac{6}{12}$

4. $\dfrac{10}{5}$
$-\dfrac{2}{5}$

5. $\dfrac{11}{9}$
$+\dfrac{9}{9}$

6. $\dfrac{14}{9}$
$-\dfrac{6}{9}$

7. $\dfrac{14}{11}$
$+\dfrac{4}{11}$

8. $\dfrac{17}{11}$
$-\dfrac{6}{11}$

9. $\dfrac{15}{12}$
$-\dfrac{4}{12}$

10. $\dfrac{16}{11}$
$+\dfrac{2}{11}$

11. $\dfrac{15}{12}$
$+\dfrac{9}{12}$

12. $\dfrac{9}{8}$
$+\dfrac{6}{8}$

13. $\dfrac{8}{7}$
$-\dfrac{4}{7}$

14. $\dfrac{9}{6}$
$-\dfrac{4}{6}$

15. $\dfrac{10}{12}$
$+\dfrac{13}{12}$

16. $\dfrac{19}{12}$
$+\dfrac{7}{12}$

17. $\dfrac{13}{9}$
$+\dfrac{8}{9}$

18. $\dfrac{12}{10}$
$+\dfrac{6}{10}$

19. $\dfrac{7}{4}$
$-\dfrac{2}{4}$

20. $\dfrac{6}{5}$
$-\dfrac{3}{5}$

21. $\dfrac{9}{5}$
$+\dfrac{3}{5}$

22. $\dfrac{10}{6}$
$-\dfrac{8}{6}$

23. $\dfrac{7}{3}$
$+\dfrac{11}{3}$

24. $\dfrac{7}{5}$
$-\dfrac{4}{5}$

25. $\dfrac{11}{9}$
$+\dfrac{10}{9}$

26. $\dfrac{19}{9}$
$-\dfrac{8}{9}$

27. $\dfrac{22}{11}$
$-\dfrac{15}{11}$

28. $\dfrac{13}{9}$
$-\dfrac{8}{9}$

29. $\dfrac{9}{8}$
$+\dfrac{6}{8}$

30. $\dfrac{6}{4}$
$+\dfrac{5}{4}$

104

Finding Decimal Equivalents

Directions: Find the decimal equivalent for each fraction by dividing the numerator by the denominator. Place a decimal point at the end of the denominator to add extra zeros as needed. Then use a calculator to check your work.

Example: $\frac{1}{5} = 1 \div 5 = 5\overline{)1\underset{\cdot}{\uparrow}0}^{0.2}$ $\frac{1}{5} = .2$

1. $\frac{2}{3}$	2. $\frac{2}{4}$	3. $\frac{3}{4}$	4. $\frac{9}{10}$
5. $\frac{2}{5}$	6. $\frac{1}{8}$	7. $\frac{1}{10}$	8. $\frac{1}{12}$
9. $\frac{4}{5}$	10. $\frac{1}{3}$	11. $\frac{1}{9}$	12. $\frac{1}{6}$
13. $\frac{5}{6}$	14. $\frac{3}{10}$	15. $\frac{1}{7}$	16. $\frac{5}{10}$
17. $\frac{3}{7}$	18. $\frac{1}{4}$	19. $\frac{3}{5}$	20. $\frac{6}{11}$

Dynamic Decimals

Facts and Reminders

Decimal Values

The single most important fact you must remember when dealing with decimals is that everything to the right of the decimal point has a value less than the whole number 1. Look at the examples. Everything below has a value less than 1.

0.5	0.23	0.487	0.67899654

It often helps to think of money as a comparison. Anything to the right of the decimal point is worth less than a single dollar.

$3.25	$0.34	$5.19	$300.03

Also, remember that any number without a visible decimal point has the decimal point at the end of the number.

234 = 234.0	2 = 2.0	98,654 = 98,654.0

Place Value for Decimals

The numbers to the right of the decimal follow this order:

tenths	0.1
hundredths	0.12
thousandths	0.123
ten thousandths	0.1234
hundred thousandths	0.12345
millionths	0.123456

The farther a digit is to the right of the decimal point, the less value it has.

0.2 is greater than 0.02
0.05 is greater than 0.005
0.27 is greater than 0.2698 (6 is less than 7)
0.009 is greater than 0.008999 (8 is less than 9)

Addition and Subtraction of Decimals

When adding decimals, line up the decimal points above one another. Insert zeros, where needed, as placeholders in the decimal and then add.

23.45 + 3.789 =

$$\begin{array}{r} 23.450 \\ + \ 3.789 \\ \hline 27.239 \end{array}$$

When subtracting decimals, place the number with the higher value on top and line up the decimal points above one another. Insert zeros, where needed, as placeholders in the decimal and then subtract.

43.9 − 2.7654 =

$$\begin{array}{r} 43.9000 \\ - \ 2.7654 \\ \hline 41.1346 \end{array}$$

Dynamic Decimals *(cont.)*

Remember the following information:

- Everything to the right of the decimal point has a value less than the whole number 1. All of the examples below have a value less than 1.

  0.27   0.0096   0.95215

- Any number without a visible decimal point has the decimal point at the end of the number.

  12 = 12.0   148 = 148.0   3,546 = 3,546.0

- The farther a digit is to the right of the decimal point, the less value it has.

  0.1 is greater than 0.01   0.004 is greater than 0.0034

Directions: Study the Facts and Reminders page on 106. Circle the number that has a greater value in each pair of decimals. The first one is done for you.

1. (0.345)
   0.3445

2. 0.211
   0.2111

3. 0.456
   0.4563

4. 0.08
   0.008

5. 0.6512
   0.5612

6. 0.098
   0.09788

7. 0.111
   0.11

8. 0.7612
   0.761

9. 0.005
   0.004987

10. 0.3009
    0.3018

11. 0.445
    0.454

12. 0.1207
    0.2107

Directions: Organize each set of decimals from greatest to least. The first one is started for you.

13. 1.6453 ___21.532___
     21.532 _____
     0.0076 _____
     0.6521 _____
     3.9854 __0.0076__

14. 0.96435 _____
     54.942 _____
     0.02 _____
     1.23 _____
     0.0023 _____

15. 0.7812 _____
     0.77982 _____
     4.86314 _____
     4.8632 _____
     32.1 _____

16. 0.006321 _____
     0.013751 _____
     0.0932 _____
     0.02632 _____
     0.021001 _____

Changing Fractions to Decimals and Decimals to Percents

- To change a fraction to a decimal, divide the numerator by the denominator.
- To change a decimal to a percentage, multiply the decimal by 100.

Directions: Complete the chart below. Write each decimal answer to the hundredths place, two places to the right of the decimal point.

Fraction	Decimal	Percent
1. $\frac{1}{2}$	$1 \div 2 = .50$	$.50 \times 100 = 50\%$
2. $\frac{1}{3}$		
3. $\frac{2}{3}$		
4. $\frac{1}{4}$		
5. $\frac{3}{4}$		
6. $\frac{1}{5}$		
7. $\frac{2}{5}$		
8. $\frac{3}{5}$		
9. $\frac{4}{5}$		
10. $\frac{1}{6}$		
11.. $\frac{5}{6}$		
12. $\frac{1}{8}$		
13. $\frac{5}{8}$		
14. $\frac{7}{8}$		
15. $\frac{1}{9}$		

Simple Word Problems with Fractions and Decimals

Bake Sale

Lauren had 4 cakes to sell at the school bake sale. "I'm going to cut these in half," she thought, "in case someone only wants half."

1. If someone wants a whole cake, how many halves will Lauren sell to the person? _____

2. How many half cakes can Lauren make out of 4 whole cakes? _____

3. Holly sold $\frac{1}{4}$ of a pie to each person who wanted a piece. She had 8 pies and they all were sold. How many people bought pieces of pie? _____

Dollars and Sense

4. There's a sale at the local grocery store.

Tomato Soup 7 cans for $0.56	Sugar 5 pounds for $0.45

How much does 1 can of tomato soup cost? _____ How much does 1 pound of sugar cost? _____

5. The Najera family ate at Heartland Café and the bill was $23.48 for four. They all ordered the same thing! What was the cost of each person's meal? _____

6. Lupe loves to garden. She paid $143.78 for a tree, $53.67 for tulip bulbs, $17.09 for tomato plants, and $11.34 for a bag of grass seed. How much did she spend in all? _____

7. Lauren's dad went on a canoe trip. He spent $37.34 on gas, $264.77 on canoe rental, $127.45 on food, $189.34 on a new sleeping bag, and $47.12 on souvenirs. How much did the trip cost? _____

8. Jessica needs 12 meters of ribbon to make 9 ties. Ribbon costs $0.89 a meter. How much change does she receive from her $20 bill? _____

9. Carson raised $1.85 per kilometer in a charity run. If she ran 20.5 kilometers, how much money did she raise? (Round to nearest hundredth). _____

Lunch!

10. How many servings of $\frac{1}{2}$ a cantaloupe can you make from 2 cantaloupes? _____ from 3 cantaloupes? _____

11. Gabriel had 3 cookies. He gave David $\frac{1}{2}$ of a cookie. How many cookies does Gabriel have left? _____

Simple Word Problems with Fractions and Percents

Directions: Solve the word problems below.

1. The Lincoln Way cheerleaders in Frankfort raised $1,000.00 during the school year.

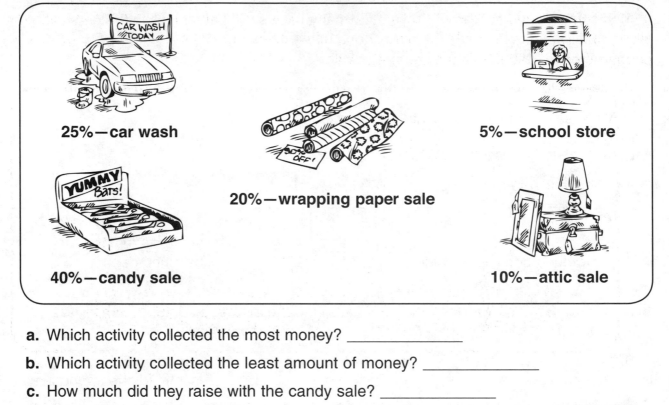

25%—car wash

20%—wrapping paper sale

5%—school store

40%—candy sale

10%—attic sale

    a. Which activity collected the most money? _____

    b. Which activity collected the least amount of money? _____

    c. How much did they raise with the candy sale? _____

    d. How much money did they raise with the car wash? _____

    e. How much money did they raise at the school store? _____

2. Mrs. Anderson's Girl Scout troop has $600 in savings. The girls collected 50% of the money by recycling aluminum cans. Fifteen percent of the money came from donations and 35% of it came from their annual auction. How much money was raised by selling cans, donations, and by having an auction? _____

3. Your purchases total $24.95. If the sales tax rate is 6%, what is the total amount that you must pay? (Round to the nearest penny.) _____

4. Art walked $1\frac{1}{4}$ miles Monday, $2\frac{3}{4}$ miles Tuesday, and $1\frac{1}{2}$ miles Wednesday. How many miles did he walk? _____

5. Andrew's dad drove 60 miles per hour to get to the amusement park. It took them 1 hour and 20 minutes. How many miles is it to the amusement park? _____

Using Fractions, Decimals, and Percents to Show Probability

Hal has gone fishing for the day. There are 7 carp (non-edible), 9 mackerel, 38 trout, and 46 catfish in the lake. Assume that he catches one fish at random. While he is fishing, his son Peter goes diving for lost treasures. He reaches into the treasure chest and randomly chooses a coin. In the treasure chest, there are 16 tin, 12 titanium, 10 bronze, 8 copper, 3 silver, and 1 gold coin. Only the gold and titanium coins are still shiny. Only the gold, silver, copper, bronze, and titanium coins are valuable.

Directions: Use the information above to show the probability as a fraction, decimal, and percent. The first one is done for you.

	Fraction	Decimal	Percent
1. Hal catches a catfish.	$\frac{46}{100}$	.46	46%
2. Hal catches a non-edible fish.			
3. Hal catches a two-syllable fish.			
4. Peter selects the gold coin.			
5. Peter selects a valuable coin.			
6. Peter selects a copper coin.			

7. Which fish is Hal least likely to catch? _____

8. Which coin is Peter most likely to grab? _____

Solving Money Problems with Decimals

Directions: Figure out the shell game. Guess which coins are under the shells. There is only one coin under each shell. The coin can be a penny, nickel, dime, or quarter. The first one has been done for you as an example.

1. __25¢__   __1¢__   = $.26

2. _____ _____ _____ _____ = $.22

3. _____ _____ _____ = $.35

4. _____ _____ _____ _____ = $.31

5. _____ _____ _____ _____ _____ _____ = $.51

6. _____ _____ _____ _____ _____ = $.85

Directions: Add.

7.
```
  $435.00
+ $921.00
_____
```

8.
```
  $8.21
+ $6.30
_____
```

9.
```
  $25,941.00
+  $6,037.00
_____
```

10.
```
  $9.75
+ $32.94
_____
```

11.
```
    $421.00
+ $6,382.00
_____
```

12.
```
  $6,931.00
+ $7,482.00
_____
```

13.
```
  $74.30
   $8.65
   $2.50
_____
```

14.
```
  $84.52
   $7.34
_____
```

15.
```
    $625.00
  $8,401.00
+    $73.00
_____
```

                   ©Teacher Created Resources, Inc.

In the Money

Directions: List the dollars and coins you would give each person below to make each amount listed. A sample has been done for you. Draw a picture, if needed, to show the money each person has.

1. $5—Brian has 4 dollars and 15 coins.   <u>4 dollars, 5 dimes, ten nickels</u>

2. $4—Lynda has 7 coins and 3 dollars.   _____

3. $10—Derek has 9 dollars and 19 coins.   _____

4. $6—Melyssa has 5 dollars and 25 coins.   _____

5. $4—Laura has 16 coins and 3 dollars.   _____

6. $15—Branden has 14 dollars and 6 coins.   _____

7. $21—Garett has 10 coins and a 20 dollar bill   _____

8. $13—Sean has 1 coin and 12 dollars.   _____

9. $15—Cade has 14 dollars and 17 coins.   _____

10. $5—Brittany has 4 dollars and 28 coins.   _____

Using Basic Math Operations in Money Problems

Directions: Solve the money problems below using the four operations—addition, subtraction, multiplication, and division.

Bob's Birdhouse Boutique just opened and here's how sales are going.

1. Bob sold 385 hanging seed feeders at $7.99 each. How much money did he make?
   _____

2. Last month, Bob made $533.61 on sales of 49 miniature birdbaths. How much did he charge for each one? _____

3. Bob earned $987.34 on birdhouse kits and $1,278.00 on feeders in April and May. How much did he earn? _____

4. Bob has a new product in—a birdhouse kid's bank for $6.39. He sold 298 of them. How much did he make? _____

5. Bob received $657.57 for sales of wild birdseed and $1,765.01 for sales of hummingbird feeders. How much more did he make on hummingbird feeders? _____

6. He sold 98 wind socks with pictures of birds on them at $11.85 each. How much money did he earn? _____

7. He sold 68 framed pictures of owls for a total of $930.92. How much did he charge for each picture? _____

8. Bob sells seeds for wildflower gardens that attract birds. He made $3,642.03 in a month selling bags of seeds at $9.87 each. How many bags did he sell? _____

Using Basic Math Operations in Money Problems (cont.)

Directions: Harold of Harold's Hardware sells boxes of nails, screws, fasteners, and other small items. He's getting tired, though, of people asking, "How much is just one?" So he made this sign. Figure out the price per unit (@ means "at").

Harold's Hardware Price List

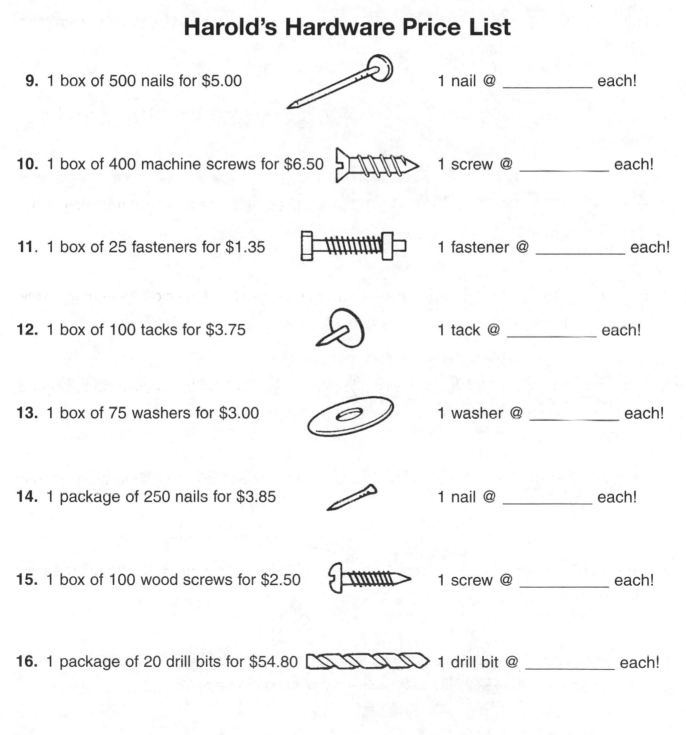

9. 1 box of 500 nails for $5.00   1 nail @ _____ each!

10. 1 box of 400 machine screws for $6.50   1 screw @ _____ each!

11. 1 box of 25 fasteners for $1.35   1 fastener @ _____ each!

12. 1 box of 100 tacks for $3.75   1 tack @ _____ each!

13. 1 box of 75 washers for $3.00   1 washer @ _____ each!

14. 1 package of 250 nails for $3.85   1 nail @ _____ each!

15. 1 box of 100 wood screws for $2.50   1 screw @ _____ each!

16. 1 package of 20 drill bits for $54.80   1 drill bit @ _____ each!

Solving Problems Involving Discounts and Sales

Directions: You have been assigned to a special TV news investigations unit looking into "Big Bill's Warehouse of Sales." Big Bill claims that everything he has is on sale and that every purchase of a sale item saves customers money. Is he telling the truth?

1. Gutter World charged Big Bill $3.67 each for 298 aluminum downspouts. He sold them all for $9.09 each "on sale," he said. How much profit did he make? _____

2. Mrs. Green wanted to buy tulip bulbs from Big Bill for $3.67 each. "You can have a dozen, little lady, for $44.00." How much did Mrs. Green save? _____

3. A man purchased 180 used hamster wheels for his new invention at $.79 each. He handed Big Bill $200 and received $47.80 in change. How much did Big Bill cheat him by? _____

4. Big Bill sold 7,000 plastic squirrels for $3.99 each. He made a $2.00 profit on each one. How much profit did he make on all 7,000 plastic squirrels? _____

5. Big Bill charged $1.79 more for each birdbath than he had paid. His price was $7.89, and he sold a truckload of 3,500 to the forest preserve district. How much extra money did he get? _____

6. Big Bill sold 4,328 bent weather vanes at $4.99 to the gift shop at the Peotone Airport. His profit was $1.45 on each one. How much money did he make? _____

7. Rick's Hardware, opposite Big Bill's, is offering a 25% off Father's Day sale on a new drill that costs $20. "I have that same drill priced at $22 but with 30% off—so there!" announced Big Bill. Which is the better buy? _____

8. Altogether, Big Bill made a profit of $243,000.00 last year. "I only keep 15% total for myself—that's $27,000.00 and another $24,300.00 for my poor old mother. All the rest goes to charity," he said, wiping a tear from his eye. How much more money than $27,000.00 of his profit did he keep? _____

Money Brain Teasers

Directions: Solve the problems.

1. Price: $3.99

Which is the better deal?

   a. 30% off any cereal

   b. Sale price today only—$2.99

2. Price: $599.00

Which is the better deal?

   a. Save $80.00

   b. $15.00 off, plus another 10% off this canoe only

3. At the Dew Drop Inn, Elmira presented the receipt below to Big Bill. "I got ketchup on it," she apologized. "I can't figure the missing amounts. Can you?"

super salad	$5.99
veggie plate	$8.95
small juice	$1.00
ice cream	$1.25
subtotal	_____
tax (7%)	$1.20
15% tip	_____
TOTAL	$21.15

Working with Money

Directions: Count the money for problems 1 and 2. For problems 3–6, answer the questions.

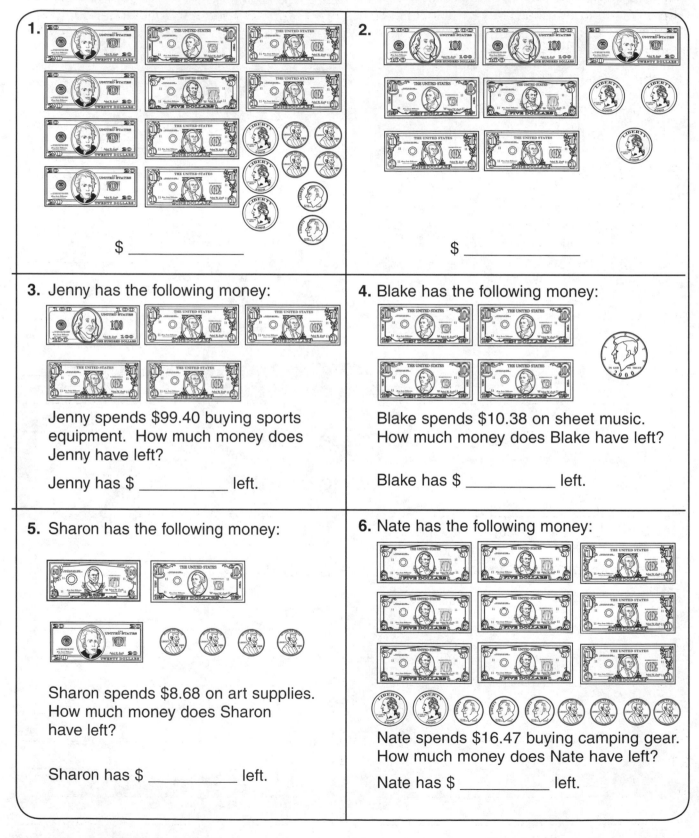

1.

$ _____

2.

$ _____

3. Jenny has the following money:

Jenny spends $99.40 buying sports equipment. How much money does Jenny have left?

Jenny has $ _____ left.

4. Blake has the following money:

Blake spends $10.38 on sheet music. How much money does Blake have left?

Blake has $ _____ left.

5. Sharon has the following money:

Sharon spends $8.68 on art supplies. How much money does Sharon have left?

Sharon has $ _____ left.

6. Nate has the following money:

Nate spends $16.47 buying camping gear. How much money does Nate have left?

Nate has $ _____ left.

Change for a Dollar

Directions: There are more than 200 ways to make change for a dollar. Work with a friend to list as many ways as you can. List the coins in order on each line, from largest to smallest. (**Hint:** Working from large to small coins will help you find more ways to make change, too.) The list has been started for you. If you need more space, continue your list on the back of this paper.

Use the following abbreviations:

hd (half dollar)	**q** (quarter)	**d** (dime)	**n** (nickel)	**p** (penny)

1. 2hd
2. 1hd and 2q
3. 1hd and 5d
4. 1hd and 10n
5.
6.
7.
8.
9.
10.
11.
12.
13.
14.
15.
16.
17.
18.
19.
20.
21.
22.
23.
24.
25.

26.
27.
28.
29.
30.
31.
32.
33.
34.
35.
36.
37.
38.
39.
40.
41.
42.
43.
44.
45.
46.
47.
48.
49.
50.

Money Word Problems

Forty-one Flavors is a popular new ice-cream parlor. Here are some of their prices.

Price List

single scoop	$0.99	regular sundae	$2.50
double scoop	$1.49	large sundae	$3.25
triple scoop	$1.95	super sundae	$4.00
quadruple scoop	$2.39	cola float	$3.50

Directions: Use your skills to solve these word problems.

Remember: All answers involving money must have a dollar sign and a decimal point.

1. Your best friend bought a triple scoop of blackberry ice cream. How much more did it cost than a double scoop? _____

2. The best player on the school basketball team bought a large sundae and a triple scoop of plum nuts ice cream. How much did the player spend altogether? _____

3. The basketball coach bought a regular sundae for all 12 of her players. What was the cost of the 12 sundaes? _____

4. The soccer coach spent $56 on super sundaes. How many super sundaes did she buy?

   _____

5. Your mother paid for a quadruple scoop, a triple scoop, and a double scoop for you and your friends. What was the total cost? _____

6. A third grade teacher bought each of her 20 students a double scoop of ice cream. How much did it cost the teacher? _____

7. Your best friend's mother spent $65 on large sundaes for a birthday party. How many large sundaes did she buy? _____

8. Elaine bought a single scoop, Darlene bought a double scoop, and Jordan bought a quadruple scoop of black 'n blueberry ice cream. How much did they spend in all?

   _____

9. A Girl Scout troop leader bought 18 cola floats for her scouts. How much did she spend?

   _____

10. How much more does it cost for a quadruple scoop than for a double scoop of ice cream?

    _____

Math

More Money Word Problems

The Holey Doughnut is a sweet success. The owner has invented several new types of doughnuts. Help him figure out how much each customer owes.

Price List			
Creamy Dream	$1.99	Doggy Doughnut	$2.49
Juicy Jelly	$2.25	Plum Nuts Filled	$1.75
Tiger Twist	$1.49	Round Mound	$2.99

Directions: Use your mathematics skills to solve these word problems.

Remember: All answers involving money have a dollar sign and decimal point.

1. Your best friend bought a Doggy Doughnut and a Plum Nuts Filled for his breakfast. How much did it cost him? _____

2. How much less does it cost for a Plum Nuts Filled than for a Round Mound? _____

3. You bought a Tiger Twist. How much change did you get for a $10 bill? _____

4. A group of 6 teenagers spent $24.60. They split the cost evenly. How much money should each teenager pay? _____

5. Your coach bought a Creamy Dream, a Juicy Jelly, and a Round Mound. How much did he spend? _____

6. A grandfather bought each of his 9 grandchildren a Plum Nuts Filled. How much did it cost him? _____

7. The fifth grade teacher bought 30 Juicy Jelly doughnuts for her class. How much did it cost her? _____

8. The girls' soccer coach bought 15 Round Mounds for her team. How much did she pay? _____

9. A group of 20 teenagers bought $98.80 worth of doughnuts and split the cost evenly among them. How much did each teenager pay? _____

10. Mike bought one of each doughnut. How much did Mike spend? _____

Money for Movies

You can rent any movie title at DVD Bonanza, which has the latest releases and old favorites, as well as classic movies.

Rental Prices			
just released	$3.99	old favorite	$2.99
recent movie	$3.50	classic	$2.50
musical	$3.25		

Directions: Use your skills to solve these word problems.

Remember: All answers involving money must have a dollar sign and a decimal point.

1. Your mother gave a DVD party for you and your friends. She rented 7 old favorites for you to choose from. How much did she spend? _____

2. As a class reward, your teacher rented the just released DVD entitled *Cheerleaders Play Football*. How much change did the teacher receive from a $20 dollar bill? _____

3. You and your friends decide to spend Friday evening watching a series of 5 horror flicks. How much does it cost to rent the 5 old favorites? _____

4. A group of girls in your class have a sleepover. One mother rents 9 musicals to match each girl's taste in music. How much did it cost to rent the DVDs? _____

5. The soccer coach rented a series of soccer movies, including 1 just released, 1 recent movie, 1 old favorite, and 1 classic. How much did the coach spend on rental fees?

    _____

6. A group of 7 friends spent $28.70 on DVD fees. They split the cost evenly. How much did each friend pay? _____

7. The school's music teacher rented 1 old favorite, 1 classic, and 1 musical for her class. How much did she spend? _____

8. The football coach rented 1 just released movie. How much change did he get from a $10 bill? _____

9. The principal spent $14.95 on rental fees. How much change did he get from a $100 bill? _____

10. Your best friend's mother rented 2 old favorites and 3 just released movies for a birthday celebration. How much did it cost her? _____

All About Lines

- A **line** goes on endlessly in both directions.
- A **line segment** is part of a line.
- A **ray** goes on endlessly in one direction.

Directions: Identify each line.

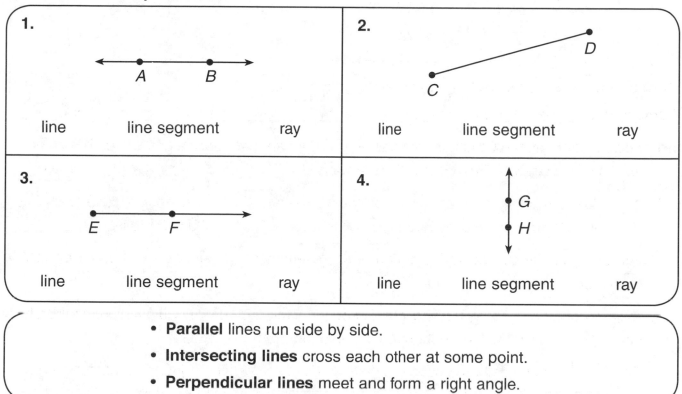

1.

line   line segment   ray

2.

line   line segment   ray

3.

line   line segment   ray

4.

line   line segment   ray

- **Parallel** lines run side by side.
- **Intersecting lines** cross each other at some point.
- **Perpendicular lines** meet and form a right angle.

Directions: Describe each pair of lines.

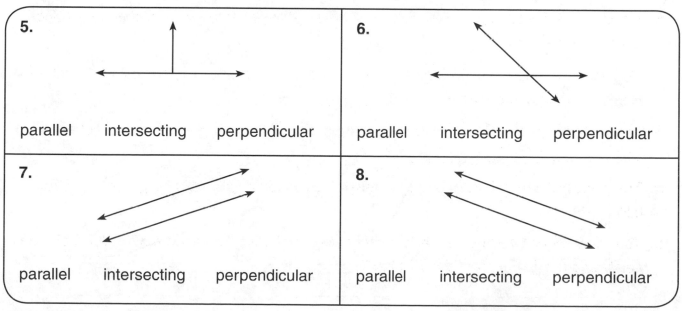

5.

parallel   intersecting   perpendicular

6.

parallel   intersecting   perpendicular

7.

parallel   intersecting   perpendicular

8.

parallel   intersecting   perpendicular

Identifying Angles

Reminders

- An acute angle measures less than 90°.
- An obtuse angle measures more than 90° and less than 180°.
- A right angle measures exactly 90°.
- A straight angle measures exactly 180°.

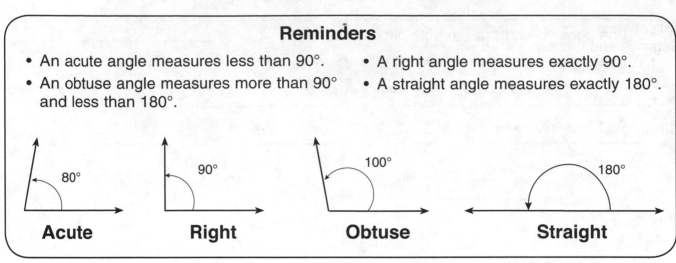

Acute   **Right**   **Obtuse**   **Straight**

Directions: Label each of these angles as acute, right, obtuse, or straight angles.

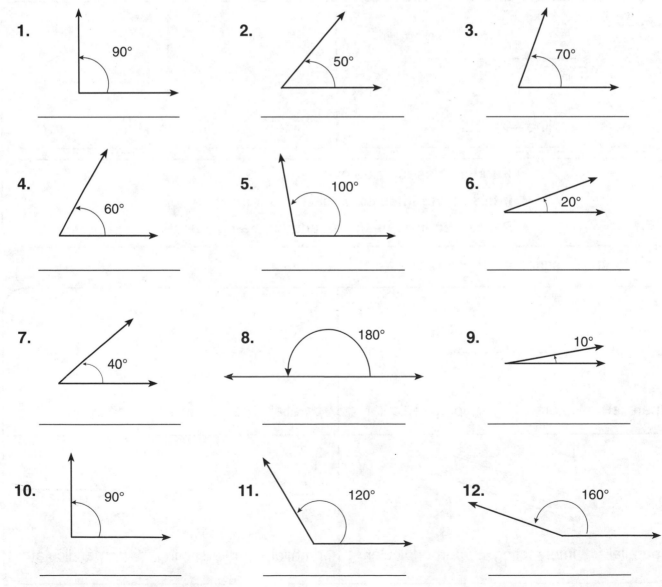

1. 90° _____

2. 50° _____

3. 70° _____

4. 60° _____

5. 100° _____

6. 20° _____

7. 40° _____

8. 180° _____

9. 10° _____

10. 90° _____

11. 120° _____

12. 160° _____

Measuring Angles with a Protractor

Directions: Use a protractor to measure each of the angles below. Write the number of degrees and the name of each angle: acute, right, obtuse, or straight.

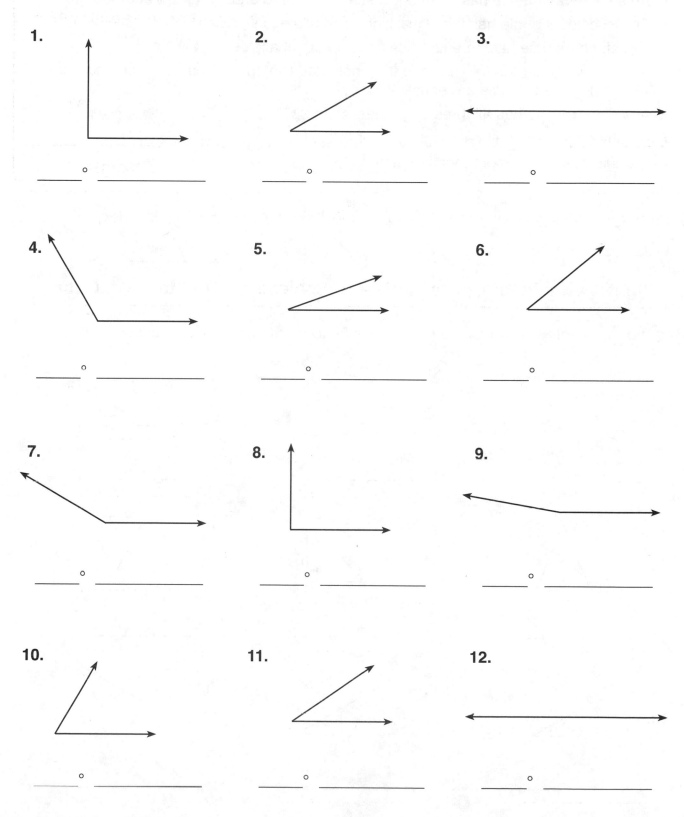

1.

_____ ° _____

2.

_____ ° _____

3.

_____ ° _____

4.

_____ ° _____

5.

_____ ° _____

6.

_____ ° _____

7.

_____ ° _____

8.

_____ ° _____

9.

_____ ° _____

10.

_____ ° _____

11.

_____ ° _____

12.

_____ ° _____

Identifying Triangles

- A right triangle has one 90° angle.
- An equilateral triangle has three equal sides and three equal angles of 60° each.
- An isosceles triangle has two equal sides and two equal angles.
- A scalene triangle has no equal sides and no equal angles.
- An isosceles right triangle has one 90° angle and two 45° angles. The sides adjacent (next to) the right angle are equal.
- An acute triangle has all three angles less than 90°.
- An obtuse triangle has one angle greater than 90°.
- Triangles can have more than one name.

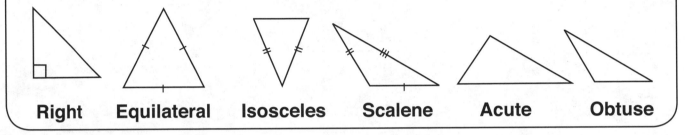

Right   **Equilateral**   **Isosceles**   **Scalene**   **Acute**   **Obtuse**

Directions: Identify each triangle. If the triangle has more than one name, use both names.

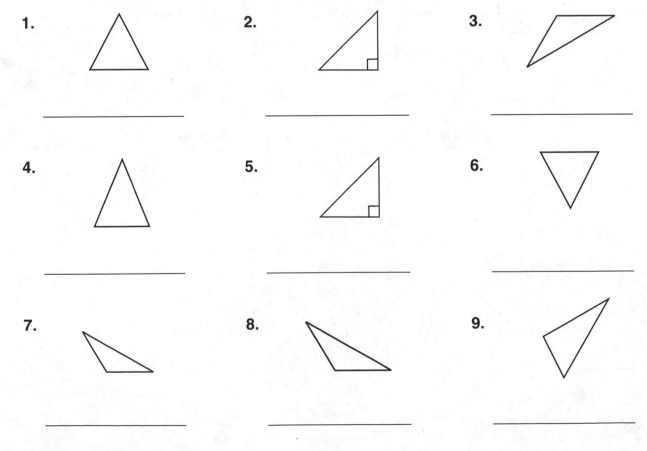

1. _____

2. _____

3. _____

4. _____

5. _____

6. _____

7. _____

8. _____

9. _____

Computing the Interior Angles of a Triangle

- The sum of the interior angles of every triangle is 180°.

- If you know two of the angles of a triangle, you can find the third angle by adding the two angles you know and subtracting the sum from 180°.

Directions: Compute the number of degrees in each unmarked angle.

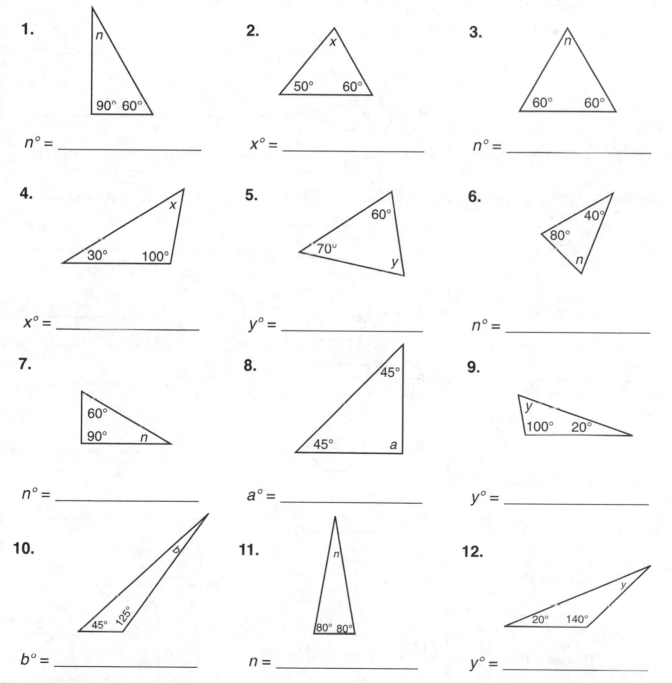

1.

$n° =$ _____

2.

$x° =$ _____

3.

$n° =$ _____

4.

$x° =$ _____

5.

$y° =$ _____

6.

$n° =$ _____

7.

$n° =$ _____

8.

$a° =$ _____

9.

$y° =$ _____

10.

$b° =$ _____

11.

$n =$ _____

12.

$y° =$ _____

Identifying Polygons

Polygon Names

Directions: Use the names listed on the left to identify each of the polygons below. Use the most specific name for each figure.

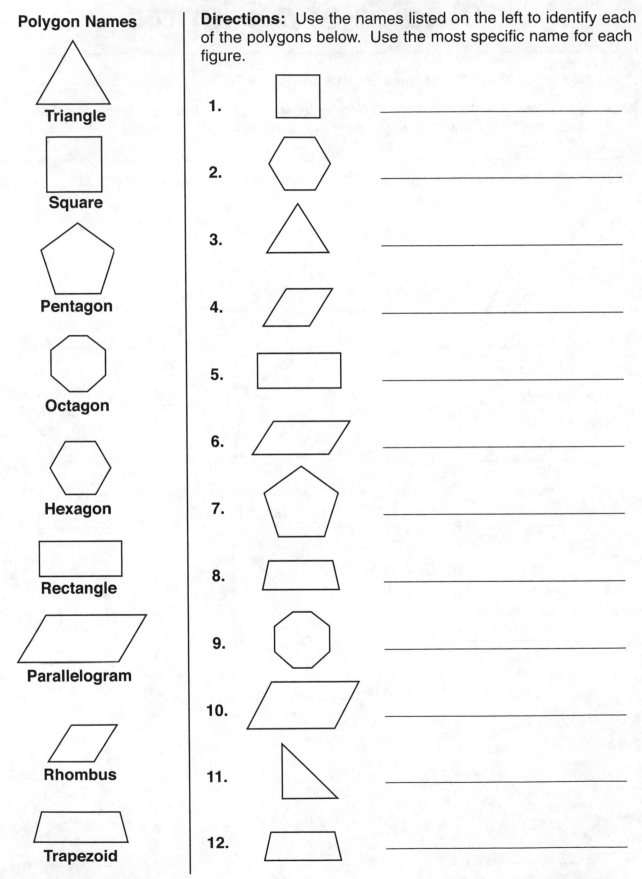

Triangle

Square

Pentagon

Octagon

Hexagon

Rectangle

Parallelogram

Rhombus

Trapezoid

1. _____

2. _____

3. _____

4. _____

5. _____

6. _____

7. _____

8. _____

9. _____

10. _____

11. _____

12. _____

Computing the Perimeter of Squares

- The perimeter of a geometric figure is the distance around the figure.
- The perimeter of a square can be computed by multiplying the length of one side of the square by four.

Directions: Compute the perimeter of these squares.

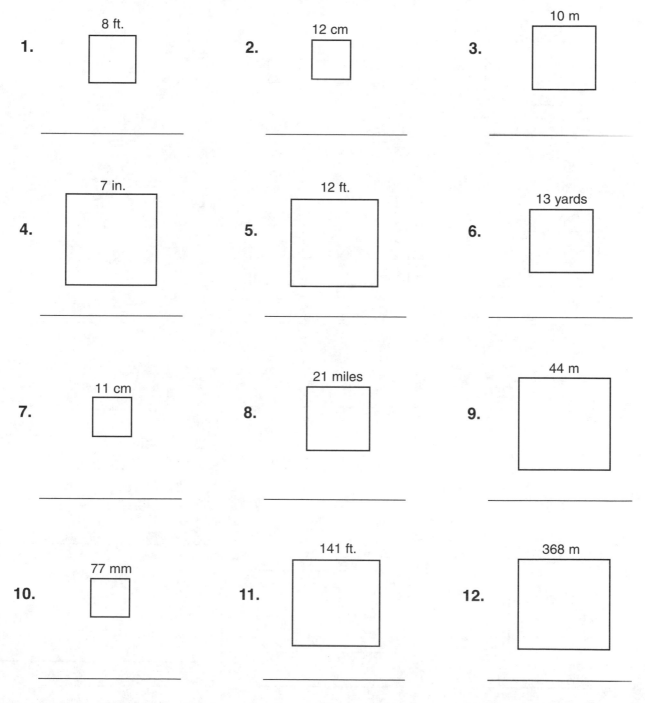

1. 8 ft.

_____

2. 12 cm

_____

3. 10 m

_____

4. 7 in.

_____

5. 12 ft.

_____

6. 13 yards

_____

7. 11 cm

_____

8. 21 miles

_____

9. 44 m

_____

10. 77 mm

_____

11. 141 ft.

_____

12. 368 m

_____

Computing the Perimeter of Rectangles

The perimeter of a rectangle is computed by adding the length plus the width and multiplying the sum times two.

P = 2 x (l + w)

Directions: Compute the perimeter of these rectangles.

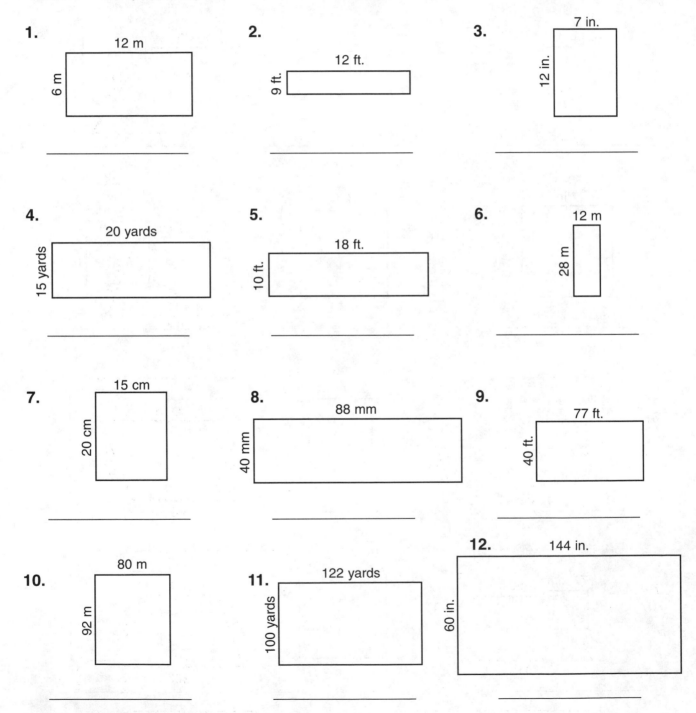

1.
12 m
6 m

_____

2.
12 ft.
9 ft.

_____

3.
7 in.
12 in.

_____

4.
20 yards
15 yards

_____

5.
18 ft.
10 ft.

_____

6.
12 m
28 m

_____

7.
15 cm
20 cm

_____

8.
88 mm
40 mm

_____

9.
77 ft.
40 ft.

_____

10.
80 m
92 m

_____

11.
122 yards
100 yards

_____

12.
144 in.
60 in.

_____

Computing the Perimeter of Other Quadrilaterals

The perimeter of figures with four unequal sides is computed by adding the lengths of each side.

Directions: Compute the perimeter of these trapezoids.

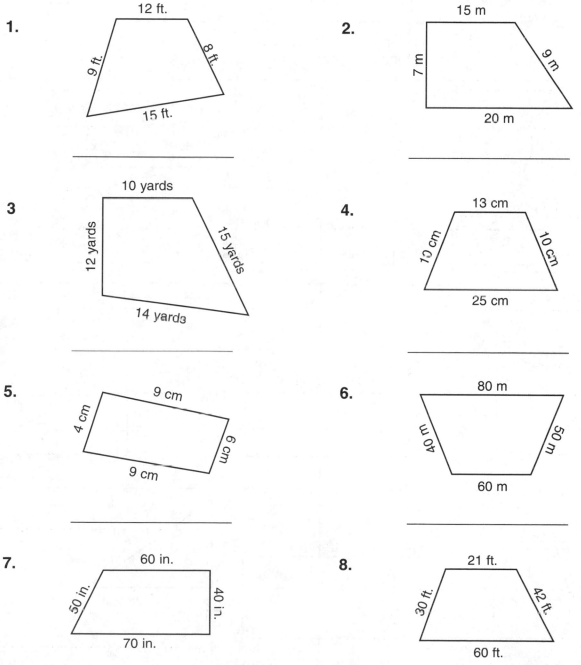

1. 12 ft. / 9 ft. / 8 ft. / 15 ft.

2. 15 m / 7 m / 9 m / 20 m

3 10 yards / 12 yards / 15 yards / 14 yards

4. 13 cm / 10 cm / 10 cm / 25 cm

5. 9 cm / 4 cm / 6 cm / 9 cm

6. 80 m / 40 m / 50 m / 60 m

7. 60 in. / 50 in. / 40 in. / 70 in.

8. 21 ft. / 30 ft. / 42 ft. / 60 ft.

Finding the Perimeter

Formulas for Finding the Perimeter (P)

Triangle:	$P = a + b + c$
Rectangle:	$P = (2 \times a) + (2 \times b)$
Square:	$P = 4 \times s$ (side)
Parallelogram:	$P = (2 \times a) + (2 \times b)$
Circle:	C (circumference) $= 3.14 \times d$ (diameter)
Trapezoid:	$P = a + b + c + d$

Directions: Identify each shape. Find the perimeter for each shape.

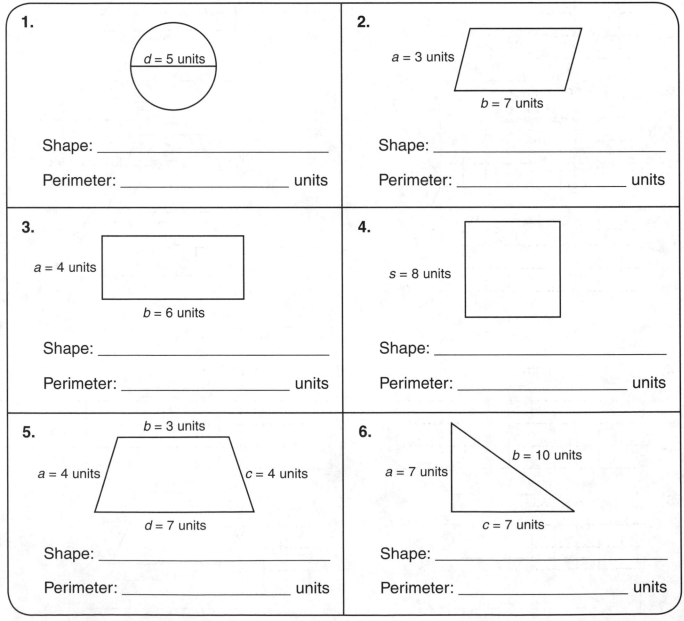

1.

$d = 5$ units

Shape: _____

Perimeter: _____ units

2.

$a = 3$ units

$b = 7$ units

Shape: _____

Perimeter: _____ units

3.

$a = 4$ units

$b = 6$ units

Shape: _____

Perimeter: _____ units

4.

$s = 8$ units

Shape: _____

Perimeter: _____ units

5.

$b = 3$ units

$a = 4$ units

$c = 4$ units

$d = 7$ units

Shape: _____

Perimeter: _____ units

6.

$b = 10$ units

$a = 7$ units

$c = 7$ units

Shape: _____

Perimeter: _____ units

132

Computing Area

The area of a rectangle is computed by multiplying the length times the width.

$$A = l \times w$$

Directions: Count the number of squares along the width of the rectangle. Count the number of squares along the length of the rectangle. Multiply the length times the width to compute the area of each rectangle.

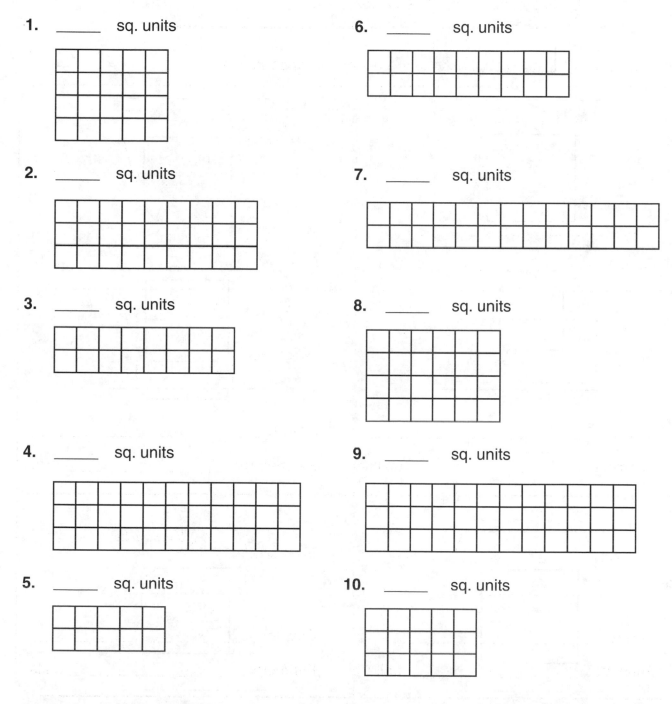

1. _____ sq. units

2. _____ sq. units

3. _____ sq. units

4. _____ sq. units

5. _____ sq. units

6. _____ sq. units

7. _____ sq. units

8. _____ sq. units

9. _____ sq. units

10. _____ sq. units

Computing the Area of Squares

The area of a square is computed by multiplying the length of one side times itself.

A = s x s or A = s^2 (Area = side squared)

Directions: Compute the area of each square.

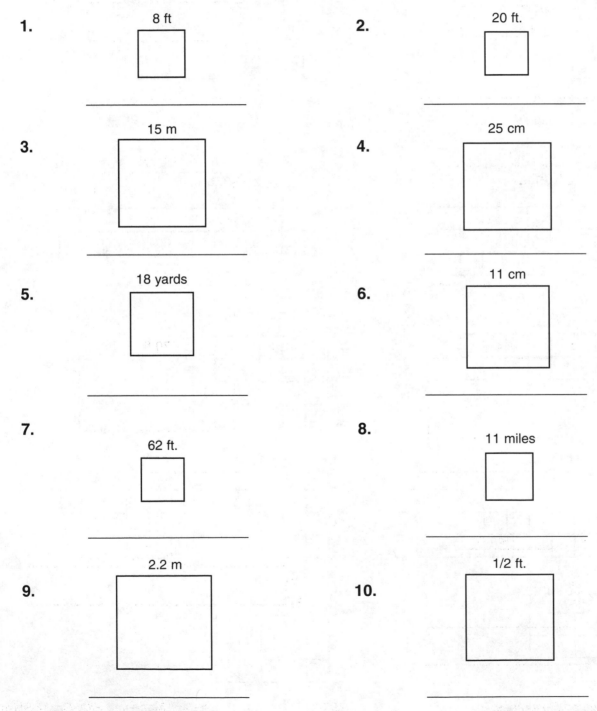

1. 8 ft

2. 20 ft.

3. 15 m

4. 25 cm

5. 18 yards

6. 11 cm

7. 62 ft.

8. 11 miles

9. 2.2 m

10. 1/2 ft.

Computing the Area of Rectangles

The area of a rectangle is computed by multiplying the width of one side times the length of an adjoining side.

A = l x w

Directions: Compute the area of each rectangle.

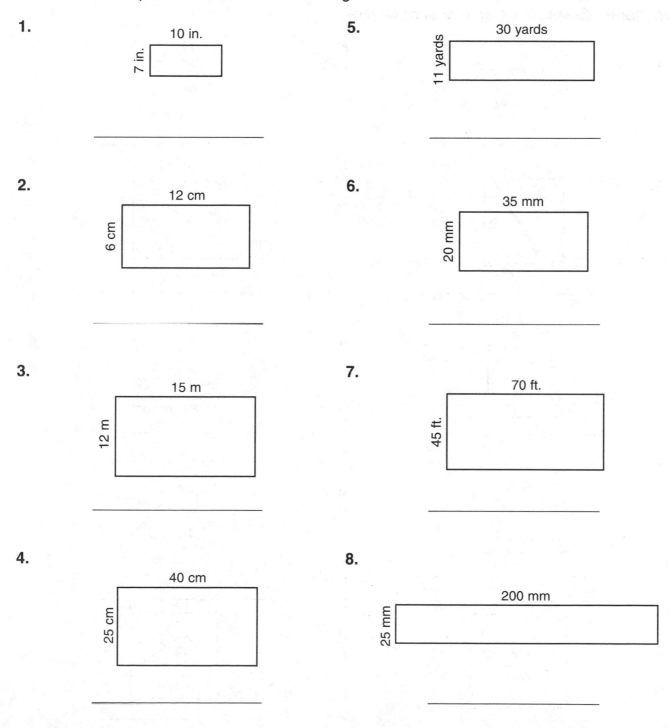

1.

10 in.

7 in.

_____

2.

12 cm

6 cm

_____

3.

15 m

12 m

_____

4.

40 cm

25 cm

_____

5.

30 yards

11 yards

_____

6.

35 mm

20 mm

_____

7.

70 ft.

45 ft.

_____

8.

200 mm

25 mm

_____

Computing the Area of Triangles

- The area of a triangle is one half the area of a parallelogram.
- To compute the area of a triangle, multiply the base times the height and divide by 2, or multiply $\frac{1}{2}$ times the base times the height.

$$A = \frac{1}{2} (b \times h)$$

Directions: Compute the area of each triangle.

1.

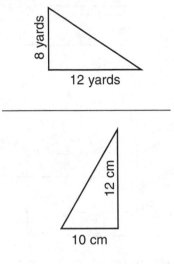

8 yards
12 yards

_____

2.

12 cm
10 cm

_____

3.

21 ft.
30 ft.

_____

4.

9 cm
16 cm

_____

5.

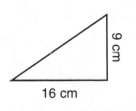

17 m
70 m

_____

6.

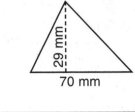

29 mm
70 mm

_____

7.

12 yards
15 yards

_____

8.

40 cm
86 cm

_____

9.

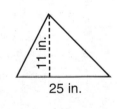

11 in.
25 in.

_____

10.

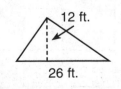

12 ft.
26 ft.

_____

136   ©Teacher Created Resources, Inc.

Computing the Volume of a Cube

The volume of a cube is computed by multiplying the length of one side times itself times itself again.

V = s x s x s or V = s³ or Volume = side cubed

Directions: Compute the volume of each cube.

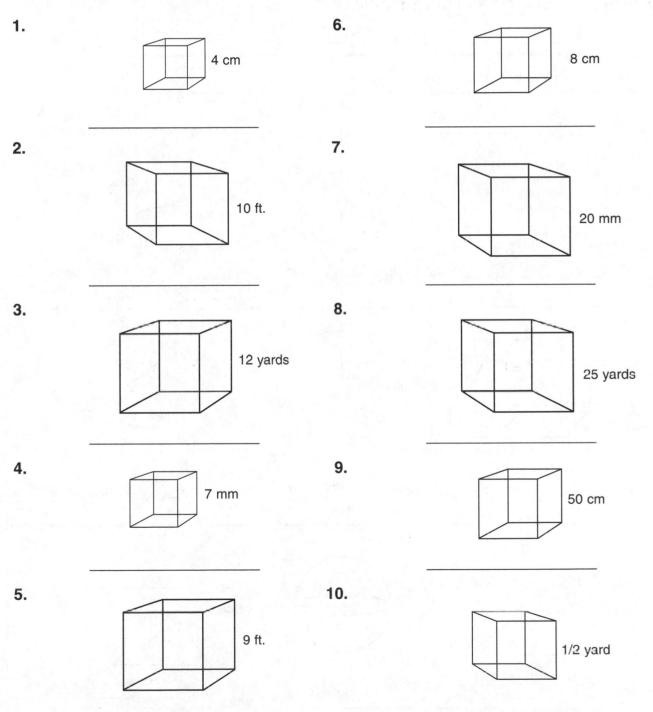

1.
    4 cm

_____

2.
    10 ft.

_____

3.
    12 yards

_____

4.
    7 mm

_____

5.
    9 ft.

_____

6.
    8 cm

_____

7.
    20 mm

_____

8.
    25 yards

_____

9.
    50 cm

_____

10.
    1/2 yard

_____

Finding the Volume

Formulas

Rectangular Solid: V (volume) = l (length) x w (width) x h (height)

Cube: $V = s^3$ (side³)

Cylinder: $V = \pi$ (3.14) x r^2 (radius²) x h

Cone: $V = \dfrac{1}{3}$ x π x r^2 x h

Sphere: $V = \dfrac{1}{3}$ x π x r^3

Directions: Find the volume for each shape.

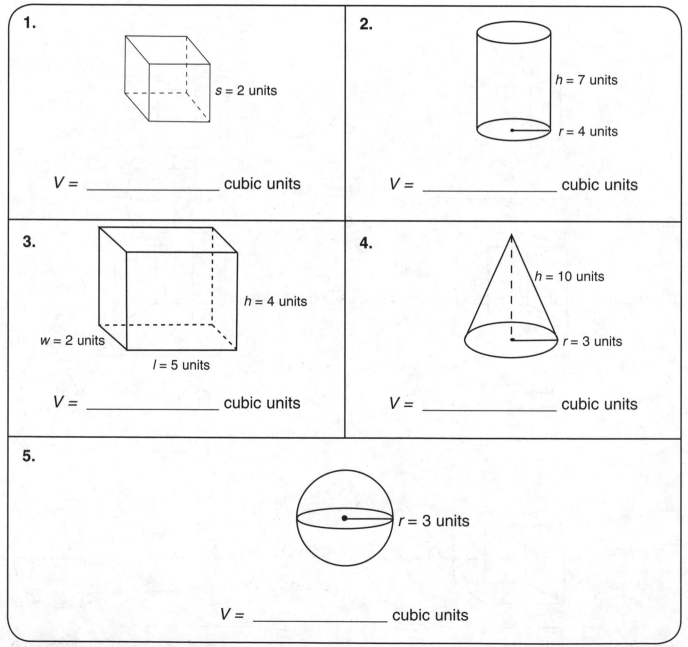

1. $s = 2$ units

V = _____ cubic units

2. $h = 7$ units $r = 4$ units

V = _____ cubic units

3. $h = 4$ units $w = 2$ units $l = 5$ units

V = _____ cubic units

4. $h = 10$ units $r = 3$ units

V = _____ cubic units

5. $r = 3$ units

V = _____ cubic units

Identifying Radius, Diameter, and Circumference

- The **circumference** is the distance around a circle.
- The **radius** is the distance from the center of a circle to any point on the circle.
- The **diameter** is a line segment extending from one side of the circle to the other through the center of the circle.
- The diameter is twice the radius.

Directions: Label the circumference, the radius, and the diameter of these circles.

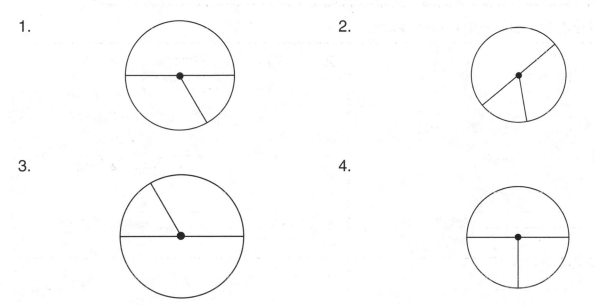

1.

2.

3.

4.

Directions: Use the information on the circles to find the values.

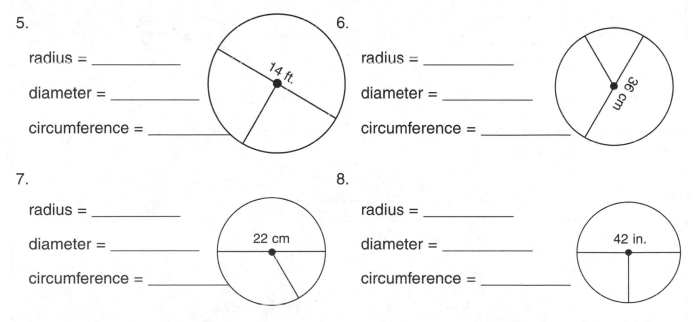

5.

radius = _____

diameter = _____

circumference = _____

6.

radius = _____

diameter = _____

circumference = _____

7.

radius = _____

diameter = _____

circumference = _____

8.

radius = _____

diameter = _____

circumference = _____

Computing Circumference

- The circumference is the distance around a circle.
- Pi (π) = 3.14
- The circumference is computed by multiplying 3.14 times the diameter.

C = πd (Pi times the diameter)

Directions: Compute the circumference of each circle.

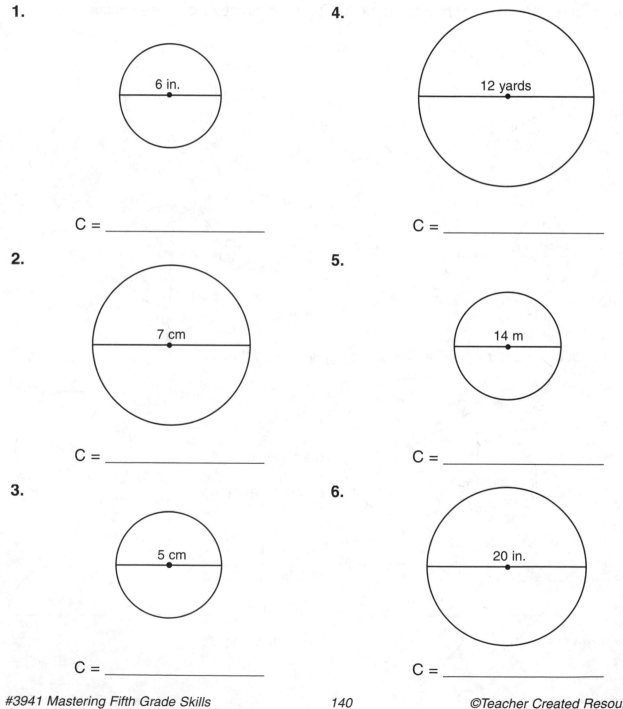

1.

6 in.

C = _____

4.

12 yards

C = _____

2.

7 cm

C = _____

5.

14 m

C = _____

3.

5 cm

C = _____

6.

20 in.

C = _____

Recognizing Symmetry

- A line of symmetry is a line drawn through the center of a flat shape so that one half of the shape can be folded to fit exactly over the other half.

- A figure may have one line of symmetry, several lines of symmetry, or no lines of

Directions: Draw one line of symmetry through the symmetrical figures below. Circle the figures which have no lines of symmetry.

1.

2.

3.

4.

5.

6.

7.

8.

9.

10.

11.

12.

Recognizing Congruence

- Congruent figures fit exactly over each other.
- Congruent figures are exactly the same in shape and size.
- Congruent figures can be turned over or around to fit.

Directions: Determine which of the figures in each set are congruent. Circle the congruent shapes.

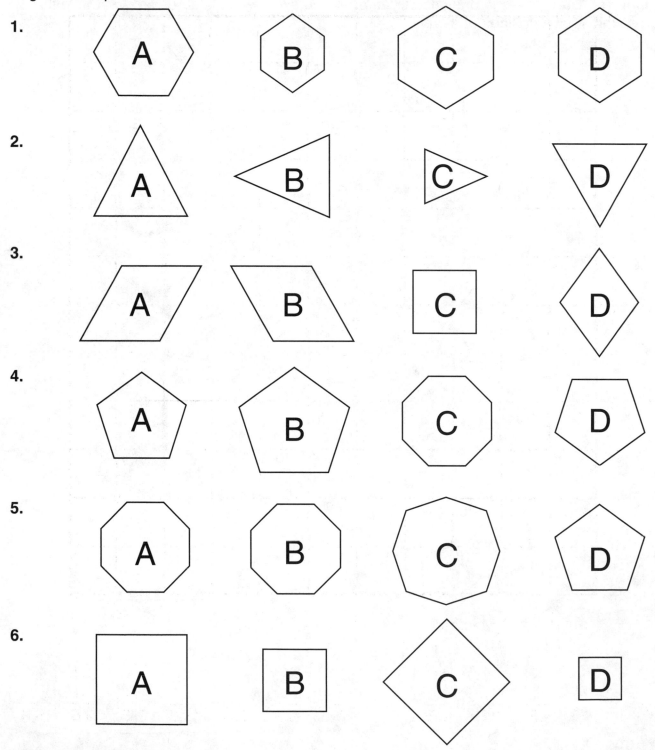

1. A B C D

2. A B C D

3. A B C D

4. A B C D

5. A B C D

6. A B C D

Locating Points on a Graph

Jim earned a terrific prize for winning first place in the community talent show. The prize he won is spelled out in this graph.

Directions: Find the points on the graph that are identified below. Can you discover what Jim won? Each point you find will give you a letter of the hidden prize.

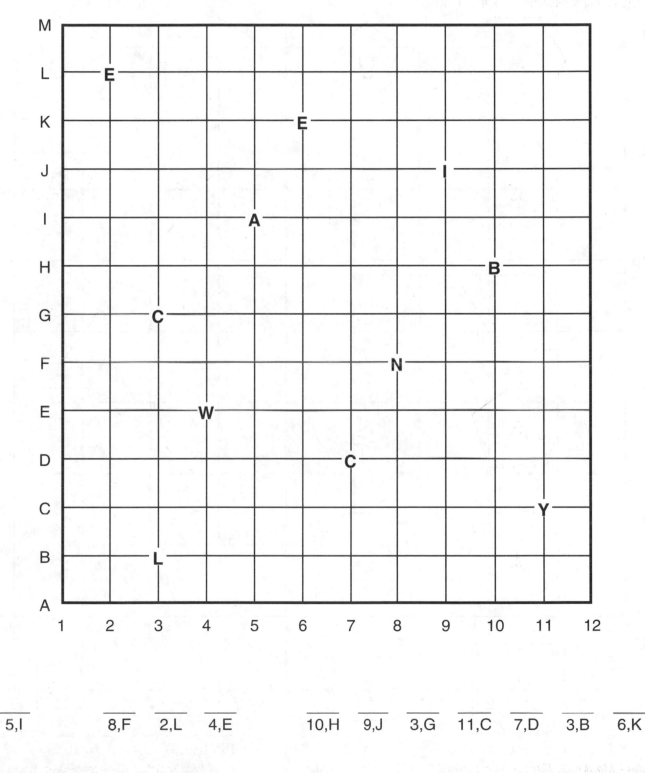

<u>　</u>　　<u>　</u>　<u>　</u>　<u>　</u>　　<u>　</u>　<u>　</u>　<u>　</u>　<u>　</u>　<u>　</u>　<u>　</u>　<u>　</u>
5,I　　　8,F　2,L　4,E　　10,H　9,J　3,G　11,C　7,D　3,B　6,K

Math

Finding Coordinates on a Graph

How Do You Make a Hot Dog Stand?

Directions: The answer to this riddle is written in a special code at the bottom of this page. Each pair of numbers stands for a point on the graph. Write the letter shown at the point near the intersection of each pair of numbers. Read numbers across and then up. The letters will spell out the answer to the riddle.

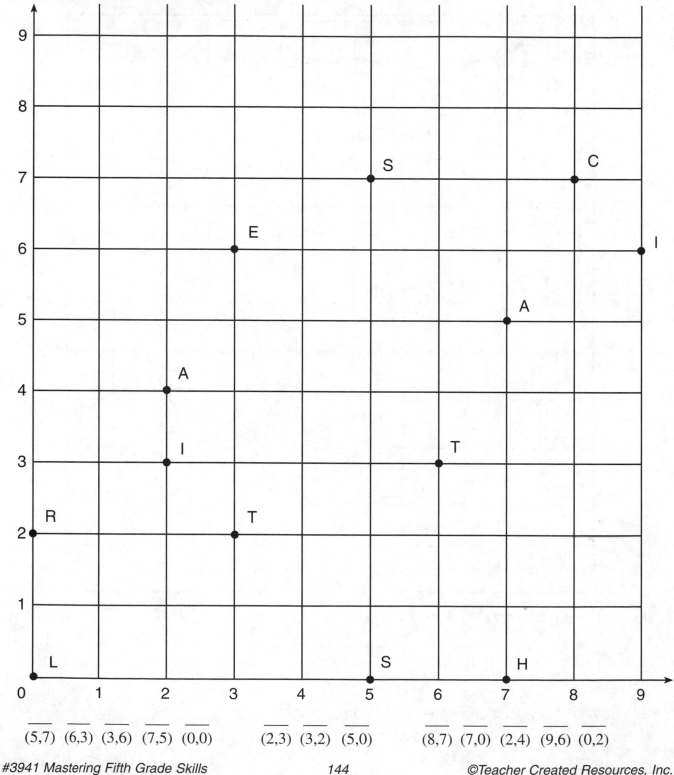

$\overline{}$ $\overline{}$ $\overline{}$ $\overline{}$ $\overline{}$ $\overline{}$ $\overline{}$ $\overline{}$ $\overline{}$ $\overline{}$ $\overline{}$ $\overline{}$ $\overline{}$
(5,7) (6,3) (3,6) (7,5) (0,0)   (2,3) (3,2) (5,0)   (8,7) (7,0) (2,4) (9,6) (0,2)

Plotting Coordinates
(Positive Numbers)

Coordinates must always be plotted using the x axis for the first number in a number pair and the y axis for the second number of each pair. (**Note:** Always go across before you go up or down.)

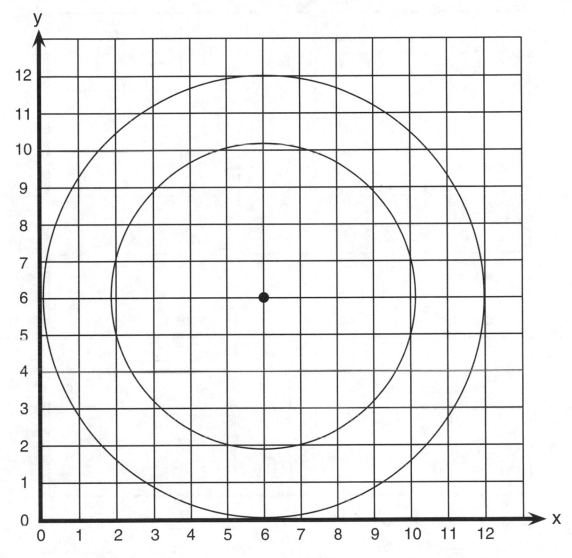

Directions: Graph the coordinate number pairs below. Connect each dot with a ruler as you proceed. (**Note:** You will go over some line segments more than once.)

A. (0, 0)	B. (12, 0)	C. (12, 12)	D. (0, 12)	E. (0, 0)
F. (12, 12)	G. (0, 12)	H. (12, 0)	I. (6, 0)	J. (6, 12)
K. (0, 6)	L. (6, 0)	M. (12, 6)	N. (6, 12)	O. (0, 6)
P. (12, 6)	Q. (9, 6)	R. (9, 9)	S. (3, 9)	T. (3, 3)
U. (9, 3)				

How many squares can you count in this design? _____

How many triangles can you count in this design? _____

Coordinate Pairs

Directions: Study the city grid shown below. Notice where landmarks such as the bank and park are located. Notice which numbers are positive and which are negative. Note how the four quadrants are labeled: I, II, III, and IV. Use the information to answer these word problems. **Remember:** Always go across before going up or down and use the point for finding the coordinate.

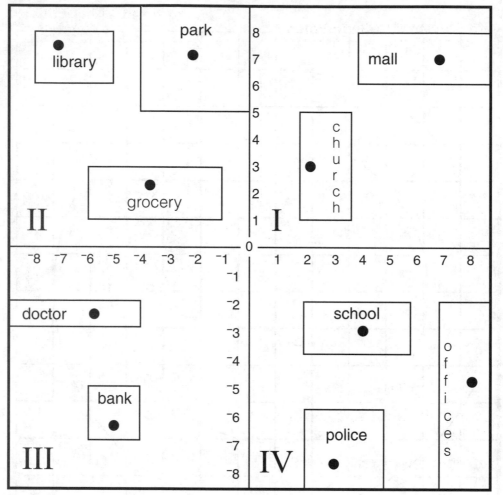

1. What feature is located at coordinates (7, 7)? _____

2. What building is located at coordinates (4, ⁻3)? _____

3. Which business is located at (⁻5, ⁻6)? _____

4. Which quadrant has all negative numbers? _____

5. Which quadrant has only positive coordinates? _____

6. What are the coordinates of the police station? _____

7. Which public building is located at coordinates (⁻7, 7)? _____

8. What are the coordinates of the church? _____

9. What public area is located at coordinates (⁻2, 7)? _____

10. Which quadrant always begins with a positive number and concludes with a negative number?_____

Bar Graphs

Directions: This bar graph illustrates the votes some states had in the Electoral College in the year 2004. The Electoral College casts 538 votes to determine the next President of the United States. A majority of 270 votes is needed to win. Study the graph and answer these questions.

Directions: This double bar graph illustrates the results of a student questionnaire about the average amount of time spent weekly on homework and watching television. Study the graph and answer these questions.

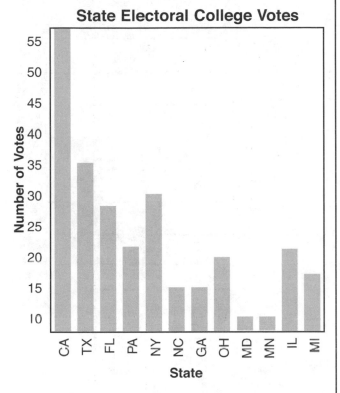

State Electoral College Votes

Average Time Spent on Homework/ Watching TV

1. Which state has the most votes in the Electoral College? _____

2. Which two states have exactly 10 votes in the Electoral College? _____

3. Which two states have 21 votes in the Electoral College? _____

4. Which state has 17 votes in the Electoral College? _____

5. How many votes does North Carolina have?

    _____

6. How many votes does Ohio have?

    _____

7. Which state has 10 more votes than Illinois? _____

8. Which grade averaged 8 hours a week of homework and 14 hours of television watching? _____

9. Which grade watched the most television? _____

10. Which grade did the most homework in one week? _____

11. Which grade did only 4 hours of homework?

    _____

12. Which grade spent almost as much time on homework as on watching television?

    _____

13. Which grade spent 14 more hours watching television than they did on homework?

    _____

14. Which grade spent 21 hours a week watching television? _____

Vertical and Horizontal Bar Graphs

The bars on a bar graph may be drawn either vertically or horizontally, depending upon what it is you are graphing. Remember, a graph is a picture, and if you can make a graph suggest what you are measuring, choose the kind of bar that will help "tell the story."

Directions: Read these graphs. Then answer the questions below them.

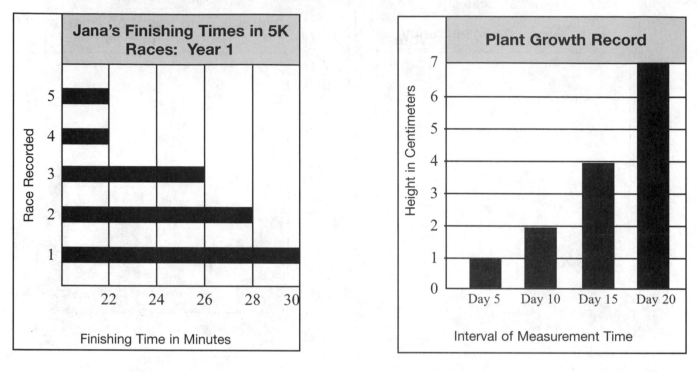

1. Why are horizontal bars used to show race results? _____

_____

_____

2. Why are vertical bars used to show plant growth? _____

_____

_____

3. What type of bar graph, vertical or horizontal, would better show the findings on these subjects:

   comparisons of world's tallest buildings? _____

   growth of a snake? _____

   distances baseballs are thrown? _____

   amount of books read by different classes in a month? _____

4. Choose ideas from question #3 and graph them as an individual, group, or class activity.

Line Graphs

Directions: A line graph illustrates change over time. This graph illustrates human life expectancies at times from 400 BCE in Greece to CE 2000 in the United States. Use the graph to answer these questions.

Estimated Life Expectancy

Directions: The double line graph shows the number of home runs hit by the home run leader in each league for a 10-year period. Study the graph and answer these questions.

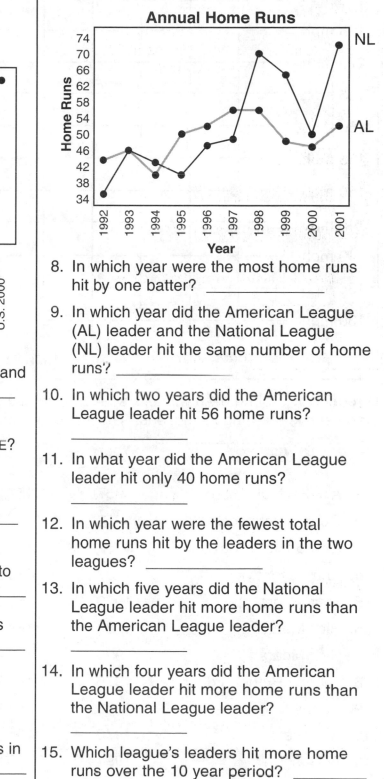

Annual Home Runs

1. What was the life expectancy in England about the year 1250? _____

2. What was the average age a person lived to in Greece in the year 400 BCE?
   _____

3. In what country and year was the life expectancy 47 years? _____

4. What is the difference in average life expectancy from Greece in 400 BCE to the United States in 2000? _____

5. In what year in the United States was the life expectancy 36 years? _____

6. In what century did life expectancy increase 30 years? _____

7. How many years did it take for life expectancy to increase from 30 years in Greece to 40 years in England? _____

8. In which year were the most home runs hit by one batter? _____

9. In which year did the American League (AL) leader and the National League (NL) leader hit the same number of home runs? _____

10. In which two years did the American League leader hit 56 home runs?
    _____

11. In what year did the American League leader hit only 40 home runs?
    _____

12. In which year were the fewest total home runs hit by the leaders in the two leagues? _____

13. In which five years did the National League leader hit more home runs than the American League leader?
    _____

14. In which four years did the American League leader hit more home runs than the National League leader?
    _____

15. Which league's leaders hit more home runs over the 10 year period? _____

Making a Line Graph

Car Speeds of Indianapolis 500 Winners

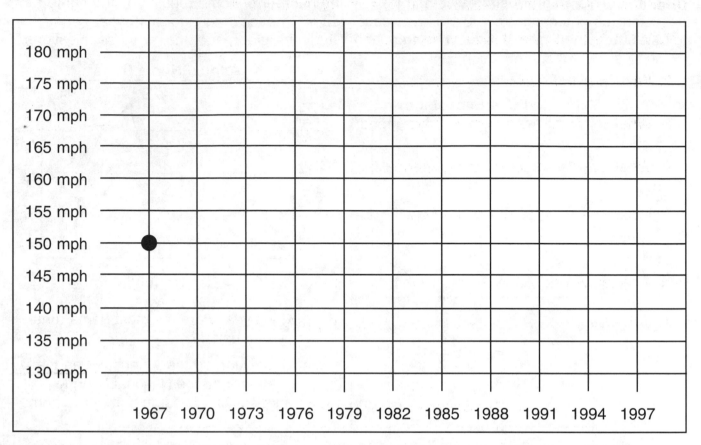

Directions: Round each winner's speed to the nearest ten miles per hour (mph). Make a line graph above showing the speeds. The first one is done for you.

Driver	Year	Speed	Rounded
1. A.J. Foyt, Jr.	1967	151.207 mph	150
2. Gordon Johncock	1973	159.036 mph	
3. Gordon Johncock	1982	162.029 mph	
4. Arie Luyendyk	1997	145.857 mph	
5. Rick Mears	1979	158.899 mph	
6. Rick Mears	1988	144.809 mph	
7. Rick Mears	1991	176.457 mph	
8. Johnny Rutherford	1976	148.725 mph	
9. Danny Sullivan	1985	152.982 mph	
10. Al Unser	1970	155.749 mph	
11. Al Unser, Jr.	1994	160.872 mph	

Using a Line and Bar Graph

Directions: Answer the questions using the line graph on page 150.

1. What year had the slowest winning speed? _____

2. What was the slowest winning speed? _____

3. What year had the fastest winning speed? _____ .

4. What was the fastest winning speed? _____

5. What was the mph difference between the slowest winning speed and the fastest winning speed? _____

6. What was Rick Mears' average winning speed? _____

7. What was Gordon Johncock's average winning speed? _____

Car Speeds of Indianapolis 500 Winners

140 mph	150 mph	160 mph	170 mph	180 mph

Directions: Make a bar graph above showing the rounded winning speeds.

8. What was the most often occurring winning speed? _____

9. Which speeds tied for the same number of wins? _____

10. Which speed was not a winning speed? _____

Pictograph and Line Plots

Directions: This pictograph represents a survey of sports preferences among grade school students in the 4th through 6th grades. Study the pictograph and answer the questions below.

Directions: This line plot illustrates the number of books read by individual students in one month. Each x stands for one student and the number of books that they read. Study the line plot and answer the questions.

Students' Favorite Sports

Baseball ○ ○ ◖

Soccer ○ ○ ○ ○ ○ ○

Football ○ ○ ○ ○ ◖

Basketball ○ ○ ○ ○ ○

Swimming ○ ◖

Bicycling ○

Key: O = 10 students

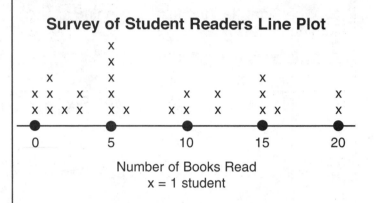

Survey of Student Readers Line Plot

Number of Books Read
x = 1 student

1. How many students prefer to play basketball? _____

2. How many students prefer bicycling as their favorite sport? _____

3. How many students prefer to play baseball? _____

4. How many students prefer football as their favorite sport? _____

5. Which are the two most favorite sports? _____ _____

6. Which are the two least favorite sports? _____ _____

7. How many more students prefer soccer to swimming? _____

8. How many more students prefer football to baseball? _____

9. What is the total number of students surveyed? _____

10. How many students read 20 books in one month? _____

11. How many students read no books in the month? _____

12. Did any students read exactly 16 books? _____

13. How many students read 12 books? _____

14. How many students read 15 books in one month? _____

15. What is the total number of students who read less than 5 books? _____

16. What is the total number of books read by all the students in the survey? _____

Pictograph: Recycling Project

The Linsdale Elementary School Earth Kids Club worked for three months collecting recyclable products. You can see the results of their efforts in this pictograph.

Earth Kids Club Recycling Project: March, April, May 2006

aluminum cans		
plastic bottles		
glass		
1 foot/30 cm high newspaper bundles		
1 foot/30 cm high paper bundles		
bags of outgrown clothing		

Key: 1 picture = 100 units

1/2 picture = 50 units

Directions: Compute the amounts of each of these products collected by the Earth Kids Club:

1. aluminum cans:_____   4. newspaper bundles: _____

2. plastic bottles:_____   5. paper bundles: _____

3. glass:_____   6. bags of clothing: _____

Which of these products could you and your friends help to recycle? _____

_____

_____

Tables and Charts

Directions: The following frequency table records the responses of fifth graders when asked to name their favorite table game. Study the table and answer the questions below.

Game	Tally	Frequency
Checkers	~~HHT~~ ~~HHT~~ ///	13
Chess	~~HHT~~ //	7
Twenty-One	////	4
War	~~HHT~~ ////	9
Hearts	//	2
Old Maid	/	1
Chinese Checkers	///	3
Solitaire	////	4
None	~~HHT~~ /	6

1. Which was the most favorite table game? _____

2. Which was the least favorite table game? _____

3. How many 5th graders liked no table game? _____

4. How many more 5th graders preferred Chess to Old Maid? _____

5. How many more students liked Checkers better than Chess? _____

6. Which two card games were preferred by 4 students? _____

7. How many students participated in the survey? _____

8. What is the total number of students that preferred the board games: Chess, Checkers, and Chinese Checkers? _____

Directions: This chart lists the wingspan (from the tip of one wing to the tip of the other wing) of some birds. Study the chart and answer the questions below.

turkey vulture	72 inches	golden eagle	92 inches
black vulture	60 inches	bald eagle	96 inches
red-tailed hawk	54 inches	red-shouldered hawk	48 inches
sparrow hawk	23 inches		

9. What is the wingspan of the sparrow hawk? _____

10. What is the wingspan of the black vulture? _____

11. Which bird on the chart has the widest wingspan? _____

12. Which bird on the chart has the shortest wingspan? _____

13. What is the difference between the wingspans of the red-tailed hawk and the black vulture? _____

Using a Pie Chart

Directions: Ginger receives a $10.00-per-week allowance. The pie chart shows how Ginger spends her money.

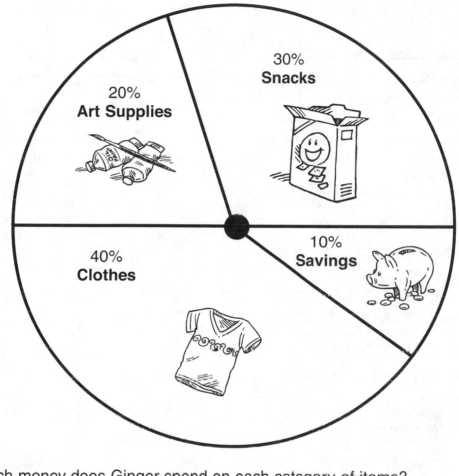

1. How much money does Ginger spend on each category of items?

   Art Supplies: _____   Snacks:_____

   Clothes: _____   Savings: _____

2. If the average month has 4 weeks, how much money does Ginger save?_____

3. If the average year has 52 weeks, how much money does Ginger spend on Art Supplies? _____

4. If Ginger uses her clothing money for a new winter coat that cost $25.00, how many weeks will it take for Ginger to have enough money to pay for it? _____

Chart the Read-a-Thon!

Students at Hudson Elementary School participated in a Read-a-Thon to raise money for their school library. Each student has tallied the number of books he or she has read and is ready to collect the pledge money.

Directions: This chart represents the reading and pledging of 15 students in the Read-a-Thon. After reading the chart, answer the questions at the bottom of the page.

Hudson Elementary School Read-A-Thon: Room 3

Student's Name	Total Books Read	Pledge per Book	Money Collected
Acevedo, Jennifer	31	10¢	$ 3.10
Adams, Joseph	5	10¢	$ 0.50
Barton, Michael	61	5¢	$ 3.05
Duran, Louis	17	15¢	$ 2.55
Edwards, Marylou	47	5¢	$ 2.35
Harrison, Trevor	11	25¢	$ 2.75
Lee, Rebecca	40	10¢	$ 4.00
Logan, Cassie	22	5¢	$ 1.10
Marshall, Barbara	9	50¢	$ 4.50
Peterson, David	102	5¢	$ 5.10
Ross, Kathryn	58	10¢	$ 5.80
Rublo, Anthony	83	5¢	$ 4.15
Shea, Sharon	39	10¢	$ 3.90
Tran, Alvan	14	10¢	$ 1.40
Yetter, Liz	75	5¢	$ 3.75
Total			

1. Which student read the most books? _____

2. What was the highest amount of money collected by one student?_____
   Which student? _____

3. Who had the highest pledge of money per book? _____

4. Was the person who read the most books the same as the person who collected the most money?_____

5. Was the person who had the highest pledge of money per book the same as the person who collected the most money? _____

6. What was the total number of books read by all the students? _____

7. How much money did these students earn for the library? _____

Would a Read-a-Thon be a good way to raise money at your school?

Columbus Didn't Discover America

Although most people think Christopher Columbus discovered America, Leif Ericsson probably arrived first. He set sail from his home in Norway around A.D.1000. He landed in Canada and named it Vinland.

SPINDLE

He went home and told others about the place. The next year men and women went to build homes in the new land. However, the Native Americans did not want the people there. They ***repeatedly*** destroyed the Norse villages. Around 1005, the Norse gave up. They left and never returned.

There's proof that this happened. A Norse spindle was dug up in Newfoundland, Canada. A woman used it to spin wool into yarn 1,000 years ago. Only the Norse used this kind of spindle. This simple tool proves that they arrived before Columbus ever set sail.

1. **What is the main idea of this article?**

   a. The Norse found America almost 500 years before Columbus.

   b. Leif Ericsson called Canada Vinland.

   c. A Norse spindle has been dug up in Newfoundland.

2. **Which statement is false?**

   a. The Native Americans welcomed the Norse settlers.

   b. In about 1005 the Norse returned to Norway.

   c. The Newfoundland spindle could only have been Norse.

3. **Of the following choices, which happened first?**

   a. Christopher Columbus came to North America.

   b. Leif Ericsson came to North America.

   c. Norse settlers came to North America.

4. **The opposite of the word *repeatedly* is**

   a. happily.

   b. frequently.

   c. rarely.

Nautical Help

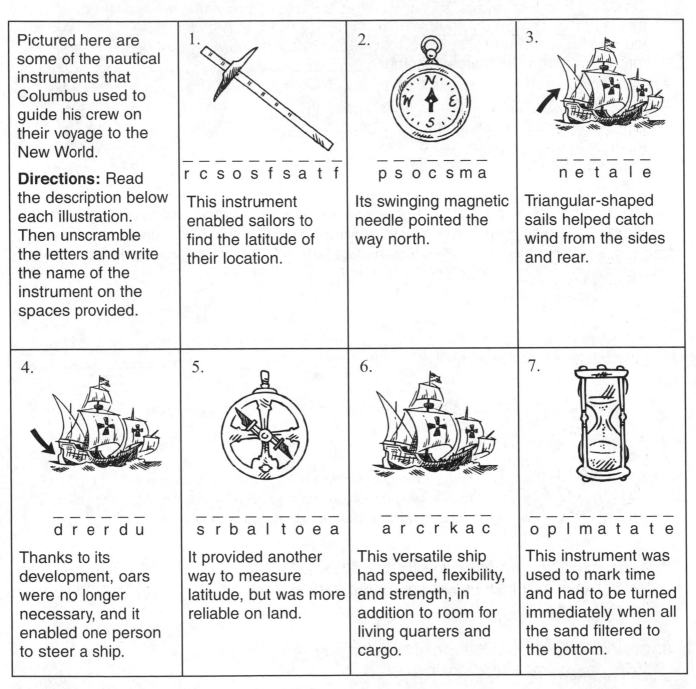

Pictured here are some of the nautical instruments that Columbus used to guide his crew on their voyage to the New World.

Directions: Read the description below each illustration. Then unscramble the letters and write the name of the instrument on the spaces provided.

1. _ _ _ _ _ _ _ _ _ _
r c s o s f s a t f
This instrument enabled sailors to find the latitude of their location.

2. _ _ _ _ _ _ _
p s o c s m a
Its swinging magnetic needle pointed the way north.

3. _ _ _ _ _ _
n e t a l e
Triangular-shaped sails helped catch wind from the sides and rear.

4. _ _ _ _ _ _
d r e r d u
Thanks to its development, oars were no longer necessary, and it enabled one person to steer a ship.

5. _ _ _ _ _ _ _ _ _
s r b a l t o e a
It provided another way to measure latitude, but was more reliable on land.

6. _ _ _ _ _ _ _
a r c r k a c
This versatile ship had speed, flexibility, and strength, in addition to room for living quarters and cargo.

7. _ _ _ _ _ _ _ _ _
o p l m a t a t e
This instrument was used to mark time and had to be turned immediately when all the sand filtered to the bottom.

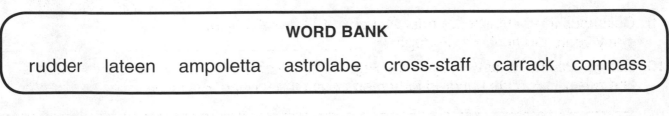

WORD BANK

rudder   lateen   ampoletta   astrolabe   cross-staff   carrack   compass

Math on Board

Directions: These math problems contain some very interesting facts about Columbus. See what you can learn when you solve the following problems.

1. On Columbus' first voyage, he commanded a fleet of three ships, the *Niña*, the *Pinta*, and the *Santa María*. The ships were quite small; they carried few men aboard on that initial journey. Forty men were on the *Santa María*, 24 on the *Niña*, and 26 on the *Pinta*. How many crewman were there altogether?_____

2. If each crewman aboard the three ships was allowed two loaves of bread per day, how many loaves would be needed for a three-day trip?_____

3. King Ferdinand and Queen Isabella offered 10,000 maradevis per year for life to the man who first spotted land. If one maradevi is worth one cent in gold, how many dollars in gold are 10,000 maradevis worth? _____

4. If the first man to see land on the voyage lived for ten more years, how many dollars in gold would he receive altogether? _____

5. A sailor's wages were 1,000 maradevis per month. How many dollars in gold is that?_____

6. Columbus determined the earth's circumference to be 20,000 miles. The actual distance is 25,000 miles. What is the difference between the actual and Columbus' measurement?_____

7. A sea league is 2.82 nautical miles. If the fleet sailed 59 leagues in one 24-hour period, how many nautical miles did they sail? _____

8. Columbus was born in Genoa, Italy, in the year 1451. He died in 1506. How old was he when he died? _____

9. Columbus lived in Lisbon, Portugal, from 1476 to 1485. How many years did he live in Portugal? _____

10. During Columbus' last voyage—the High Voyage—only 116 men were left after deaths and desertions. One hundred forty men began the voyage. How many died or deserted?

Voyage Math

Directions: Solve each problem below. Then write the answer in the blank to learn some intriguing facts about the early explorers and their voyages.

1. 25 x 140 Columbus thought the distance between Spain and the Indies was only _____ miles.	7. 434 ÷ 7 Hernán Cortés died at the age of _____.
2. 224 ÷ 16 Vasco da Gama led _____ warships to battle the Arab fleet.	8. 102 ÷ 6 Marco Polo and his family stayed in China for _____ years.
3. 50 x 5 Magellan led a fleet of _____ men through the Strait of Magellan.	9. 270 ÷ 3 Pizarro received more than _____ million dollars in gold and silver from the Incas.
4. 152 ÷ 4 It took Magellan _____ days to pass through the strait.	10. 144 ÷ 12 The *Santa María* was only _____ feet wide.
5. 5 x 83 Cortés and his _____ soldiers and horsemen amazed the Tlascalans.	11. 25 x 10 Only 18 of the _____ men survived Magellan's voyage around the world.
6. 520 ÷ 13 Columbus was _____ years old when he began his first voyage in 1492.	12. 5 x 16 The *Santa María* was 70 or _____ feet long.

Social Studies

Are You Accustomed
to Their Customs?

Directions: Listed below are the manners and customs of the Pilgrims for meal time. Compare those customs with those in your own home. How are they alike and/or different?

Pilgrim Customs	Your Customs
Use fingers instead of a fork to eat.	
Only take food given to you by your parents.	
Napkin tied around neck and hangs down to knees.	
Only the father sits in a chair; others sit on stools; children sometimes stand.	
Allowed to keep hat on during dinner.	
Never scratch at the table.	
Bones are piled neatly on the table.	
Everyone drinks from the same cup.	

Triangle Trade

The enslavement of African men, women, and children developed into an economic institution that became the main workforce for plantation societies. Sugar plantations established by Spain and Portugal in the Mediterranean used slaves purchased from African traders to work their fields. When these countries colonized the West Indies, they took the slave system with them to the new sugar plantations. Plantation owners first tried to use local "Indians" as slaves, but they died from the European diseases and sometimes revolted or were rescued by their tribal members. So the Spaniards sought other plantation workers and decided Africans would be the perfect choice since they were hard workers, and they would be too far from home to be rescued by their families or tribes.

Eventually, the English colonies copied this economic system for their plantations and for their household servants. South Carolina and Georgia became dependent on slave labor for their huge sugar, rice, and indigo plantations where producing these crops required heavy, back-breaking work. Other colonial landowners purchased household and farm slaves.

Soon there were entire fleets of ships involved in sailing to the coast of Africa where they would load up captured slaves. A unique Triangular Trade system evolved which had three stops. A ship leaving New England with a cargo of rum and iron would stop by Africa to trade these commodities for slaves. The ship full of slaves would continue on to the West Indies where the slaves would be sold for molasses to make rum. Then the ship would return to New England to start the route all over again.

1. **Spain and Portugal used slaves to work on their . . .**
   a. sugar plantations.
   b. cotton plantations.
   c. tobacco plantations.
   d. rice plantations.

2. **The English colonies used slavery as an economic system . . .**
   a. before the European countries had established it.
   b. after the European countries had established it.
   c. at the same time as the European countries established it.
   d. never in their history.

3. **A ship leaving New England for Africa carried . . .**
   a. slaves.
   b. molasses.
   c. servants.
   d. rum and iron.

4. **What were slaves sold for in the West Indies?**
   a. cotton to make clothes
   b. rum to use in cooking
   c. molasses to make rum
   d. other slaves

162

Triangle Trade (cont.)

Maps

The maps below illustrate two versions of the triangle trade which colonists conducted. Both trade patterns involved slaves.

Assignment

Use the maps to answer the following questions.

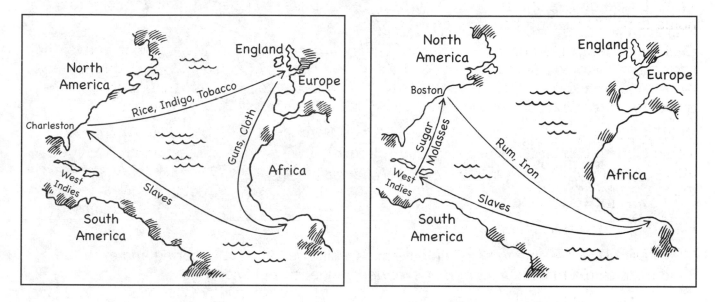

Map 1   **Map 2**

Map 1

1. What was the destination of a ship leaving Charleston? _____

2. What did a ship leaving Charleston carry? _____

3. What did a ship carry from Africa to Charleston? _____

4. What did a ship carry from England to Africa? _____

Map 2

5. What was the destination of a ship leaving Boston? _____

6. What did a ship leaving Boston carry? _____

7. What did a ship carry from Africa to the West Indies? _____

8. What did a ship carry from the West Indies back to Boston? _____

9. What ocean did all of these ships cross? _____

10. What three continents were involved in this trade? _____

Triangle Trade (cont.)

Maps (cont.)

Look carefully at the map. Notice the three-sided figures made by the lines between the colonies, Europe, and Africa. The resulting triangles made up what is known as "triangular trade." All of the countries were interconnected by slave trade. In addition, goods from the colonies were traded in England. From there, ships traveled to Africa to trade goods for slaves. Then ships went back to the West Indies and the home port.

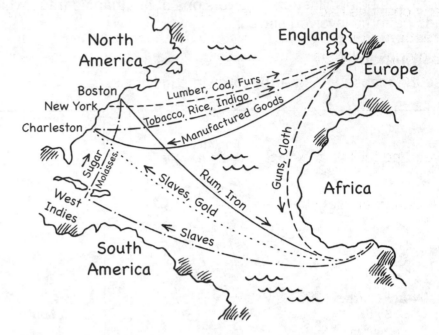

Directions: Use the map to help you determine which goods were imported and exported. Read each clue and write *imported* or *exported* on the lines provided.

1. Rum and iron were _____ to Africa.

2. Slaves were _____ from Africa to the West Indies.

3. Lumber, cod, and furs were _____ by England.

4. Sugar and molasses were _____ to Boston from the West Indies.

5. Manufactured goods were _____ by the colonies from England.

6. Gold and slaves were _____ from Africa to the colonies.

7. Tobacco, rice, and indigo were _____ from Charleston to England.

8. Guns and cloth were _____ by England.

Impact

The first meeting between the Europeans and the natives of the "new world" resulted in changes that profoundly affected both peoples. Some changes benefited the Europeans, but many changes had a negative impact on the Native Americans.

Directions: Find out more about these changes by reading the paragraph below. Unscramble the groups of letters to make words that will complete each sentence. If you need help, use the Word Bank at the bottom of the page.

Some Europeans became (eltwayh) _____ from all the gold,

silver, and fur that they obtained from the (altvNe) _____Americans.

The European diet changed as new foods such as corn, (ocaoc) _____ ,

and (moselalo) _____ were introduced.

The Native Americans, however, did not fare well. Contagious (sedasesi) _____

were passed on to them by the explorers. (plamSlxo)_____ killed

close to (enysvet-vfie) _____ percent of the Native Americans who

once inhabited both North and South (rAicmea) _____ . Many

others died when they were forced to (bolar) _____ in mines and on farms.

Their lives were changed forever as they acquired European (solot)_____ ,

weapons, and cooking (slenutis)_____ ; began to breed horses,

cows, and (heicksnc)_____ ; and grew wheat and rice.

Word Bank

diseases	Smallpox	utensils	tomatoes
tools	chickens	wealthy	America
Native	labor	cocoa	seventy-five

Pocahontas

Born around 1595, the daughter of Indian Chief Powhatan was affectionately called Pocahontas, which means "playful one." Pocahontas' relationship with the Jamestown colonists proved invaluable to the struggling community.

One autumn, reports came that white men were building a fort near the James River. Months later, news of a fierce battle came from Powhatan's brother, Opechancanough; some Indians had been taken prisoner. Captain John Smith promised to set the Indians free only if corn was brought to Jamestown. Powhatan agreed to the demands.

Weeks later, Opechancanough's men captured Captain Smith himself during another skirmish and took him to Powhatan at the village of Werowocomoco.

When Captain Smith was delivered by his captors, however, he was honored by the villagers. Opechancanough was furious! Two of his braves had been killed; the young chief demanded Smith's life in exchange. Yielding to his younger brother's demands, Chief Powhatan ordered Smith beaten to death. As the popular—and much-debated—story goes, guards raised their war clubs, but Pocahontas dashed forward and laid herself upon Smith to save him. A displeased Chief Powhatan gave in to his daughter's wishes and ordered the guards to drop their weapons.

Two days later, Smith was told that they were now friends. Indeed, Pocahontas brought food to the settlers when they were starving; in 1609, she warned Smith of an impending ambush. In turn, Smith taught the Indian princess English words.

When Smith was seriously injured in a gunpowder explosion in 1609, he returned to England before the severe winter and "the starving time" set in. Hoping to improve relations with the Powhatans, Captain Samuel Argall kidnapped Pocahontas and took her to Jamestown. There she was made to live at Reverend Alexander Whitaker's residence in Henrico, a town upriver from Jamestown. Pocahontas was taught how to read and given instruction in the English ways. When she was baptized into Christianity, she was given the name Rebecca.

In 1614, she married John Rolfe, a plantation owner. This marriage brought peace among the settlers and the Native Americans. One year after the birth of Thomas, the Rolfes' only child, the family traveled to England to promote the Jamestown colony.

Known to the English as Lady Rolfe, Pocahontas was presented at the court of King James I. Unfortunately, Pocahontas's health began to fail, most likely because Native Americans had little resistance to European diseases. After regaining some strength, Pocahontas and her family boarded a ship bound for America in 1617. As the ship was anchored in the Thames River, Pocahontas became weak and died at the age of 21. She was buried at Gravesend on March 21, 1617.

Pocahontas Crossword Puzzle

Directions: Write the words in the proper spaces on the crossword puzzle below. Answers to these clues can be found in the story on page 166.

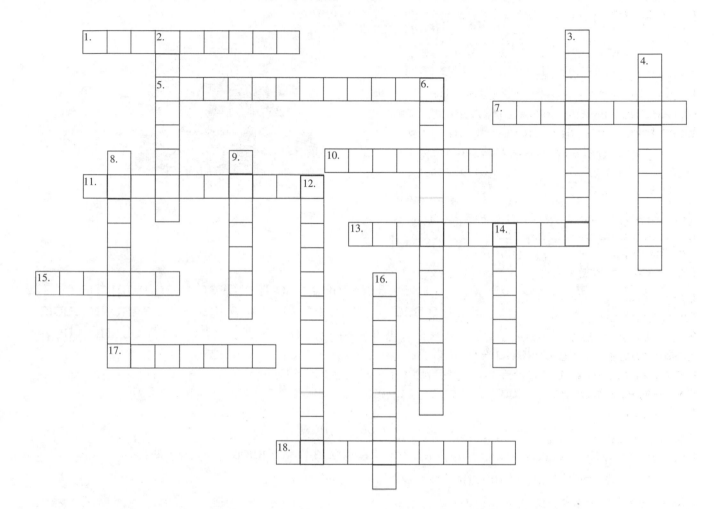

Across

1. Smith was injured in a _____ explosion.
5. Powhatan's village
7. Pocahontas had no resistance to European _____.
10. Pocahontas' Christian name
11. daughter of Powhatan
13. John Rolfe owned a _____.
15. name of the Rolfes' child
17. town where captured Pocahontas was taken
18. meaning of Pocahontas

Down

2. Pocahontas' father
3. where Pocahontas visited Captain Smith
4. age at which Pocahontas died
6. Powhatan's brother
8. Pocahontas saved the life of this captain.
9. country toured by the Rolfe family
12. captain who captured Pocahontas
14. river where ship anchored in England
16. Pocahontas' English title

Iroquois Native Americans

Directions: Read the passage below and answer the following questions.

The Native Americans called the Iroquois had a well-established nation. Several families, all related through the mother, lived in bark-covered long houses. They hunted for deer, fish, turkeys, and other wild animals with bows and arrows. They also grew squash, corn, beans, and berries. All food was shared among the members of the tribe so that everyone had enough to eat. When they were sick, their medicine men used herbal cures to make them well.

Women had an important role. They assigned and removed men from their tribal government. Five tribes joined to form an **alliance** known as the Iroquois League. They agreed that the five tribes would not fight with each other. They also promised to defend each other against outside attacks.

1. **You can conclude that in the Iroquois nation. . .**

    a. men were the only ones who had a say in how things were done.

    b. women were the only ones who had a say in how things were done.

    c. both men and women had a say in how things were done.

2. **After the Iroquois League formed,**

    a. it weakened the member tribes a great deal.

    b. it made it more risky for other tribes to attack them.

    c. it caused friction between the member tribes.

3. **Part of the Iroquois diet included. . .**

    a. raccoon.   b. ice cream.   c. chocolate.

4. **The word *alliance* means groups. . .**

    a. that are at war with each other.

    b. joined in a common cause.

    c. becoming independent of each other.

About the Navajo

The Navajo is the largest Native American tribe living in America today. There are about 140,000 and most live on the Navajo Reservation. The reservation is located in the northeast corner of Arizona, a small part of Utah, and a part of New Mexico.

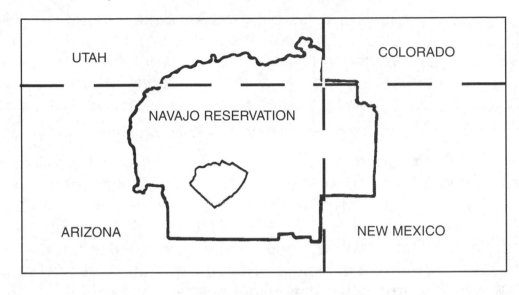

To the Navajo their land is sacred. It includes four sacred mountains—a white mountain, a turquoise blue mountain, a yellow mountain, and a mountain of jet black. The land is a mixture of desert, tall mountains, and deep canyons.

It is believed that the original Navajo people came to North America across the Bering Strait more than 20,000 years ago. These ancestors then migrated from what is now Alaska and Canada to the southwestern United States. They are closely related to the Apache. They settled near the Pueblos who taught them to farm. Early Spanish explorers called them "Apache de Nabaju"—the Apache of the Cultivated Fields. The Navajo call themselves Dine (Din-ay) which means The People.

The Navajo are a bright and adaptable people. They raise sheep which they learned from the Spanish. The art of weaving was learned from the Pueblo. A Navajo rug is a work of art and can sell for several thousand dollars. Silversmithing was learned from Mexican craftsmen. Navajo jewelry is now famous throughout the United States and Mexico.

Directions: Use complete sentences to answer the following questions.

1. Which states touch the Navajo reservation?_____

   _____

2. How do the Navajo feel about their land? _____

   _____

3. Where did the Navajo come from originally? _____

   _____

4. For what two crafts are the Navajo known? _____

   _____

Sacagawea Helped to Explore America

When Sacagawea was just 12 years old, Red Arrow kidnapped her. He took her to live with his tribe. Instead of her tipi, she had to live in a dark, earth-covered dome. Every day she worked in the fields. She never left the village until Red Arrow lost her in a bet. A fur trapper named Charbonneau won her. Sacagawea became his third wife. He and his other wives treated her as their slave. No one could guess the important role this young woman would play in U.S. history.

President Jefferson made the Louisiana Purchase in 1803. He asked Lewis and Clark to explore this land west of the Mississippi River. Jefferson hoped that they would find a water route to the Pacific Ocean. Lewis and Clark hired Charbonneau to help them. They asked to take Sacagawea, too. She went along, carrying her newborn baby on her back. Seeing her made Native Americans less afraid of the explorers. They did not attack. Both Lewis and Clark wrote in their journals that they might not have survived their trip to the West Coast without her.

While the men rode in a boat, Sacagawea often walked along the riverbanks, picking plants for food. She asked the Shoshone tribe to give them horses and tell them how to **traverse** the Rocky Mountains. She greeted other Native Americans using a language like their own. She also acted quickly when their boat tipped over. She grabbed their journals, instruments, and medicines before they sank or floated away. She made their 7,500-mile trip a success.

Lewis and Clark's long journey opened the West to white settlers. America started to expand from the East Coast to the West Coast. In Sacagawea's honor, the U.S. put her image on a one-dollar coin.

Sacagawea Helped to Explore America (cont.)

Comprehension Questions

1. **Who hired Charbonneau?**

   a. President Jefferson

   b. Sacagawea

   c. Red Arrow

   d. Lewis and Clark

2. **On a historical time line, what happened second?**

   a. Charbonneau married Sacagawea.

   b. Red Arrow kidnapped Sacagawea.

   c. Sacagawea had a baby.

   d. Sacagawea helped Lewis and Clark.

3. **How are modern parents like Sacagawea?**

   a. They often carry their babies in backpacks.

   b. They take their newborns on long journeys.

   c. They carry their babies through an unknown wilderness.

   d. They search riverbanks for food and medicine.

4. **The word _traverse_ means. . .**

   a. enjoy.

   b. find.

   c. travel across.

   d. go under.

5. **What disappointed Jefferson about Lewis and Clark's journey?**

   a. They never reached the Pacific Ocean.

   b. They could not find a water route to the West Coast.

   c. When their boat tipped over, they lost all of the maps and journals they had made.

   d. He didn't like the fact that Lewis and Clark had taken Sacagawea along.

6. **Picture Lewis and Clark's boat. What don't you see?**

   a. oars

   b. sails

   c. a wood frame

   d. paddle wheel

7. **Would you have liked to go with Sacagawea on Lewis and Clark's trip? Explain.**

   _____

   _____

   _____

Map of Native American Tribes

The map below shows the location of Native American tribes in terms of present-day state boundaries. Where tribes lived changed, depending upon circumstances such as hunting and war.

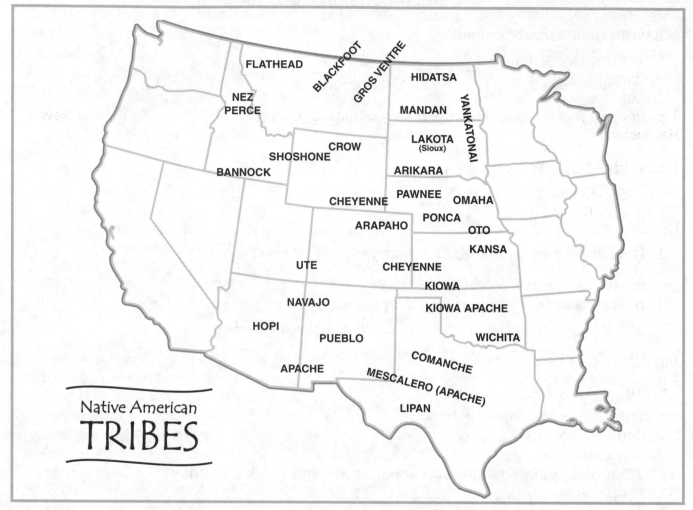

Directions: Listed below are states that became part of the United States as the country expanded westward. Using the map above and a current U.S. map, write down one Native American tribe that lived in each of these states. (Some states have more than one tribe.)

1. Arizona _____

2. Colorado _____

3. Idaho _____

4. Kansas _____

5. Montana _____

6. Nebraska _____

7. New Mexico _____

8. North Dakota _____

9. Oklahoma _____

10. South Dakota _____

11. Texas _____

12. Wyoming _____

172

The Thirteen Colonies

The New England Colonies

Most settlers in the New England colonies did some farming, but the land was actually poor for growing crops. It was strewn with rocks and tree stumps, and the growing season was short. There were many fine harbors, however, and many colonists were involved in fishing, shipbuilding, and shipping goods to and from other colonies and England. There were many merchants, artisans, and skilled workers in these towns.

Most families lived near a village, shopped regularly, and attended weekly church services. Many of the citizens were Puritans or other dissenters from the official Church of England. The New England colonies included Massachusetts, Connecticut, Rhode Island, and New Hampshire.

The Middle Colonies

New York, Delaware, New Jersey, and Pennsylvania comprised the middle colonies. There were many English settlers but also people from Germany, Sweden, Scotland, the Netherlands, and other countries. These colonies were often more free about practicing unpopular religions and were open to Quakers, Catholics, Jews, and dissenters from established churches in Europe. Most people owned small farms, although some wealthy landowners had huge holdings, especially in New York and New Jersey. The most powerful Indian tribe was the Iroquois, a powerful confederation of tribes in New York.

The Southern Colonies

Agriculture dominated the economy of the southern colonies. Large plantations were established by successful landowners and used to grow cash crops, which were exported rather than sold to the local population. Tobacco, rice, wheat, and indigo (a blue dye) were the main cash crops. This kind of economy required a large supply of cheap labor. Although indentured servants were used in the early years of settlement, the importation of black slaves from Africa soon became the source of cheap labor. The southern colonies included Virginia, Maryland, Georgia, North Carolina, and South Carolina. Charleston, South Carolina, and Savannah, Georgia, were thriving ports where crops could be exported and supplies imported.

List each of the Colonies below.

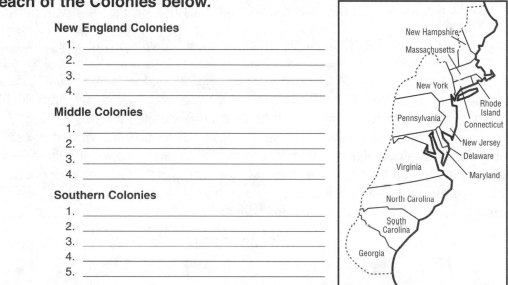

New England Colonies

1. _____
2. _____
3. _____
4. _____

Middle Colonies

1. _____
2. _____
3. _____
4. _____

Southern Colonies

1. _____
2. _____
3. _____
4. _____
5. _____

The American Colonies Before the Revolution

The New England Colonies

The first English settlements in New England were in the colony of Massachusetts. The Pilgrims founded the Plymouth community on the Massachusetts coast in December 1620. Another group of Puritans founded the Massachusetts Bay Colony in 1630. Despite extreme privations and the loss of many lives in the first years, these Puritans settled 130 communities by the mid-1600s. The colony of Rhode Island was created by religious dissidents who did not approve of Puritan religious practices or the mistreatment of Native Americans. Another group of dissidents founded Connecticut in the 1630s.

New Hampshire, which was settled by religious dissidents, farmers, fishermen, and traders, became a separate colony in 1680. The New England colonists engaged in several bitter wars with Native American tribes. People in the New England colonies took over the land and gradually killed or pushed the native people off their land. They cleared land for farms and established towns occupied by craftsmen who made everything from barrels and baskets to axes and plows. These hardy New England settlers survived bitter cold winters, famines, epidemics, wars, and deep personal and political conflicts over religion. Boston, the largest city in the New England colonies, was a very successful seaport with over 16,000 residents and many craftsmen, newspapers, and businesses.

The Middle Atlantic Colonies

The Middle Atlantic colonies were settled by other Europeans. The Dutch founded New Netherland in the 1620s, and Sweden started several settlements in what is now Delaware and New Jersey. The Dutch were forced to surrender New Netherland to a British naval force in 1664, and it was renamed New York. Portions of the southern half of this area were given to English landlords, who named their settlement New Jersey. Pennsylvania was founded in 1681 by William Penn, who was given the land by his friend the King of England to repay a debt. Penn intended the colony to become a **haven** for Quakers, a group of religious dissenters who disapproved of the Church of England.

The Middle colonies prospered because they had fertile soil. Farmers shipped wheat, farm animals, and other crops to New York and Philadelphia, the two largest cities, for sale overseas. These two cities used their seaports to develop thriving trading and shipping businesses. Many crafts and small industries developed in these colonies. New York City and Philadelphia had over 25,000 citizens and were the largest cities in the English colonies.

The Southern Colonies

The first permanent English settlement in North America was founded at Jamestown, Virginia, in 1607. After several years of severe famine, Indian warfare, and failure, this colony survived and flourished. Lord Baltimore founded Maryland as a refuge for Catholics, who were political dissidents in England, and to make a fortune in the tobacco business. Carolina was founded as a business venture in 1663. Political disputes caused it to split into two colonies in 1729. Georgia was founded as a refuge for dissident religious groups and debtors, who were allowed to leave prison in Britain and start new lives in the colonies. All of the southern colonies were devoted primarily to large-scale agriculture, which included growing cash crops such as tobacco, rice, and indigo (a plant that produces a bright blue dye). The labor-intensive nature of farming in the south led to the development of large plantations owned by rich landowners and worked by imported black slaves.

The American Colonies Before the Revolution (cont.)

Comprehension Questions

Directions: Read page 174 about the American colonies before the Revolution. Answer the questions below by circling the correct answer.

1. **In which colony were the first English settlements in New England located?**
   a. Connecticut
   b. Rhode Island
   c. Virginia
   d. Massachusetts

2. **Which religious group founded Plymouth Colony and the Massachusetts Bay Colony?**
   a. Puritans
   b. Church of England
   c. Catholics
   d. Quakers

3. **William Penn intended his colony to be a *haven* for Quakers. What does haven mean?**
   a. farm land
   b. church
   c. place of safety
   d. seaport

4. **Which was the largest city in the New England colonies?**
   a. New York
   b. Boston
   c. Philadelphia
   d. Baltimore

5. **In which colony was the first permanent English settlement in North America located?**
   a. Massachusetts
   b. Pennsylvania
   c. Virginia
   d. Maryland

6. **Georgia was founded as a refuge for which group of people?**
   a. Quakers
   b. debtors
   c. Puritans
   d. Catholics

7. **In which year did Carolina split into two colonies?**
   a. 1607
   b. 1729
   c. 1620
   d. 1663

8. **Which plant produces a blue dye?**
   a. indigo
   b. tobacco
   c. wheat
   d. rice

9. **Which colony was renamed New York?**
   a. New Jersey
   b. New Sweden
   c. New Netherland
   d. New England

10. **Which group of colonies grew cash crops on plantations and used black slaves for farming?**
    a. Southern
    b. Middle Atlantic
    c. New England
    d. New York

The Declaration of Independence

The Second Continental Congress

As the American colonies became more and more incensed by British efforts to impose taxes and exercise authority over them, some colonists were beginning to believe that only a complete separation from Great Britain would be acceptable. The Second Continental Congress met in May 1775 with the Colonies in a state of crisis. The Intolerable Acts had inflamed American anger not only in Boston but also throughout all of the colonies. Armed men in all of the colonies organized into **militias** to prepare for the coming conflict. The Continental Congress attempted to ward off the impending conflict by sending a petition to King George III suggesting a peaceful solution, but he refused to even read it.

The Committee of Five

In June 1776, Richard Henry Lee of Virginia presented a resolution in the Congress seeking full independence from Great Britain. At the time only seven colonies voted to support it. Some colonies needed the approval of their legislatures, and others were undecided. On June 11, 1776, five members of Congress were appointed to draft a declaration of independence to be voted on by the full Congress. John Adams of Massachusetts and Roger Sherman of Connecticut represented the northern colonies. Benjamin Franklin of Pennsylvania and Robert Livingston of New York represented the middle colonies. Thomas Jefferson of Virginia represented the southern colonies.

Jefferson Chosen to Write the Document

The Committee of Five had several meetings and chose Thomas Jefferson to write the original draft. He was well known as a gifted writer and a strong supporter of independence. Adams was particularly blunt in his reasons for supporting Jefferson. He was a Virginian, and they needed southern support for the resolution. Jefferson was also popular and well liked, as opposed to Adams who characterized himself as "obnoxious, suspected, and unpopular." Thirdly, Adams said that Jefferson could write 10 times better than he could.

Jefferson spent about two-and-a-half weeks writing his draft, mostly in the evenings. He had other congressional sessions and committee meetings to attend during the day. Jefferson showed his final draft to the other committee members, in particular Franklin and Adams, who made a few suggestions and changes. The document was submitted to Congress on June 28, 1776. For two days the Congress discussed Jefferson's draft. About 80 changes were made in the text, sometimes changes in wording or punctuation and sometimes the deletion of entire paragraphs. Jefferson, a slaveholder himself, wanted to declare an end to slavery, but some southern representatives would not accept this.

The Signing

In late afternoon on July 4, the delegates were satisfied with the Declaration and ready to sign it. John Hancock signed the document as president of the Continental Congress, and that made it legal. He wrote in a very large script, he claimed, so that King George could read it without his spectacles. The document was quickly printed and proclaimed throughout the colonies. Later, 55 other members of Congress signed the document pledging their lives, their fortunes, and their sacred honor to secure their liberty.

The Declaration of Independence Quiz (cont.)

Comprehension Questions

Directions: Read page 176 about the Declaration of Independence. Answer the questions below by circling the correct answer.

1. **Who introduced a resolution in the Continental Congress calling for independence from Great Britain?**
   a. George Washington
   b. John Hancock
   c. Thomas Jefferson
   d. Richard Henry Lee

2. **Which member of the committee who was chosen to write the Declaration of Independence characterized himself as "obnoxious, suspected, and unpopular"?**
   a. John Adams
   b. Thomas Jefferson
   c. John Hancock
   d. Benjamin Franklin

3. **How many changes in Jefferson's draft of the Declaration did Congress make?**
   a. none
   b. 2
   c. about 80
   d. about 12

4. **How long did Jefferson take to write the draft of the Declaration?**
   a. 4 years
   b. 2 days
   c. 2 months
   d. 2½ weeks

5. **How many members of Congress signed the Declaration of Independence?**
   a. 300
   b. 56
   c. 80
   d. none

6. **Who wrote his signature in a large script so that King George could read it without his spectacles?**
   a. Thomas Jefferson
   b. George Washington
   c. Benjamin Franklin
   d. John Hancock

7. **What are *militias*?**
   a. writers
   b. public speakers
   c. citizen soldiers
   d. legislators

8. **What would southern representatives in the Continental Congress not accept as part of the Declaration?**
   a. the idea of natural rights
   b. separation from Great Britain
   c. an end to slavery
   d. taxes on tobacco

9. **Which colony did Roger Sherman represent on the Committee of Five?**
   a. Connecticut
   b. Rhode Island
   c. Pennsylvania
   d. Virginia

10. **What were the signers of the Declaration prepared to pledge?**
    a. their children
    b. their futures
    c. their sacred honor
    d. their land

To Oregon or Bust!

Between 1800 and 1860 many people moved west. Farmers had heard of the rich soil and open land for animals to graze. The West also had supplies of gold, silver, coal, iron, copper, and timber.

The people usually followed trails that fur trappers or Native Americans had made. The Oregon Trail was one of the most well traveled. It went from Missouri to Oregon. It took about five months to travel its 2,000 miles. Some settlers followed the bumpy dirt path on horses. Others rode in wagons pulled by mules or oxen. These wagons had wooden boxes covered by a canvas tarp. The people packed bedding, guns, tools, and food in the wagons. To keep the weight down, they left behind anything that wasn't necessary. Still, when an animal died or got too weak to keep pulling the heavy wagon, the pioneers had to drop things beside the trail.

Families formed wagon trains. Each train had 30 to 70 wagons. The group hired a man as a guide and leader. Usually he had been a fur trapper who knew the trail well. Even in a big group, people faced **jeopardy** on the Oregon Trail. The settlers had to face heat, dust storms, and tornadoes. They entered a land that the Native Americans had lived in for thousands of years. Native Americans attacked the pioneers. So did thieves and wolves. Illnesses and a lack of medicine and proper food killed many people. Graves along the trail marked those who didn't make it.

The pioneers had to cross the Great Plains. Then they had to get through the Rocky Mountains before winter. Otherwise, they'd get stuck in the mountains. Snow would block the narrow passages. They could starve or freeze to death.

In spite of all of these hardships, thousands of people reached Oregon. Then they faced new challenges as they tried to build a life in the wilderness.

To Oregon or Bust! (cont.)

Comprehension Questions

Circle the letter to the best answer. You may look back at the story on page 178.

1. **Each wagon train wanted to get beyond the Rocky Mountains before. . .**

   a. fall.

   c. spring.

   b. winter.

   d. summer.

2. **What happened first?**

   a. The group found a leader.

   b. The people loaded their wagons.

   c. The people followed the Oregon Trail.

   d. People got together who wanted to go west.

3. **What caused so many people to travel west in the 1800s?**

   a. Diamonds were found.

   b. Free cattle were given to anyone who went.

   c. There was lots of land for growing crops and livestock.

   d. The West was a place of great natural beauty.

4. ***Jeopardy* means**

   a. danger.

   c. games.

   b. sadness.

   d. noise.

5. **If a family had to lighten their load along the Trail, what would they probably drop beside the path?**

   a. guns

   b. furniture

   c. food

   d. tools

6. **Picture yourself on the Oregon Trail long ago. What don't you see?**

   a. fields of grass waving in the wind

   b. tall mountains

   c. wide rivers

   d. farms

7. **What do you think was the biggest danger on the Oregon Trail? Explain.**

   _____

   _____

   _____

The Westward Movement

Heading West

The Westward movement of the American people across the continent from the Atlantic colonies to the Pacific coast was one of the greatest migrations in human history. Millions of settlers, American-born and immigrants from other lands, moved from the original 13 states across the nation. They eventually reached the Pacific coastline, and some then backtracked to settle in the Great Plains in the center of the country. The first major movement away from the coastal colonies along the Atlantic Ocean began just as the nation was beginning to rebel against British rule. The Wilderness Road, blazed by Daniel Boone and his companions in 1775, provided a route for pioneers to get through the Appalachian Mountains. Settlers also moved southwest into what would become Alabama, Mississippi, and Florida when the Spanish gave up this land to the U.S. in 1819.

Manifest Destiny

Many Americans felt the nation had a Manifest Destiny, an obligation to expand and settle the continent from the Atlantic Ocean to the Pacific Ocean. Expansion was seen as an irresistible historical tide. When Texas became an independent nation—separating from Mexico—settlers streamed into this new country and helped it become a state. The rush to Oregon and California began in the 1840s and continued for 20 years. The last westward push was to the Great Plains, first thought of as useless desert and then drawing many farmers and settlers to its rich soil.

Do It Yourself

People on the frontier had no one to rely upon but themselves. They were separated from relatives and friends living in settled communities. These pioneers had to build their own homes and farms. They built homes of logs, sod, or adobe depending on what was available. They treated themselves when sick because doctors were rarely available. Children learned to take responsibility early in life. They grew up quickly, married young, and raised large families.

New frontiers were usually populated by poor people looking for a fresh start. The leaders they elected to run the government or local military forces were men of action who had not inherited land or wealth. Men like Andrew Jackson and Davy Crockett were elected to public office because they lived just as other pioneers did. Their followers admired the courage and success of men like these.

Leaders had to pay attention to the demands of their **constituents** if they wanted to be successful. This could be good because people felt an immediate connection with their government. It had negative results too. In many cases it led to legislation against Native Americans, minorities, and foreigners which restricted their lives and liberties.

The Role of Women

On the frontier, women worked beside their men. They endured the sufferings of the wagon train. They helped with farm work and ran the farm if the man of the family was injured or died. Wives helped build log cabins and sod houses. On occasion, women fought Native Americans and outlaws. They operated mills, stores, and inns. Although the father was considered the head of the family, the fact that they shared the work tended to give women influence in family decisions and a voice in community life. It is no accident that the first states where women achieved the right to vote were western states like Montana and Wyoming.

The Westward Movement (cont.)

Comprehension Questions

Directions: Read page 180 about the Westward Movement. Answer the questions below by circling the correct answer.

1. **Through what mountains did the Wilderness Road provide a route?**

   a. Appalachian

   b. Rockies

   c. Sierra Nevada

   d. Cascade

2. **What term describes the idea that the United States would extend from the Atlantic to the Pacific Ocean?**

   a. migration

   b. Manifest Destiny

   c. democracy

   d. immigration

3. **Which man symbolizes a frontier leader?**

   a. George Washington

   b. John Adams

   c. Davy Crockett

   d. Thomas Jefferson

4. **Which of these materials was not used to build frontier homes?**

   a. cement

   b. logs

   c. sod

   d. adobe

5. **Which area was the last to be settled?**

   a. Oregon

   b. California

   c. Ohio

   d. Oklahoma

6. **Which of the following jobs did women do on the frontier?**

   a. operated stores

   b. built cabins

   c. fought Indians

   d. all of the above

7. **Which state was among the first to allow women to vote?**

   a. New York

   b. Tennessee

   c. Montana

   d. California

8. **Which of the following was generally true of young people on the frontier?**

   a. They married young.

   b. They accepted responsibility.

   c. They played a lot.

   d. Both a and b

9. **What does the word *constituents* mean?**

   a. hunters

   b. voters

   c. miners

   d. politicians

10. **When did the Spanish give Florida and parts of Alabama and Mississippi to the United States?**

    a. 1819

    b. 1899

    c. 1776

    d. 1789

Western Trails Map

The map below shows the trails that were used to travel west across the United States. Use this map to answer the questions on the next page.

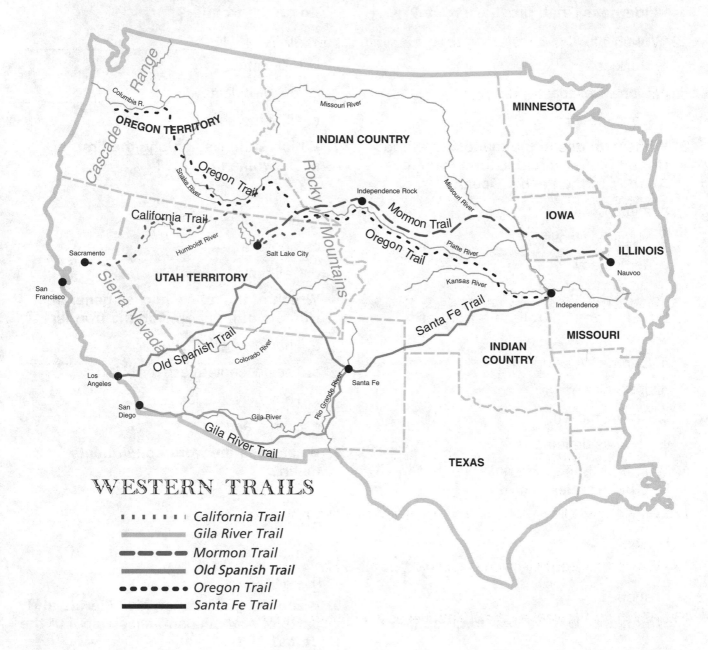

Social Studies

Western Trails Map (cont.)

Directions: Use the map on the previous page to answer the questions below.

1. What are the six major trails used for the westward migration of the American people?

   _____

2. Which city was the starting point for most of the trails? _____

3. In which two states did most of the trails end? _____

4. Where did the Mormon Trail begin? _____

5. Where did the Mormon Trail end? _____

6. Which trail went from Santa Fe to Los Angeles? _____

7. Which trail went from Santa Fe to San Diego? _____

8. Which trail was the longest? _____

9. Which two western mountain ranges did the California Trail cross? _____

10. Which two trails crossed the Rio Grande River? _____

11. Which trail followed the Humboldt River part of the way? _____

12. Which trail went over the Cascade Mountain Range? _____

13. Which trail went over the Sierra Nevada Mountain Range? _____

14. Which two trails followed the Platte River for a long distance? _____

   _____

U.S. Expansion Map

The map below shows the land acquisitions of the United States and the years in which territories were acquired.

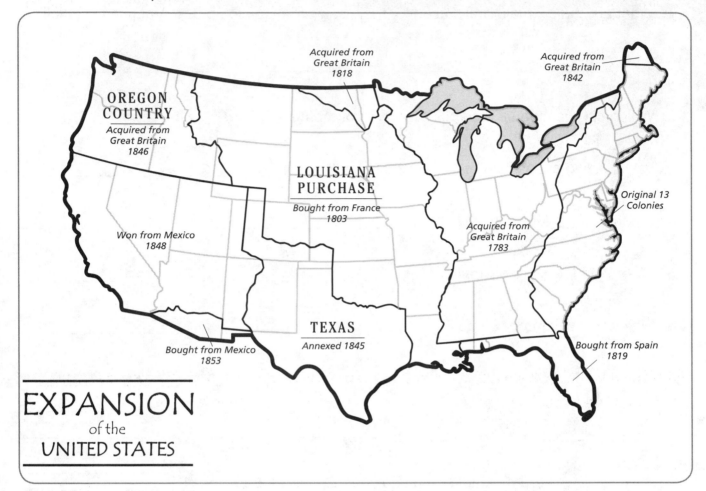

Directions: Use the map above and a current U.S. map to answer the following questions.

1. What seven U.S. states were partially or entirely created from land acquired by a treaty with Mexico in 1848? _____

2. Which three states were formed entirely from the Oregon Country? _____

3. What 14 states were formed in whole or in part from the Louisiana Purchase? _____

   _____

   _____

4. Which three states were formed in whole or in part from land acquired from Spain in 1819?

   _____

Frontier Railroads Map

The first transcontinental railroad was the Central Pacific and the Union Pacific. Later railroads were the Great Northern, the Atchison, Topeka, Santa Fe, and the Texas and Pacific (which connected New Orleans and Los Angeles).

Directions: Use the above map and a current U.S. map to answer the following questions.

1. Name five states the Central Pacific and Union Pacific passed through. _____
   _____

2. List seven cities on the Central Pacific/Union Pacific route. _____
   _____

3. Name five states the Southern Pacific passed through. _____
   _____

4. List five cities on the Southern Pacific route. _____
   _____

5. Name six states along the Great Northern route. _____
   _____

6. Name seven states through which the Atchison, Topeka, & Santa Fe traveled. _____
   _____

7. Give three states that the Texas & Pacific went through. _____
   _____

Frontier Words

Frontier living generated many new words that were commonly used by the pioneers. Figure out these words by reading the clues first. Then find the coordinates on the grid below.

Directions: Write the letter that is in that space on the proper lines. (To find the coordinates, go across the first number of spaces. From there, count up the second number of spaces.)

4	l	d	s	i	g	e	m	c	p	s	u	g	l	a	t
3	f	e	a	n	r	o	i	u	i	h	e	u	o	n	d
2	p	o	h	e	m	a	s	f	c	y	m	t	p	r	s
1	c	a	e	y	l	t	g	r	o	n	d	o	a	f	s
0	1	2	3	4	5	6	7	8	9	10	11	12	13	14	15

1. __ __ __ __ __   a prairie sod house
  3,4 13,3 2,4 11,1 10,2

2. __ __ __ __   __ __ __ __ __ __ __   also known as johnnycakes
  8,4 9,1 5,3 4,3   15,3 2,2 2,4 5,4 6,4 14,2 7,2

3. __ __ __ __ __ - __ __ __ __ __ __   they rushed to California to find gold
  8,2 12,1 8,1 15,4 4,1   4,3 7,3 10,1 3,1 5,3 10,4

4. __ __ __ __ __   dried buffalo manure used for fires
  8,4 3,2 9,3 13,2 3,4

5. __ __ __ __ __ __ __ __ __   settlers of the western frontier
  4,2 7,4 4,4 7,1 5,3 2,1 14,3 6,1 7,2

6. __ __ __ __   disease now known as malaria
  6,2 12,4 8,3 11,3

7. __ __ __ __ __ __ __ __   thieves who stole cattle
  5,3 11,4 15,2 6,1 13,4 2,3 8,1 15,1

8. prairie __ __ __ __ __ __ __ __   nickname for covered wagon
  7,2 1,1 10,3 2,2 9,1 14,3 3,1 5,3

Abraham Lincoln

Abraham Lincoln was born February 12, 1809, in a log cabin in the backwoods of Kentucky. When he was seven years old, his family moved to southwest Indiana where Lincoln helped to clear the fields and plant crops. His mother died when he was nine years old and his father remarried about a year later. He got along well with his stepmother and her three children. The family made another move to Illinois in 1830. Abraham was 21 years old and six feet four inches tall. He was muscular and physically powerful.

Abraham once said he went to school by "the littles"—a little now and a little then. He enjoyed reading and was a self-taught prairie lawyer. His political future began to take shape with his successful legal career in Springfield, Illinois. He ran for public office several times and served in the Illinois legislature and as a member of the U.S. House of Representatives.

He married Mary Todd on November 4, 1842. They had four children, Robert (the only one who lived to adulthood), Edward, William, and Thomas (Tad).

In 1858 he was the Republican candidate for the Senate. Though he was not an abolitionist, he was morally against slavery, a practice he had seen years before while visiting New Orleans. He ran against Stephen Douglas, and though Lincoln did not win, their debates made him famous. He was devoted to the cause of personal freedom for all people.

In 1860 Abraham Lincoln was elected president of the United States. As expected, the Southern (slave) states withdrew from the Union and formed the Confederate States of America. He led the North through the Civil War and wrote the Emancipation Proclamation, freeing the slaves. At Gettysburg, he gave one of his most famous speeches, declaring that government "of the people, by the people, for the people, shall not perish from the earth."

The war ended just as he was beginning his second term as president. He was planning the reconstruction of the United States. Within days of his second inauguration, Lincoln was assassinated by John Wilkes Booth. He died early on the morning of April 15, 1865.

1. **Going to school by "the littles" means . . .**
   a. learning a little now and a little then.
   b. being taught by a teacher named Mrs. Little.
   c. going to school in a little schoolhouse.
   d. not learning very much at all.

2. **According to the passage, Lincoln was a member of the U.S. . . .**
   a. army.
   b. Red Cross.
   c. House of Representatives.
   d. post office.

3. **What document freed the slaves?**
   a. The Gettysburg Address
   b. The Constitution
   c. The Bill of Rights
   d. The Emancipation Proclamation

4. **The Civil War ended just as Lincoln was beginning his . . .**
   a. legal career.
   b. second term as president.
   c. debates with Stephen Douglas.
   d. married life with Mary Todd.

Emancipation and Reconstruction

In the South many people believed that loyalty to their particular state was more important than loyalty to the Union. The Southern cotton plantations relied on slave labor, while the North was becoming industrialized and believed that slavery was wrong. Politicians could not agree on whether new states should permit slavery. It was this conflict between two basic ways of life that led to the start of the Civil War.

Soon after the election of Abraham Lincoln in 1860, the state of South Carolina seceded from the Union. Six other states, Alabama, Florida, Georgia, Louisiana, Mississippi, and Texas followed shortly thereafter. They formed a new government, the Confederate States of America, and elected Jefferson Davis their president. Lincoln believed that no state had the right to leave the Union, but in an effort to keep peace, he offered to continue slavery in states where it was not already illegal.

The North was superior in both resources and manufacturing. It had control of shipping but still had a difficult time occupying the Southern states and ending the struggle. The Southern strategy was to make the war so costly (in terms of money and lives) that the people would want to give up.

The Civil War began when the South fired on Fort Sumter (which was federal property) in Charleston, South Carolina. The battle ended with a Union surrender, though there were no soldiers killed on either side. Shortly after that, four more slave states, Arkansas, Tenneessee, North Carolina, and Virginia joined the Confederacy. General Robert E. Lee was commander in chief of all the Confederate forces. In 1864, Brigadier General Ulysses S. Grant was made general in chief of all the Union armies.

The land and sea battles claimed over 600,000 lives. After the Union victory at Antietam (1863), Lincoln issued the Emancipation Proclamation that declared slaves in the Southern states were free. (They actually were not freed until the war was over in 1865.) Another important Union victory was at Gettysburg, Pennsylvania, where Lincoln delivered his famous Gettysburg Address.

Lee surrendered to Grant on April 9, 1865, at Appomattox Court House after defeats at Vicksburg, Richmond, and Petersburg. Five days later, Abraham Lincoln was assassinated by a Southern sympathizer, John Wilkes Booth, while watching a play at Ford's Theatre in Washington.

After Lincoln's death, a plan for reconstruction was undertaken by Andrew Johnson, the new president. It was most important to reunite the states. The states had to approve the Thirteenth Amendment, which abolished slavery. By the end of 1865, all the Confederate states (but Texas) had reentered the Union. In March 1865, Congress established the Freedmen's Bureau to provide freed slaves with food and medical care. They also set up schools and helped former slaves find jobs. Slaves could be legally married, and their children belonged to them, not the slave owner.

The South was ruled by the Union army until it formed new state governments. The new state legislatures had to adopt two new amendments to the Constitution. The Fourteenth Amendment said all people born in the United States were citizens and would be treated equally under the law. The Fifteenth Amendment said no citizen could be denied the right to vote, regardless of color or race. Southerners were unhappy with the changes.

Emancipation and Reconstruction (cont.)

Comprehension Questions

1. **According to the passage on page 188, what led to the start of the Civil War?**
   a. People in different states disagreed on what new states to add to the Union.
   b. People in different states disagreed on the subject of slavery.
   c. People in different states disagreed about the country's flag.
   d. People in different states disagreed about whether to grow cotton or a different kind of crop.

2. **The Civil War began when . . .**
   a. the South fired on Fort Sumter.
   b. South Carolina seceded from the Union.
   c. Jefferson Davis was elected president.
   d. the North became more industrialized.

3. **Who were the two generals in charge of the armies in the Civil War?**
   a. Abraham Lincoln and Jefferson Davis
   b. Stephen Douglas and George Washington
   c. Robert E. Lee and Ulysses S. Grant
   d. Andrew Johnson and John Wilkes Booth

4. **What are two things the Freedmen's Bureau provided to former slaves?**
   a. food and drink
   b. blankets and bandages
   c. beds and bathrooms
   d. food and medical care

5. **The Fourteenth Amendment said that all people born in the United States . . .**
   a. had to move to one of the new states.
   b. were citizens and would be treated equally under the law.
   c. had to help rebuild the South through Reconstruction.
   d. were allowed to vote.

6. **The Fifteenth Amendment gave all citizens the right to . . .**
   a. bear arms.
   b. live.
   c. vote.
   d. pray.

World War II Submarines

America entered World War II after the Japanese attacked Pearl Harbor. Since the attack was a complete surprise, it destroyed most of the American warships there.

Japan is an island in the Pacific Ocean. It has few natural resources. All of its fuel came by ship. So did all the materials needed to build planes, ships, and submarines for the war.

Of course, Americans did not want the Japanese to get fuel or supplies. Yet for the first months of the war, the U.S. only had submarines that were able to fight. So the subs were sent to sink the ships carrying goods to Japan. They did an amazing job. Even though subs had less than 2% of the Navy's **manpower**, they caused more than half of Japan's shipping losses: 5.3 million tons of materials and fuel.

U.S. subs also gathered information. Later in the war, they rescued American pilots who had their planes shot down over the ocean. The first President George Bush was one of the Navy pilots saved in this way.

Life on a submarine was not easy. The air was stuffy. It was crowded. There was no place to be alone. In the main aisle of the sub, each man had to frequently pause while someone squeezed past. Each person's bunk was barely big enough to lie down on. Serving on a sub was scary, too. If an enemy discovered a sub, the sailors had to shut down its engines and hope that the depth charges fired on them would miss.

Due to the many hardships, everyone on a sub was a volunteer. Before going down, these men had to pass a lot of physical and mental testing. They had to convince doctors that they wouldn't crack under the pressure of being thousands of feet below water with no chance for escape or rescue.

Many men on subs lost their lives in World War II. More than 3,600 Americans lie in watery graves where their submarines sank.

World War II Submarines (cont.)

Comprehension Questions

1. **The Japanese needed supply ships because . . .**
   a. the ships were so reliable and always delivered all of the goods.
   b. they didn't have the money to develop their own resources.
   c. it was cheap to import fuel.
   d. they didn't have the supplies on their own island.

2. **On a historical time line, what happened second?**
   a. U.S. subs picked up downed American pilots.
   b. U.S. subs attacked supply ships.
   c. The Japanese lost World War II.
   d. The Japanese attacked Pearl Harbor.

3. **Why are so many submariners on the bottom of the ocean instead of in a cemetery?**
   a. Their families didn't want their bodies returned to them.
   b. They asked to be buried at sea.
   c. It was too difficult to find them and bring them back to the surface.
   d. People in wars aren't buried; their bodies are left lying wherever they die.

4. **Manpower means . . .**
   a. the number of men minus the number of women.
   b. something that works when people push it.
   c. the number of people working.
   d. having a manual instead of an automatic transmission.

5. **Why did each submariner have to go through so much testing?**
   a. to be sure the man could stay calm under high stress and fear
   b. to keep out men who didn't like swimming
   c. to know which men truly wanted to volunteer
   d. to keep out men who came from small families

6. **Picture a World War II submarine under water. How can the captain best see what is happening on the surface?**
   a. only by bringing the submarine up to the surface
   b. by having some men swim to the surface
   c. by opening a hatch
   d. by using a periscope

7. **Would you have volunteered to serve on a World War II submarine? Explain.**

   _____

   _____

   _____

Final Days of World War II

On April 25, 1945, Harry Truman learned that the United States had a new weapon of "almost unbelievable destructive power." President Roosevelt had authorized the secret "Manhattan Project" which produced a bomb that could destroy an entire city.

The war in Europe was over, and the Nazi government under Adolf Hitler had surrendered. Secretary of War Henry Stimson suggested that the atomic bomb would quickly end the war with Japan.

Truman met with Allied leaders in Potsdam, Germany, on July 16. On July 26, the Allied leaders sent an ultimatum to Japan. The Japanese ignored warnings and refused to surrender because they did not know about the A-bomb. Some scientists felt that the bomb should not be used to shorten the war; however, President Truman believed that if American soldiers would be saved, it should be used.

Despite widespread death and destruction, the atomic bomb dropped on Hiroshima on August 6, 1945, did not make the Japanese surrender. President Truman ordered a second bomb to be dropped three days later on Nagasaki. World War II was over.

1. Describe the power of the atomic bomb. _____

   _____

2. Who was Henry Stimson? _____

   _____

3. How did he want to end the war with Japan? _____

   _____

4. How did Japan respond to the warnings of Allied leaders? _____

   _____

5. How did President Truman justify using the A-bomb? _____

   _____

6. Name the two Japanese cities that were bombed to end World War II.

   _____ and _____

7. Do you admire President Truman's ability to make difficult decisions? Do you think Franklin Roosevelt would have decided to bomb Japan if he had been alive? Explain.

   _____

   _____

Brown v. Board of Education

This case is one of the most important in the history of the Supreme Court. It directly affected segregated schools in twenty-one states and proved that separate schools cannot be truly equal.

There were three cases combined in *Brown v. Board of Education.*

In the first, Oliver Brown of Topeka, Kansas, sued the Board of Education because his daughter Linda was forced to cross railroad tracks and take a bus to school when a better white school was only five blocks from her home. In the second suit, *Briggs v. Clarendon County*, twenty black parents sued the Clarendon County, South Carolina, School District because they spent $43 per year on black students and $179 per year on white students. The third case, *Davis v. County School Board of Prince Edward County*, was filed by the NAACP on behalf of 117 black high school students who were angry about conditions in their school. These three suits were combined when they went before the Supreme Court.

The Supreme Court listened to NAACP lawyer Thurgood Marshall argue for the children, saying that separating people makes them feel inferior. On the other side, John W. Davis argued that the Constitution did not prevent separation and that states had the right to make their own decisions in social matters like segregation. The Court considered the problem for a year. During that time, the chief justice died, and President Eisenhower appointed Earl Warren to take his place.

Earl Warren was able to convince the Supreme Court that the "separate but equal" position had no place in public education.

The Court was unanimous in its decision.

Summarize what you know about *Brown v. Board of Education.*

The three cases and details:

1. _____

   _____

2. _____

   _____

3. _____

   _____

The two lawyers and their positions:

1. _____

2. _____

The decision: _____

Amazing Weather Facts

Directions: Each 2-digit number stands for a letter. The tens digit numbers are printed vertically. The ones digit numbers are across the top. A = 11, B = 12, F = 21, and so on. Here is an example:

Example: A = 11, R = 43

$$\frac{r}{43} \quad \frac{a}{11} \quad \frac{i}{24} \quad \frac{n}{34}$$

	1	2	3	4	5
1	A	B	C	D	E
2	F	G	H	I	J
3	K	L	M	N	O
4	P	Q	R	S	T
5	U	V	W	X	Y

Fact 1: The world's highest average precipitation occurs in $\overline{13}\ \overline{35}\ \overline{32}\ \overline{35}\ \overline{33}\ \overline{12}\ \overline{24}\ \overline{11}$ which has a whopping 524" $\overline{43}\ \overline{11}\ \overline{24}\ \overline{34}$ each year.

Fact 2: The world's lowest average precipitation is not in a $\overline{14}\ \overline{15}\ \overline{44}\ \overline{15}\ \overline{43}\ \overline{45}$! The $\overline{14}\ \overline{43}\ \overline{24}\ \overline{15}\ \overline{44}\ \overline{45}$ place on Earth is in the $\overline{11}\ \overline{34}\ \overline{14}\ \overline{15}\ \overline{44}$ $\overline{33}\ \overline{35}\ \overline{51}\ \overline{34}\ \overline{45}\ \overline{11}\ \overline{24}\ \overline{34}\ \overline{44}$ of $\overline{13}\ \overline{23}\ \overline{24}\ \overline{32}\ \overline{15}$, where there's just 0.03" of rainfall annually.

Fact 3: What's really surprising is that $\overline{12}\ \overline{35}\ \overline{45}\ \overline{23}$ of these $\overline{13}\ \overline{35}\ \overline{51}\ \overline{34}\ \overline{45}\ \overline{43}\ \overline{24}\ \overline{15}\ \overline{44}$ are on the same $\overline{13}\ \overline{35}\ \overline{34}\ \overline{45}\ \overline{24}\ \overline{34}\ \overline{15}\ \overline{34}\ \overline{45}$! They are located on the $\overline{53}\ \overline{15}\ \overline{44}\ \overline{45}$ $\overline{13}\ \overline{35}\ \overline{11}\ \overline{44}\ \overline{45}$ of $\overline{44}\ \overline{35}\ \overline{51}\ \overline{45}\ \overline{23}$ $\overline{11}\ \overline{33}\ \overline{15}\ \overline{43}\ \overline{24}\ \overline{13}\ \overline{11}$.

Fact 4: The most $\overline{14}\ \overline{11}\ \overline{34}\ \overline{22}\ \overline{15}\ \overline{43}\ \overline{35}\ \overline{51}\ \overline{44}$ month when the majority of $\overline{23}\ \overline{51}\ \overline{43}\ \overline{43}\ \overline{24}\ \overline{13}\ \overline{11}\ \overline{34}\ \overline{15}\ \overline{44}$ strike Mexico, the Caribbean, and the U.S.A. is $\overline{44}\ \overline{15}\ \overline{41}\ \overline{45}\ \overline{15}\ \overline{33}\ \overline{12}\ \overline{15}\ \overline{43}$.

Weather Words

Directions: Find and circle the different types of weather listed in the Word List.

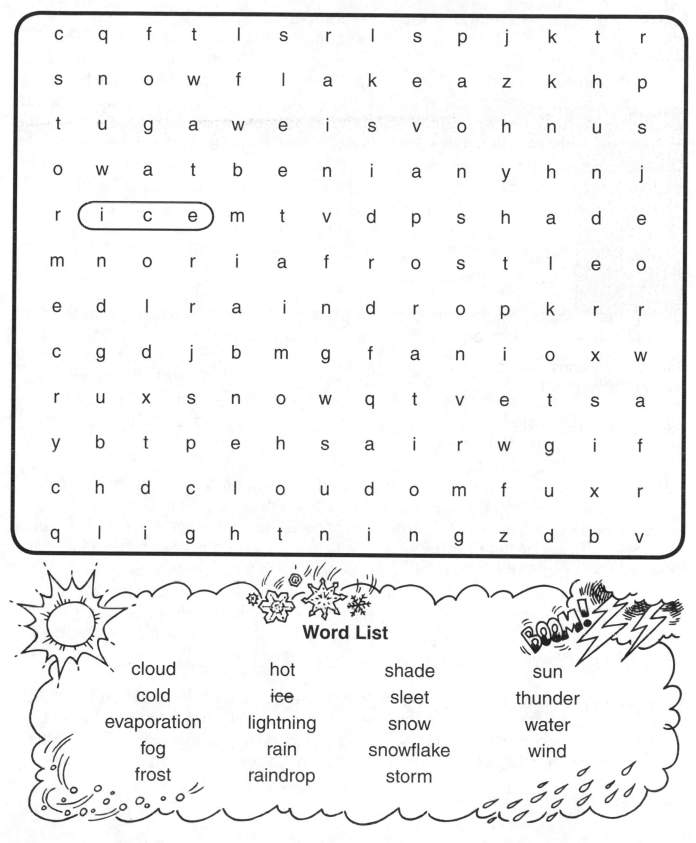

c q f t l s r l s p j k t r
s n o w f l a k e a z k h p
t u g a w e i s v o h n u s
o w a t b e n i a n y h n j
r i c e m t v d p s h a d e
m n o r i a f r o s t l e o
e d l r a i n d r o p k r r
c g d j b m g f a n i o x w
r u x s n o w q t v e t s a
y b t p e h s a i r w g i f
c h d c l o u d o m f u x r
q l i g h t n i n g z d b v

Word List

cloud	hot	shade	sun
cold	~~ice~~	sleet	thunder
evaporation	lightning	snow	water
fog	rain	snowflake	wind
frost	raindrop	storm	

El Niño Brings Weird Weather

Did you know that a change in the water temperature near South America can affect your weather? It's true. An ocean current runs along the shore of Peru. It normally flows from south to north. Each year in late December it changes direction and flows north to south. When that happens, warmer waters flow along the coast. Sometimes when this happens, the water gets too warm for the fish. They must leave the area to find food. This causes problems for the people in Peru who rely on the fish for food. Without the fish, many seabirds starve. Their bodies fall into the ocean and rot. This makes a chemical called hydrogen sulfide. This chemical combines with the salt in the water to form an acid so strong that it removes the paint on boats. The wind carries this acid through the air and ruins the paint of the houses on shore, too. It also damages crops and other plants. The people of Peru call this weather event El Niño, Spanish for "little child."

During the 1800s, scientists studied the personal journals of people who lived in Peru hundreds of years ago. They wrote about these **mysterious** events. Their diaries helped scientists to figure out answers to some of their questions about this strange change in the ocean. In the early 1900s Sir Gilbert Walker wanted to predict dangerous monsoons. Monsoons are strong storms that bring wet, warm weather to India each year. Walker did research and found that El Niño caused the weather to change in India. But no one believed him.

It took another 50 years for scientists to really understand that a strong El Niño current near Peru meant weak monsoons on the other side of the world in India. A weak El Niño current meant strong monsoons. In the years when El Niño is especially strong or the current lasts a long time, it can cause weird weather all around the world. This happens because the current changes the location of the warmest ocean waters. Powerful thunderstorms develop over the warmest water. These storms determine where the winds blow. El Niño can cause areas that usually have little rain to get lots of it. Places that need rain for crops may have a bad dry spell.

Most scientists think that a strong El Niño comes every three to seven years. So far no one can really predict which years the current will have the most effect. When the El Niño current is strong, its effects can last up to a year. During the past 40 years the people who study weather have recorded 10 strong El Niños.

196

El Niño Brings Weird Weather (cont.)

Comprehension Questions

1. Strong El Niños usually occur. . .

a. once a decade.

b. every year.

c. once a century.

d. every 3–7 years.

2. During a year with a strong El Niño, what would happen second?

a. Dead birds fall into the ocean.

b. Many fish leave the area.

c. The current changes direction.

d. Hydrogen sulfide and salt water make a strong acid.

3. A weak El Niño causes. . .

a. more rain to fall in India.

b. less rain to fall in India.

c. forest fires in the U.S. Midwest.

d. floods in the African deserts.

4. *Mysterious* means. . .

a. dangerous.

b. exciting.

c. not understood.

d. predictable.

5. What do you think most Peruvian fishermen do during strong El Niño seasons?

a. They have a celebration.

b. They starve to death.

c. They stop fishing and start farming.

d. They go farther away from home to catch fish.

6. Picture a monsoon approaching the coast of India. What don't you see?

a. pleasure boats

b. flooding

c. heavy rainfall

d. lightning

7. What is your favorite type of weather? Explain.

_____

_____

_____

Blizzard! (cont.)

A blizzard is more than just a bad snowstorm. It's a powerful snowstorm with strong, cold winds. Blizzards usually come after a spell of warm winter weather. A mass of cold air moves down from the Arctic Circle. This cold, heavy air drops down while the warmer, moist air rises. This forms a cold front. The result is a heavy snowfall whipped by bitter north winds.

The National Weather Service of the United States defines a blizzard as a snowstorm with winds of 35 miles per hour (56 km/h). The blowing snow makes it hard to see even a foot or two ahead. During a really severe blizzard, winds gust at over 45 miles per hour (72 km/h). Then **visibility** is zero. Temperatures can drop to 10°F (-12°C).

A huge blizzard in March 1888 covered the eastern U.S., choking New York City. It took more than a week to dig the city out. During that time many people froze to death inside their homes. Blizzards caused trouble for the settlers in the West, too. The dangerous weather came without much warning. People had to rush to get themselves and their animals indoors. Otherwise they would die. Sometimes people were found frozen just a few feet away from their house or barn. They just couldn't see well enough to find shelter. It was risky to be out in a storm, yet someone had to feed the animals. So people tacked one end of a rope to their barn. They nailed the other end of the rope to their house. They went back and forth holding the rope. This kept them from getting lost in the blinding snow.

Blizzards happen in the U.S. Northern Plains states, in eastern and central Canada, and in parts of Russia. The high winds can blow snow into huge drifts 15 feet (5 m) high. These snowdrifts often stop all transportation. Schools and businesses close down for days until the snow gets cleared away. During that time, if a person needs to get to the hospital, an ambulance cannot help. Instead the person must go in a snowplow!

Blizzard! (cont.)

Comprehension Questions

Directions: Circle the letter next to the best answer. You may look back at the story on page 198 for help.

1. **How does a blizzard differ from a regular snowstorm?**
   a. A blizzard has high winds that blow lots of snow around.
   b. A blizzard has lots of snow but no wind.
   c. A blizzard has high winds but no snow.
   d. No one knows when a blizzard is coming.

2. **What would happen first?**
   a. The ambulance sent a snowplow to help Ms. Ramirez.
   b. Ms. Ramirez called an ambulance.
   c. There was a blizzard.
   d. Ms. Ramirez had a medical emergency.

3. **Why does transportation usually halt during a blizzard?**
   a. The snowdrifts bury all vehicles.
   b. Winds blow the vehicles right off the road.
   c. It's too cold for any engine to run.
   d. People can't see well enough to drive or to fly.

4. ***Visibility* means. . .**
   a. the ability to smell.
   b. the ability to see.
   c. the ability to hear.
   d. the ability to feel.

5. **Why do blizzards occur in the areas stated in the passage?**
   a. because these places are far from the Arctic Circle
   b. because these places are near the Arctic Circle
   c. because these places are south of the Equator
   d. because these places are near Antarctica

6. **Picture yourself watching the weather on TV. The weather forecaster says that a blizzard will hit your area tonight. You can expect that tomorrow you will most likely**
   a. have no light, heat, water, or phone service.
   b. go to school.
   c. go to the grocery store for food.
   d. stay at home.

7. **Do you think that modern weather forecasting has helped more people to survive blizzards? Explain.**

   _____

   _____

   _____

Twisters

Directions: Read the paragraph below and answer the questions.

Twisters, or tornadoes, are dark spinning clouds with winds as high as 300 miles per hour. These deadly storms are caused by a combination of warm air, wind, and high humidity. These factors create strong thunderstorms called supercells.

Although they can happen at any time, tornadoes usually strike from April to June. They occur most often in the Midwest. There they roar across the plains.

Every year about 1,000 tornadoes strike the U.S. This is more than any other nation. Most are not serious. However, each year about three dozen cause **significant** damage. Small twisters reach 112 miles per hour. They uproot trees and tip over cars. The strongest tornadoes can pick up a house and smash it or drop it as far as a mile away.

1. **One of the states most apt to be hit by tornadoes is. . .**
   a. Kansas.

   b. Maine.

   c. Alaska.

2. **It would be most unusual for a tornado to occur during the month of. . .**
   a. May.

   b. July.

   c. December.

3. **You can conclude that twisters are the direct result of. . .**
   a. warm winds.

   b. supercells.

   c. low humidity.

4. **The word *significant* means. . .**
   a. occasional.

   b. minor.

   c. major.

Windy Weather

1. When Joyce woke up, she heard a strong wind blowing. Thinking of the word "blowing" made her think of this word puzzle:

   Joyce wrote the word "blowing." The wind blew one of the letters away, leaving behind another word: "bowing." Then the wind continued to blow one letter away at a time, each time leaving behind a word. The last word had only one letter.

   <u>blowing</u> _____

   <u>bowing</u> _____

   _____

   _____

   _____

   _____

2. What are three small words spelled in order within the word "tornado"?

   _____ _____ _____

3. Can you change one letter at a time to make "front" into "cold"? Each step must produce a real word. Here's how you could do it:

   > front → font → fond → fold → cold

4. Now you try! Change "wind" into "warm." Remember, each step must produce a real word.

   _wind___ → _____ → _____ → _____ → _warm__

Wild Weather

You've probably heard the saying, "It's raining cats and dogs!" That's just an expression to say that it's raining hard. But would you believe that one day in France it really rained frogs?

It started out as just a typical rainy day in a small town near Paris. People went out with raincoats and umbrellas. Everything seemed normal. Suddenly, frogs started falling from the sky. They smashed through car windows. They bounced off people's heads. Everyone was scared. What was happening?

Scientists believe a waterspout made the frogs fall. Waterspouts are like tornadoes that form over large lakes or oceans. A waterspout forms when warm, moist air meets cold, dry air and creates a thick, spinning cloud. This cloud has wind speeds of about 50 miles per hour (80 km/h). It can reach up to four miles (6.4 km) high in the atmosphere. Just like a land tornado, a waterspout lifts things up and swirls them around, sometimes dropping them far away. A waterspout lasts longer than a tornado, but it loses power as it moves over land. As its strength **diminishes**, the things it sucked up from the water drop to the ground— sometimes up to 100 miles (160 km) away from where they were collected.

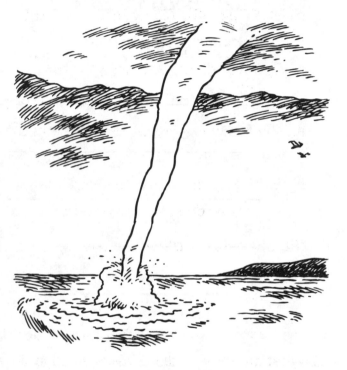

Most waterspouts occur in the tropics, but America has had its share of them. Snails fell in Pennsylvania in 1869. Seven years later, hundreds of large snakes fell in Tennessee. In Louisiana thousands of fish plunged to the ground in 1949. In more recent years a waterspout picked up a five-ton (4.5 metric tons) houseboat and flung it on the ground in Florida.

Wild Weather (cont.)

Comprehension Questions

Directions: Use the story from page 202 to answer the questions below.

1. **Snakes fell from the sky in. . .**

   a. Louisiana.

   b. Pennsylvania.

   c. Tennessee.

   d. Florida.

2. **In the formation of a waterspout, what would happen third?**

   a. Water animals are snatched up out of the water.

   b. Warm air and cold air meet over water.

   c. A spinning funnel cloud forms.

   d. Animals fall from the sky.

3. **How do tornadoes and waterspouts differ?**

   a. The winds in waterspouts spin faster than those in tornadoes.

   b. Waterspouts can't move over land; tornadoes can.

   c. Tornadoes cause less damage than waterspouts.

   d. Tornadoes don't form over water; waterspouts do.

4. **The opposite of *diminishes* is. . .**

   a. changes.

   b fades.

   c. increases.

   d. decreases.

5. **Even with modern weather forecasting,**

   a. no one can predict when a waterspout will occur.

   b. no one has ever seen a waterspout.

   c. no one knows how waterspouts form.

   d. no one knows when a waterspout has happened.

6. **Picture a waterspout over the ocean. What is it most likely to suck up?**

   a. frogs

   b. fish

   c. snails

   d. snakes

7. **Would you like to experience a waterspout? Explain.**

   _____

   _____

   _____

Weather Crossword Puzzle

Directions: Use the clues below to solve the crossword puzzle.

Across	Down
4. partly frozen rain	1. heavy winds and rain
6. drops of water from a cloud	2. source of light and heat
7. cirrus or cumulous	3. frozen rain drops
9. blowing air	5. loud boom
10. cold and white	8. rain protection
11. degrees	
12. electricity in the sky	

Weather Wise

Directions: Hidden in each sentence is a word that a meteorologist might use in a weather report. Each "weather word" can be found either in the middle of a word or by combining the end of one word with the beginning of the next. Underline the "weather word" in each sentence. Here is an example: **He is now in fifth grade. (*weather word = snow*)**

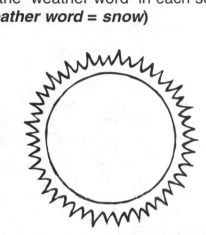

1. There was mildew in the bathroom.

2. They had to move the show indoors.

3. The cannon was shot during the Civil War.

4. The tamales were pretty spicy.

5. I'd like to sail the seas on an inner tube!

6. She is unlikely to pass the test.

7. They were about to scold Jess for being late.

8. Heather is learning to speak Spanish.

9. I sprained my ankle at the game.

10. The Thunderbird car is made by Ford.

11. In public, loud noises can be distracting.

12. The monster has torn a door off of its hinges.

13. It has clearly annoyed the dog.

14. Threats of war might encourage the two countries to negotiate.

Predicting Earthquakes

Earthquake Probability

Materials

- copies of pages 207 and 208
- pencil
- colored pencils or crayons
- calculator (optional)

Procedure

First, complete the math calculations below for the San Andreas Fault. Explain to students that the solutions (quotients) to these problems yield a percentage that indicates the probability of earthquakes in the places listed. Then write the percentages on the Probability Map (page 207). Finally, create a bar graph (page 208) that shows the areas along the San Andreas Fault in California where the probability of an earthquake is more likely.

Fundamental Facts

Seismologists predicted a major earthquake would hit somewhere along the San Andreas Fault around the year 2000. Earthquake research shows that a major earthquake has occurred in California about every 150 years. Seismologists can predict the place and magnitude of a probable earthquake, but the time of occurrence can only be established within 30 years.

Percentage Math

Percentage calculations are used by scientists to evaluate data. After analyzing the data, it can be used to predict an earthquake.

Complete the following math calculations and convert them to percentages. Add the percentages to the cities on the Probability Map. Then complete the Probability Graph and questions on page 208.

1. $27 \div 45 =$._____ or _____% San Bernardino	**2.** $173 \div 346 =$._____ or _____% Eureka	**3.** $54 \div 90 =$._____ or _____% Los Angeles
4. $19 \div 21 =$._____ or _____% Parkfield	**5.** $116 \div 172 =$._____ or _____% San Francisco	**6.** Sacramento, the capital of California, is located in the same region as San Francisco. Create a percentage calculation that will equal 59% probability for Sacramento.

Predicting Earthquakes *(cont.)*

Probability Map

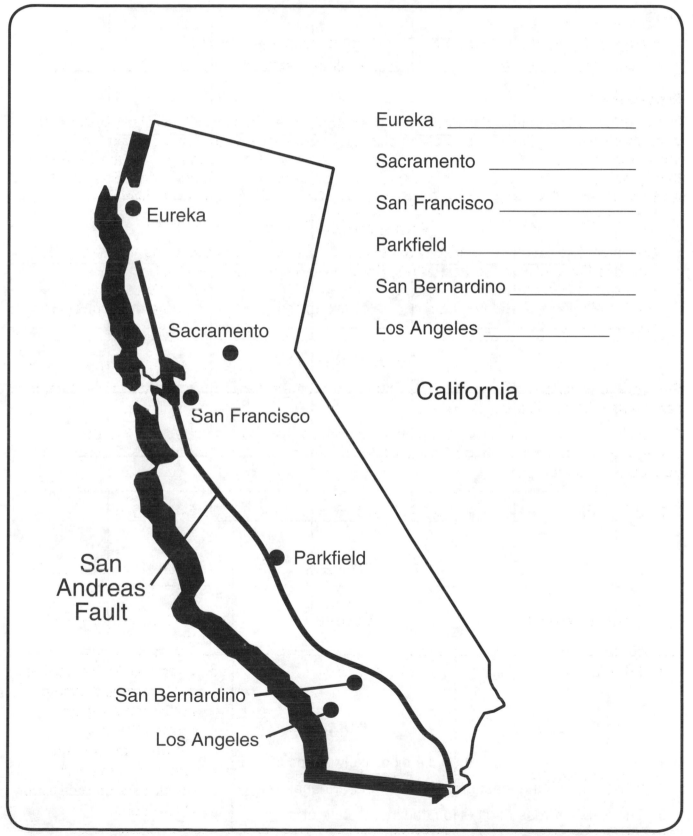

Eureka _____

Sacramento _____

San Francisco _____

Parkfield _____

San Bernardino _____

Los Angeles _____

California

Predicting Earthquakes (cont.)

Probability Graph

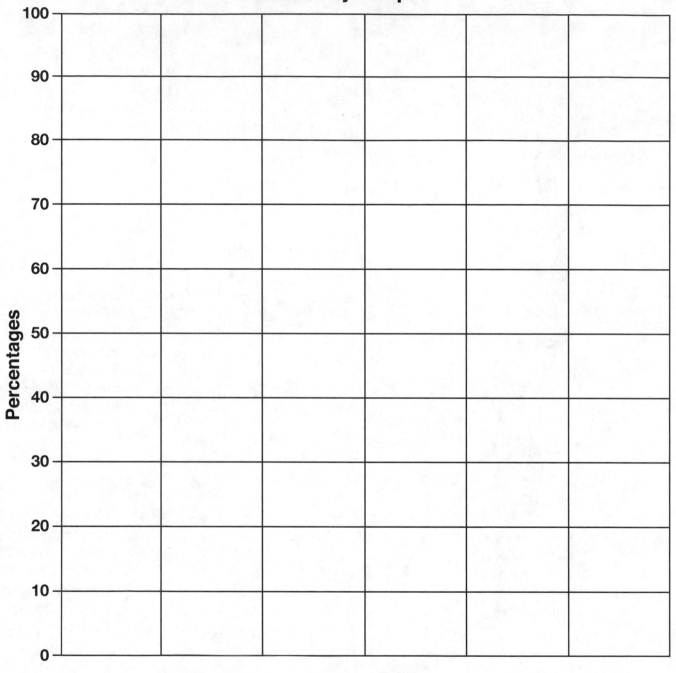

Cities

1. Near what city is an earthquake most likely to occur? _____

2. What city has the least probability of an earthquake? _____

3. The San Andreas Fault is located in the state of _____ .

Volcanic Reactions

A **volcano** is an opening in the earth's crust. **Ashes**, hot gases, **lava** and pieces of rock erupt through this opening when underground **magma chambers** become heated. Lava is a **molten**, or liquid, form of **rock** that flows down the side of a volcano in **fiery** rivers. As it cools, the lava hardens into various **formations**. Although many volcanoes are **cone-shaped**, some are **fissures**, or cracks, in the ground. Volcanoes may occur on **continents**, on **islands**, at the bottom of the sea, and even on some **planets** other than earth. These eruptions are often **violent** and result in the loss of many lives and widespread destruction of **property**.

Central Vent

Directions:
Read the paragraph about volcanoes, left. Then, find all of the bold words in the word search below. Words may be found across, down, diagonally, or backwards.

Challenge:
Find out about some famous volcanoes such as Mt. Vesuvius, Mt. St. Helens, Krakatau, or Mt. Kilauea.

```
Y E N R I Q U V A L A P A M O L T E N C
T D A V A I F O R M A T I O N S A A D O
R A D I C A A L A R A S A D R A C K A N
E A S E A T A C A R E E D A G A P C A E
P A Y A W A S A Z A Q H A N A V A O A S
O F C R A T A N S J A S A M A K A R A H
R A P A E A O O A H A L A J A L A K A A
P A P N A I I A C A E A G A S A S A H P
A W A N A Q F R A M E S E A S E A I A E
H L O C K E S R E B M A H C A M G A M D
P A V I O L E N T Y I S F U N A N D E A
X C I T I N G T H E A D F I S S U R E S
W A A V A L N E G R R E E T Z Y G R A N
T F U H R S T N E N I T N O C W F U H A
```

Birth of an Island

Islands aren't born very often. Sometimes islands are created when a volcano erupts below the surface of the ocean. The lava cools and builds up the volcano. When the volcano gets tall enough, it pokes through the surface of the ocean. In the Atlantic Ocean, both Iceland and the Canary Islands were formed this way. Some islands, like Hawaii in the Pacific Ocean, are still being formed!

In 1963, a crew on a fishing boat was present when one island was being born. Early one morning the boat was sailing near the coast of Iceland. The crew awoke to what smelled like rotten eggs. No one knew what the source of the smell was. Suddenly, the boat began rocking back and forth. The sea began to boil like a pot of dark stew. Smoke started to rise out of the water. An underwater volcano was erupting right in front of their eyes!

The captain and his crew moved the vessel and watched from a distance. The volcano spit rock and lava into the air. It looked like the sky was raining rocks. The volcano erupted for days. Finally the fires burned themselves out. The top of the volcano stuck up out of the ocean. When the lava on top of the volcano cooled, a new island sat where only water had been before.

Scientists were very excited because they had never seen a brand-new island. The scientists named the new island Surtsey, after the Icelandic god of fire. It was the perfect name for such a fiery island.

But the new island did not look much like other islands. It was only a pile of bare rock. There were no plants or animals on it. Scientists wondered how life would come to an empty island. They set up camp and watched and waited. Finally, after many months, a single plant began growing on the rocks. Scientists found that birds would often land on the island and drop plant materials that had been trapped in their feathers and claws. Sometimes, the birds would drop seeds and a plant would begin to grow.

Today, there are a lot of birds and plants living on Surtsey. Humans are not allowed to go there except for a few scientists. The island is protected so that it can be studied. Surtsey is the perfect place to learn how plants and animals spread to new places around the earth.

Birth of an Island *(cont.)*

Directions: After reading the story, answer the questions. Circle the correct answer.

1. The author compares the sea to . . .

   a. a pot of stew.

   b. raining rocks.

   c. the god of fire.

   d. rotten eggs.

2. How was Surtsey formed?

   a. A volcano erupted below the surface of the ocean.

   b. Birds would drop plant material in the same spot.

   c. The sky rained rocks until it was formed.

   d. The Icelandic god of fire created it.

3. Studying Surtsey is important because . . .

   a. underwater volcanoes have never before erupted.

   b. it teaches scientists how plants and animals spread to new places.

   c. humans are not allowed to go there.

   d. scientists had never before studied volcanoes

4. Which of these best describes the scientists' feelings when they first visited the new island of Surtsey?

   a. scared

   b. confident

   c. excited

   d. upset

5. Which of these sentences best explains what scientists think about Surtsey?

   a. The captain and his crew moved the vessel and watched from a distance.

   b. Today, there are a lot of birds and plants living on Surtsey.

   c. Surtsey is a rare opportunity to study what had never been studied before.

   d. It was the perfect name for such a fiery island.

6. What is the probable reason the new island was named after a god of fire?

   a. The island has many forest fires.

   b. The island was a pile of bare rocks.

   c. The island was made by a volcano.

   d. The island is really hot in the summer.

Your Remarkable Body

Your body is an amazing machine. Just as a machine's many parts work together to make it run, your body systems work together to keep you going. These systems include the skeletal system and the muscle system.

All of the bones in your body make up your skeletal system. Bones meet at joints. Moveable joints, like those in the fingers, let the body move. Fixed joints, like those found in the skull, do not let the bones move. Your teeth are bones with a very specific job: chewing food. The other bones form a frame that supports your body and protects its internal organs. Bones do several other tasks, too. Some bone cells take calcium out of the blood and add it to the bone. Calcium makes the bones strong so that they will not break easily. The soft inner part of a bone, called bone marrow, makes and releases new blood cells. The most obvious job that bones do is work with your muscles to let you move.

Your muscle system lets your body move and allows your internal organs to work. You have skeletal muscles and smooth muscles. Skeletal muscles move bones and are voluntary muscles that you can control. These muscles move by pulling. Each muscle can only pull in one direction. One end of each skeletal muscle connects to a bone. This bone does not move when the muscle pulls. The other end of that muscle attaches to another bone. This bone does move when the muscle pulls. One set of muscles pulls the bones in one direction; the other set pulls the bone in the other direction. This means that you use one set of muscles to lift your arm up and another set of muscles to move it back down.

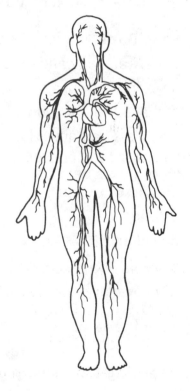

Smooth muscles make up most of the body's internal organs. Smooth muscles move food through the digestive system, air through the lungs, and blood through veins and arteries. Since you cannot control these muscles, they're called involuntary muscles. Smooth muscles cannot move as fast as skeletal muscles, but they work **continuously**. Your heart is a smooth muscle. It beats about 75 times each minute, and it will never rest as long as you live.

Your Remarkable Body (cont.)

Comprehension Questions

Directions: Use the passage on page 212 to answer the questions.

1. **You have control of the movement of. . .**

   a. some of your body's muscles.

   b. all of your body's muscles.

   c. none of your body's muscles.

   d. just your arm and leg muscles.

2. **While you are young, the part of the skeletal system that has its bones replaced by brand new bones is. . .**

   a. the skull.   c. the teeth.

   b. the feet.   d. the hands.

3. **Which is an example of voluntary muscles?**

   a. your lungs breathing

   b. your heart beating

   c. your legs walking

   d. your intestines digesting food

4. **Another word for *continuously* is. . .**

   a. rarely.   c. rapidly.

   b. often.   d. constantly.

5. **When you break an arm bone, which of these systems is affected?**

   a. the voluntary muscle system

   b. the involuntary muscle system

   c. the respiratory system

   d. the digestive system

6. **Picture a skeleton. Where do you see moveable joints?**

   a. in the skull   c. in the ribs

   b. in the knee   d. in the teeth

7. **Which body system do you find the most interesting? Explain.**

   _____

   _____

   _____

Inside the Body

Directions: Use the clues below to solve the crossword puzzle.

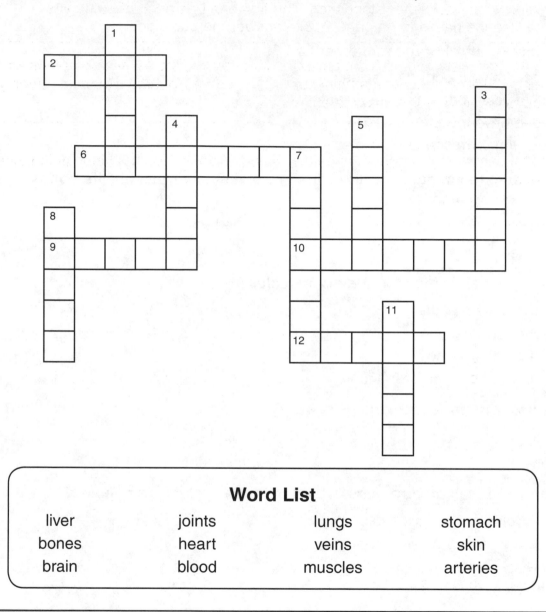

Word List

liver	joints	lungs	stomach
bones	heart	veins	skin
brain	blood	muscles	arteries

Across

2. outer layer on a body
6. carries blood throughout body
9. helps us breathe
10. makes us strong
12. pumps blood

Down

1. next to kidneys
3. connect bones together
4. carries blood to heart
5. parts of skeleton
7. belly
8. red fluid
11. thinking spot

Human Body Systems

Directions: Several of the human body systems are written in code below. Solve the code by determining what each letter stands for. The first one has been done for you.

> **Hint:** Whenever you see an "s," it always stands for "r." The "o" always stands for "e." Fill in all the letters in the words below using the letters from the example. When you figure out a letter, write it everywhere it appears.

Next, look at the body parts in the box below. Find the body part that belongs in each system. Write the letter of that body part in the box to the left of each number.

[E] 1. <u>s</u> <u>k</u> <u>e</u> <u>l</u> <u>e</u> <u>t</u> <u>a</u> <u>l</u>
        r   d   o   e   o   z   k   e

[ ] 2. ___ ___ ___ ___ ___ ___ ___
        y   s   b   g   k   s   u

[ ] 3. ___ ___ ___ ___ ___ ___ ___
        g   o   s   w   h   y   r

[ ] 4. ___ ___ ___ ___ ___ ___ ___ ___
        f   y   r   m   y   e   k   s

[ ] 5. ___ ___ ___ ___ ___ ___ ___ ___ ___
        o   g   n   h   m   s   b   g   o

[ ] 6. ___ ___ ___ ___ ___ ___ ___ ___ ___
        n   b   q   o   r   z   b   w   o

[ ] 7. ___ ___ ___ ___ ___ ___ ___ ___ ___ ___ ___
        m   b   s   m   y   e   k   z   h   s   u

[ ] 8. ___ ___ ___ ___ ___ ___ ___ ___ ___ ___ ___
        s   o   r   j   b   s   k   z   h   s   u

A. arteries	C. hormones	~~E.~~ bones	G. lungs
B. stomach	D. muscles	F. spinal cord	H. kidneys

Healthy Analogies

Directions: Look at the two words that are given. How are they alike? Find their relationship to each other. Use that relationship to find the word in the box that will complete the analogy.

exhale	dairy	~~engine~~	vegetable
touch	saliva	esophagus	digestive
blood			

Example: body systems is to human as _____ engine _____ is to truck

Reasoning: Body systems keep a human going. An engine keeps a truck running.

1. taste is to mouth as _____ is to hand

2. tears is to eyes as _____ is to mouth

3. cherry is to fruit as carrot is to _____

4. food is to intestines as _____ is to heart

5. pasta is to carbohydrates as yogurt is to _____

6. trachea is to lungs as _____ is to stomach

7. exercise is to rest as inhale is to _____

8. urinary is to kidney as _____ is to stomach

The Food Chain

Plants and animals have an interdependent relationship. Insects, fungi, and micro-organisms act as decomposers and provide **chemicals** for green plants. In turn, plants provide **food** for **plant**-eaters which provide food for **meat-eaters**. Plants, plant-eaters, and meat-eaters all supply **waste** materials for **decomposers**.

When this chain is broken, consequences can be serious. For example, if **green** plants were destroyed in great numbers by pesticides, deforestation, or forest fires, there might be no food for the plant-eaters. Then the plant-eaters would have to move away or they could face starvation.

Directions: Find out more about the food chain. Label the diagram with the **boldfaced** words from the paragraph above.

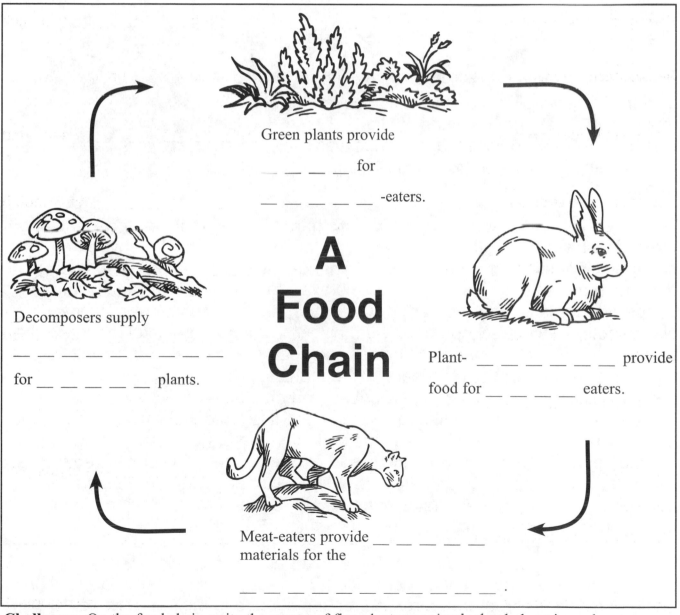

Green plants provide

_ _ _ _ for

_ _ _ _ _ _ -eaters.

A Food Chain

Decomposers supply

_ _ _ _ _ _ _ _ _

for _ _ _ _ _ plants.

Plant- _ _ _ _ _ _ provide

food for _ _ _ _ eaters.

Meat-eaters provide _ _ _ _ _ materials for the

_ _ _ _ _ _ _ _ _ _ .

Challenge: On the food chain write the names of five plants or animals that belong in each category.

Changing with the Environment

Every plant and animal is designed to live in a specific environment, or biome. A cactus would die in a swamp, just as a cattail would die in a desert. These plants are meant to live in different biomes. The cattails grow in the swamp because they need standing water. The cactus likes the high heat and little rainfall of a desert. It stores water inside itself.

Sometimes the environment changes. Then the plants and animals that are suited only to a specific place are suddenly in trouble. They must change in order to survive. Many people believe that a change in environment explains what happened to the dinosaurs. The theory states that a meteor struck Earth millions of years ago and caused a climate change. The world immediately got a lot colder. The cold-blooded dinosaurs needed more heat. They ate the kinds of plants that grew in warm places. The change was too sudden. The dinosaurs couldn't adapt. They all died out.

We have theories about dinosaurs, but it's hard to prove many of the ideas about them. We have seen other plants and animals die out when the environment changed. Some species can adapt, or change, quickly in response to changes humans make to their environment. One example happened in Britain with the peppered moth. During the early 1800s most peppered moths were white with black spots. Only a few odd ones were black. The white moths blended in with tree trunks. The black ones could easily be seen. Since the birds usually ate them, they did not get to reproduce. The population of white peppered moths stayed large; the population of black peppered moths stayed very small. Then in the mid 1800s people built a lot of factories. The factories' smokestacks sent lots of ashes into the air. These ashes darkened the bark on the trees where the moths lived. Now the white moths no longer blended in with the tree trunks. As a result, the birds saw and ate them. They did not get to reproduce. The number of white peppered moths **dwindled**. More and more black peppered moths survived. Today, most peppered moths in Britain are black.

Unfortunately, most plants and animals cannot adapt so quickly. Many species have become extinct. More die off each day. This is especially true in rainforests, where creatures rarely adapt to a change in their environments.

Changing with the Environment (cont.)

Comprehension Questions

1. **The dinosaurs may have died because of . . .**

   a. a lack of medicine.

   b. a climate change.

   c. a biome.

   d. a theory.

2. **On a historical time line, what happened second?**

   a. Most peppered moths were black.

   b. Most peppered moths were white.

   c. Factories were built in Britain.

   d. The peppered moth population started to change.

3. **Which is an example of people making a big change to a biome?**

   a. growing a crop

   b. filling in a swamp

   c. opening a beach

   d. repairing a road

4. **A synonym for *dwindled* is. . .**

   a. darkened.

   b. lightened.

   c. increased.

   d. decreased.

5. **Which is a biome?**

   a. the temperature

   b. the sky

   c. the ocean

   d. the sun

6. **Picture a bird searching for peppered moths. Where is it looking?**

   a. on tree trunks

   b. in the grass

   c. under the dirt

   d. high in the sky

7. **What environmental change do you think would be the easiest for an animal to adapt to: temperature, length of seasons, amount of water available, or kinds of food available? Explain.**

   _____

   _____

   _____

Naming the Planets

There are nine planets. Do you remember all the names? They are Mercury, Venus, Earth, Mars, Jupiter, Saturn, Uranus, Neptune, and Pluto. Here is a quick easy way to remember the names of the planets:

My   **V**ery   **E**ducated   **M**other   **J**ust   **S**erved   **U**s   **N**ine   **P**izzas!

The first letter of each word in this sentence represents a planet. This is called a mnemonic aid. Can you think of another sentence you can write using the first letters of each planet? Memorize this sentence to help you remember the names and order of the planets.

M _____ V _____ E _____ M _____

J _____ S _____ U _____ N _____

P _____ !

Directions: Label the planets on the solar system diagram below:

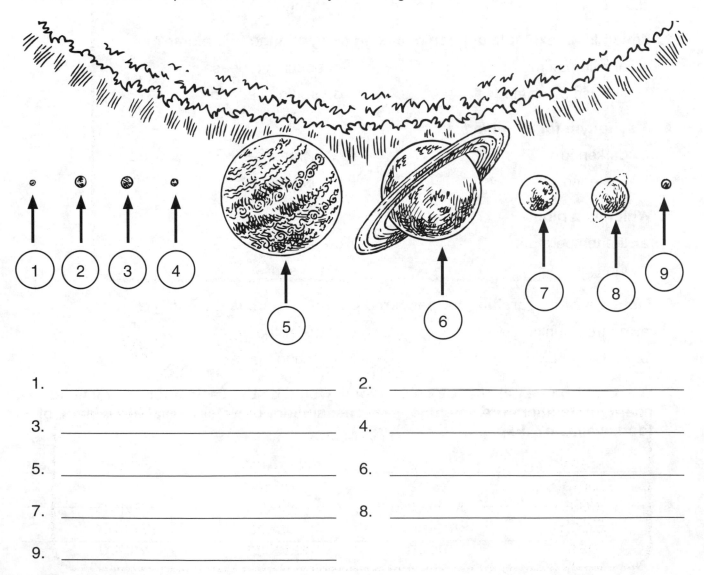

1. _____   2. _____

3. _____   4. _____

5. _____   6. _____

7. _____   8. _____

9. _____

Solar System

Directions: Our solar system is a busy place, with planets, the sun, space probes, and satellites. See how many of the words in the word list you can find.

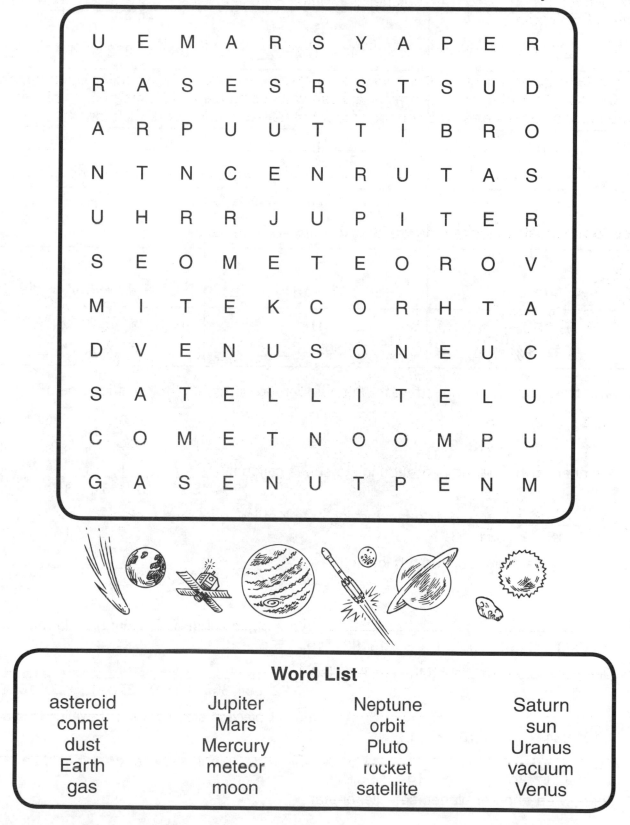

| U E M A R S Y A P E R |
| R A S E S R S T S U D |
| A R P U U T T I B R O |
| N T N C E N R U T A S |
| U H R R J U P I T E R |
| S E O M E T E O R O V |
| M I T E K C O R H T A |
| D V E N U S O N E U C |
| S A T E L L I T E L U |
| C O M E T N O O M P U |
| G A S E N U T P E N M |

Word List

asteroid	Jupiter	Neptune	Saturn
comet	Mars	orbit	sun
dust	Mercury	Pluto	Uranus
Earth	meteor	rocket	vacuum
gas	moon	satellite	Venus

Space Math Facts

Step #1: Complete the math equations to find out which numbers stand for which letters.

A	B	C
24 x 15 = _____	144 + 177 = _____	238 ÷ 14 = _____

D	E	G
117 − 78 = _____	756 + 78 = _____	26 x 13 = _____

H	I	L
356 − 298 = _____	.25 x 12 = _____	198 ÷ 22 = _____

M	N	O
11 x 11 = _____	97 + 79 = _____	97 −79 = _____

P	R	S
0 x 3 = _____	41 − 19 = _____	9.43 + 9.57 = _____

T	U	V
169 ÷ 13 = _____	777 − 399 = _____	50 x 6 = _____

Step #2: Now substitute the letters for the numbers to complete the questions below.

1. The sun is a ___ ___ ___ ___.
   19 13 360 22

2. A planet's oval-shaped path around the sun is called an ___ ___ ___ ___ ___.
   18 22 321 3 13

3. A ___ ___ ___ ___ ___ is a fast-moving chunk of ice, dust, and rock.
   17 18 121 834 13

4. Between Mars and Jupiter, a huge belt of ___ ___ ___ ___ ___ ___ ___ ___ ___ orbits the sun.
   360 19 13 834 22 18 3 39 19

5. ___ ___ ___ ___ ___ ___ ___ ___ ___ ___ are objects that orbit around a planet.
   19 360 13 834 9 9 3 13 834 19

6. One complete path around the sun is called a ___ ___ ___ ___ ___ ___ ___ ___ ___ ___.
   22 834 300 18 9 378 13 3 18 176

7. A ___ ___ ___ ___ ___ ___ ___ ___ ___ is a small piece of stone or metal traveling in space.
   121 834 13 834 18 22 18 3 39

8. An ___ ___ ___ ___ ___ ___ ___ occurs when one planet, satellite, or star casts a
   834 17 9 3 0 19 834
   shadow on another planet, satellite, or star.

Star Struck

Directions: Each group of letters below is a jumbled word about space. Write the correct word on the line to the right of the jumbled word. Correctly written, seven of the terms require capital letters.

1. setaletsil _____

2. nentpeu _____

3. ecpsa _____

4. klmiy ayw _____

5. stlepna _____

6. eemosettri _____

7. peclsie _____

8. yumrerc _____

9. ecpsa nottsai _____

10. otlpu _____

11. disatreos _____

12. omno _____

13. sneuv _____

14. axygal _____

15. etrah _____

16. oonarc _____

17. tlethus _____

18. rats _____

19. oplola _____

20. rim _____

21. ustnorasta _____

Word List

Mir	corona	galaxy	Venus
asteroids	star	Apollo	planets
earth	eclipse	astronauts	Pluto
shuttle	Milky Way	moon	meteorites
satellites	Neptune	space	space station
Mercury			

Water Is an Amazing Matter

Everything consists of matter. Matter is any **substance** that has weight and takes up space. Matter can be a liquid, a solid, or a gas.

Water can be found in all three forms. When water is a liquid, we drink it or take a shower. When water is a solid, we put cubes of it into a drink to keep it cool. We like to sled, ski, or skate on solid water. When water is a gas, we call it water vapor. When water boils, at least some of it changes into a gas. When a teakettle whistles, steam—which is water vapor—comes out of it.

Water vapor also evaporates from the ground. This happens when the sun shines after it rains. The water vapor collects into clouds. The wind blows the clouds around. With the right conditions, the cloud vapor turns back into liquid. Then it falls to the ground as rain, snow, hail, or sleet.

What makes water change its form? It all depends on the water's temperature. When water is cold—0°C or 32°F or less—it is a solid, such as ice or snow. When water is warmer, it is a liquid. When water boils—at 100°C or 212°F or more—it becomes vapor. Some people think that the amount of water changes when the water moves from one state to another. They believe that some of the water gets lost during the change. Actually, the amount of water always stays the same, no matter which state the water is in. People are tricked due to the amount of space the water uses in its different forms. Solid ice takes up more space than liquid. Water vapor takes up the least amount of space.

224

Water Is an Amazing Matter (cont.)

Comprehension Questions

Directions: Circle the letter next to the best answer. You may look back at the passage on page 224.

1. **When water boils it becomes. . .**
   a. a liquid.
   b. a solid.
   c. a vapor.
   d. another substance.

2. **Think about the water cycle. Starting with water in a lake, which of the following happens last?**
   a. Snow falls.
   b. Water vapor rises into the atmosphere.
   c. The water vapor turns into snow.
   d. Water vapor collects into clouds.

3. **What happens when you add ice cubes to a drink?**
   a. The ice cubes make the drink bubbly.
   b. The ice cubes melt.
   c. The drink heats up.
   d. As the ice cubes melt, the drink overflows the glass.

4. ***Substance* means. . .**
   a. object.
   b. liquid.
   c. material.
   d. solid.

5. **A glacier is water in what form?**
   a. solid
   b. gas
   c. liquid
   d. vapor

6. **Picture looking into a pot of boiling water. How can you tell if the water is boiling?**
   a. The water smells different.
   b. The water has turned solid.
   c. The water has changed color.
   d. The water is bubbling.

7. **What food do you like that needs boiling water to prepare? Explain.**

_____

_____

_____

Light

Light is a form of energy. Without it we could see nothing. A ray of white light contains all of the colors of the rainbow. It travels in a straight line from its source. If something opaque (such as a box) gets into the light's path, the light bounces off its surface. It scatters, or spreads out. The light beams cannot go through the object, so opaque things cast well-defined shadows. We can see opaque things the most easily. For example, grass looks green because it scatters green light from its surface. The grass absorbs the other colors of white light. The colors black and white do not follow this rule. Black absorbs all of the colors of white light. That's why it looks black. White absorbs none of the colors of white light, which is why it looks white.

You can see through transparent objects. They let all light rays pass through them. They cast no shadow. Air, water, and glass are all transparent. However, water and glass are not completely transparent. That's why we can't see air, but we can see water and glass. Translucent objects, such as a cloud or a lampshade, let some light through. They cut down the light's glare and cast fuzzy shadows. Light does not travel as quickly through translucent objects as it does through transparent ones.

Another interesting quality of light is refraction. When you put a drinking straw into a clear glass of water, the straw appears to bend beneath the water's surface. You know that the straw is really still straight. The bend you see comes from refraction. The way that light travels through transparent items causes refraction. Since air particles are far apart, air is not dense. Light can move the most rapidly through air. Water is a liquid because its particles are closer together. Because it's denser, it slows the light down. Glass is the densest of the three. As a solid, the particles in glass are very close together. Light must slow down as it moves through these dense particles. This makes the ray of light bend, which causes the **illusion** of the bent straw.

A mirror only works when light hits it. A mirror is anything with such a smooth surface that it can reflect images. Most often a mirror is a piece of glass with a silver backing, but it can also be a clear, still body of water or a piece of shiny metal. So how does your bathroom mirror reflect? A ray of light shines through the glass in the front. It reaches the shiny silver and bounces back through the glass.

Light (comt.)

Comprehension Questions

Directions: Circle the letter next to the best answer. You may look back at the story.

1. The color black absorbs. . .
   a. one of the colors of white light.
   b. the dark colors of white light.
   c. none of the colors of white light.
   d. all of the colors of white light.

2. What happens last?
   a. The ray of light travels in a straight line.
   b. You turn on a light in a dark room.
   c. The chair casts a shadow.
   d. The ray of light hits a chair.

3. You look into the mirror in your bathroom, but you can't see yourself. Why?
   a. The mirror is too old to reflect.
   b. There isn't enough light for the mirror to reflect.
   c. The mirror is cracked.
   d. The mirror is hanging crooked on the wall.

4. *Illusion* means. . .
   a. something is not really the way that it looks.
   b. something that looks like clear glass.
   c. fabric you can see through.
   d. something that looks fancy.

5. What are sheer curtains?
   a. transparent   c. opaque
   b. translucent   d. invisible

6. Picture a tree on a sunny day. Now picture it on an overcast day when you can't see the sun. What's different on the overcast day?
   a. The tree is dry.   c. The tree doesn't cast a shadow.
   b. The tree is a different color.   d. The tree's leaves are drooping.

7. One dark night the power goes off at your house. Would you rather have a candle or a flashlight? Explain.

_____

_____

_____

Looking for New Ways to Make Electricity

Think of how you used electricity today. Did you cook breakfast in the microwave? Did you turn on a light? Did you use a computer? All of these things used electrical power.

Electrical power must be made. Usually this means that a power plant burns gas, oil, or coal to generate electricity. But these are all fossil fuels. Just like fossils, these fuels formed deep underground over millions of years. Dead plants and animals rotted. After millions of years and lots of pressure from the weight of the ground above, they changed into gas, oil, or coal. People have used fossil fuels for energy for more than 100 years. Burning them causes a lot of pollution. Also, the Earth is running out of fossil fuels. And we certainly can't wait a million years for more to be made!

What will we do? Scientists are trying to figure that out. They want to find new ways to make electricity. They'd like the new ways not to cause pollution. They hope to find **renewable** energy sources. This means that, unlike fossil fuels, they can never run out. What could possibly meet those demands? The sun and the wind can.

Right now no one knows the best way to capture the sun's rays and turn them into electrical power. Still, Japan and other countries have built houses with solar roof tiles. The tiles collect sunshine even on overcast days. So far these tiles have worked so well that they have made all of the electricity the family needs each day. Some cars have already been built that use solar tiles for part of their power.

For hundreds of years, people in the Netherlands have used windmills for their energy. Today's windmills are taller and have lightweight blades to catch more wind. Some have propellers mounted on heads that can turn. This lets the windmill get the most wind possible, no matter which way the wind blows. In the driest parts of the western U.S., wind farms have sprung up. Hundreds of windmills stand on otherwise unused land. The electricity they generate powers homes and businesses in cities many miles away.

Looking for New Ways to Make Electricity (cont.)

Comprehension Questions

Directions: Circle the letter next to the best answer. You may look back at the story.

1. **Why do we need to find non-fossil fuel methods of making electricity?**
   a. Fossil fuels don't work with modern engines.
   b. No one knows the best way to use fossil fuels.
   c. The world is running out of fossil fuels.
   d. Fossil fuels are too expensive to use.

2. **What happens last?**
   a. Layers of rocks and mud cover dead plants.
   b. People remove the fossil fuel from underground.
   c. The dead plants are under a lot of pressure.
   d. After a long time, the dead plants turn into gas, oil, or coal.

3. **If we run out of fossil fuels, we will . . .**
   a. need to use another source of energy.
   b. need to find a cleaner source of water.
   c. make more fossil fuels.
   d. stop using electricity.

4. ***Renewable* means . . .**
   a. computerized.
   b. abundant.
   c. inexpensive.
   d. able to be used repeatedly.

5. **Which energy source is the best for our environment?**
   a. oil
   b. coal
   c. sunshine
   d. trees

6. **Visualize food cooking in a microwave. How is the oven getting power?**
   a. from microwaves in the air
   b. from a wall outlet
   c. from the sun
   d. from the food being cooked inside of it

7. **Which do you think is the best way to generate electricity? Explain.**

_____

_____

_____

Electricity

Directions: Read the passage and answer the questions below.

We use electricity every day. We use it to light lamps, run the dryer, and toast our bread. We need it for our computers and TVs. There are times that we need more electricity than can be made. All electricity gets generated in a power plant. When we try and use more electricity than the plant can produce at one time, we have blackouts. The power goes off completely.

Wires carry electricity from power plants to your home. Some things, like copper, let electricity flow through them. These are called conductors. Electric wires are copper. Other things, like rubber, stop electricity. Power does not pass through them. These are called insulators. Copper wires have rubber covers to keep the electricity from leaving the wire.

Lightening is natural electricity. A single lightning bolt has **tremendous** power. It could light up a city for one year. Scientists want to find a way to tap into this natural energy source.

1. **What is a machine that would still work during a power outage (blackout)?**
   a. an air conditioner
   b. a battery-powered radio
   c. a refrigerator
   d. a television

2. **Why would a large demand for electricity cause a blackout?**
   a. People can't pay enough money to get the amount of electricity they need.
   b. A high demand for power creates an explosion at a power plant.
   c. When the power plant is overwhelmed by demand, it shuts down.
   d. When the power plant is overwhelmed by demand, it starts using lightning for power.

3. **Of the following choices, which would make a good insulator?**
   a. rubber boots
   b. a metal pan
   c. a lightning rod
   d. copper wires

4. **The word *tremendous* means . . .**
   a. very little.
   b. surprising.
   c. enormous.
   d. tiny.

Answer Key

Page 8

1.
a. skull   g. brass
b. louse   h. pansy
c. peach   i. onion
d. trout   j. bread
e. raven
f. tiger

2.

colored boxes:
barrel   leather
eel   sofa
falcon   ferret
orchid   vinegar
pitcher   canal
silk   envelope
bugle

3.   Answers will vary.

Page 9

1.
a. Japan
b. September
c. Henry Hudson
d. Nile
e. Tuesday
f. Miami

2.

Monday   April
Vanessa   Tony
San Francisco
California   Seahawk
Long Beach
Friday

3.
a. countries
b. months
c. planets
d. mountains
e. oceans
f. states

Page 10

1.
a. the girl's dress
b. the tiger's stripes
c. the boy's pencil
d. the lady's handbags

e. the tree's leaves
f. the flower's petals
g. the clown's antics
h. the police officer's uniform

2.
a. the girls' dresses
b. the donkeys' ears
c. the men's books
d. the horses' saddles
e. the women's houses
f. the boys' pencils
g. the birds' nests
h. the sailors' ship

Page 11

1.
a. bit
b. listened
c. tapped
d. read
e. ate
f. wandered

2.
a. gushed
b. scowled
c. pounced
d. wiped
e. pruned
f. searched

3.
a. slithers
b. gallops
c. gambols
d. leaps
e. struts
f. waddles
g. soars
h. scampers

Page 12

1.
a. has
b. is
c. are
d. was
e. am
f. have

2.   *underline/circle*
a. going/am
b. painting/is
c. helping/was
d. run/will
e. read/has
f. seen/have

3. Answers will vary.

4. Answers will vary.

Page 13
Helping
1. is
2. has
3. is
4. will
5. has
6. have
7. are
8. can
9. will

Action
1. raising
2. learned
3. drawing
4. drink
5. taken
6. seen
7. going
8. ride
9. eat

Page 14
Answers will vary.

Page 15

1.
a. broad
b. fragile
c. circular
d. childish
e. perilous
f. careful

2.
a. interesting
b. clever
c. rusty
d. delicious
e. woolen
f. sunny
g. ripe
h. savage

3. thick
fat
sour
high
strong
minute
scared
big

Page 16
1. quick, quickly
2. happy, happily
3. hungry, hungrily
4. shy, shyly
5. angry, angrily

6. nice, nicely
7. calm, calmly

Page 17

1.
a. carefully
b. tightly
c. brightly
d. neatly
e. busily
f. angrily
g. softly
h. gracefully

2.
a. when
b. how
c. when
d. when
e. how
f. when
g. where
h. where
i. how
j. where

3.   Answers will vary.

Page 18
1. she
2. they
3. he
4. she
5. they
6. it
7. they
8. it

Page 19

1.
a. she
b. its
c. she/he
d. they
e. her
f. him

2.   *colored boxes*
we
their
them
they
yours
us
you
my
she
he
mine

Answer Key (cont.)

Page 20
1. When I went to the store, I saw my teacher, Mrs. Dorner.
2. I am reading a book named *Pride and Prejudice.*
3. In May, we will be able to go and visit my Grandma Clark.
4. My brother said, "Why does Sarah always get to sit in the front?"
5. The Andersons, our neighbors, will go to visit Paris, France next year.
6. Heidi had a birthday, and we sang "Happy Birthday to You."
7. On Thursday, he will go see Dr. Frank the orthodontist.
8. My sister Anne loves to write stories.
9-12 Remaining answers will vary.

Page 21
1. *colored boxes*
   Michelle
   England
   Wednesday
   Swan Lake
   Uranus
   Asia
   Shamrock Hotel
   October
   Pacific Ocean
   Easter
   Vietnam
   Christmas
   Canada
   Kansas City
   Murray River
   Mount Everest
   London
   Rialto House
   Wattle Street
2. Answers will vary.
3.
   a. Last Saturday Julie went to Chicago.
   b. At Christmas we are going to Italy which is a country in Europe.
   c. The wedding will take place at St. Patrick's Church in Greensboro.

Page 22
1.
   a. Wheat, rice, and corn
   b. Roses, daffodils, and hyacinths
   c. Skunks, zebras, and penguins
   d. Scissors, pliers, and hammers
   e. Ash, sycamore, and eucalyptus
2.
   a. the capital of South Australia
   b. a Swedish astronomer
   c. a featureless spot in a freezing wilderness
   d. according to a 17th century encyclopedia
   e. one of this class's finest writers
   f. the first international crime fighting organization

Page 23
1.
   a. has not
   b. we have
   c. of the clock
   d. did not
   e. we will
   f. cannot
   g. it is
   h. it was
2.
   a. I'm
   b. I've
   c. I'd
   d. I'll
   e. couldn't
   f. you've
   g. who's
   h. it's
   i. he's
   j. weren't
3. That's, we'll
   There's, It's
   We're, you'd
   They're, we've
   They'll, they're

Page 24

1.
   a. wail
   b. roam
   c. soft
   d. shake
   e. large
   f. lose
   g. bravery
   h. clap
   i. serious
   j. taste
2.
   a. get
   b. sly
   c. wet
   d. ill
   e. fat
   f. odd
   g. old
   h. gem

Page 25 and 26
1. a
2. b
3. b
4. c
5. a
6. b
7. b
8. a
9. c
10. b
11. c
12. c
13. a
14. b
15. a
16. c
17. a

Page 27

1.
   a. cheap   f. awkward
   b. timid   g. loosen
   c. coward   h. leave
   d. south   i. smile
   e. build   j. swallow
2.
   a. light   e. entrance
   b. smash   f. feeble
   c. divide   g. solid
   d. deceitful h. fake

Page 28 and 29
1. a   8. a
2. c   9. c
3. b   10. b
4. c   11. b
5. a   12. a
6. b   13. b
7. c   14. a

Page 30
1. capital
2. bear
3. passed
4. it's
5. Who's
6. led
7. peace
8. their, two
9. fair, fare
10. right, write, rite
11. patience, patients
12. dessert, desert

Page 31

Answer Key (cont.)

Page 31 *(cont.)*
1.

a. find   f. waist
b. bawl   g. guest
c. taught   h. hymn
d. flee   i. vain
e. medal   j. mayor

2.

boys   been
creek   berry
find   week
some   road
male   which
deer

3.

a. guessed   d. pour
b. flower   e. pier
c. hare

Page 32
1. examine   9. OK
2. OK   10. OK
3. OK   11. OK
4. OK   12. excitement
5. OK   13. exercise
6. excuse   14. OK
7. OK   15. except
8. exception

Page 33
1. expected
2. expand
3. expert
4. exciting
5. excellent
6. extremely
7. excuse
8. exercise
9. exclaimed
10. except
11. exception
12. exchange
13. explorer
14. examine
15. excitement

Riddle: the numeral six

Page 34
Part I
1. not skid
2. not fiction
3. not stop
4. not fat
5. not profit
6. not stick
7. not toxic
8. not returnable
9. not verbal
10. not flammable

Part II
1. nonexistent
2. nonsense
3. nonresident
4. nonstandard
5. nonessential
6. nonviolent
7. noncredit
8. nonsmoker
9. nontaxable
10. nondairy
11. nonfiction
12. nonvoter

Page 35
Part I
1. nontoxic
2. nonstop
3. nonviolent
4. nonflammable
5. nonskid
6. nonprofit
7. nonfat
8. nonstick
9. nonfiction
10. nonreturnable
11. nontaxable
12. nonverbal

Part II
Answers will vary.

Page 36
1. television
2. Midwest
3. midsection
4. telecast
5. midsummer
6. telethon
7. midweek
8. telemarketing
9. midst
10. telecommunications
11. midterm
12. telecommute

Page 37
Part I
1. monarch
2. monopoly
3. quadruplets
4. monorail
5. quartet
6. quadrilateral
8. quarter

Part II
1. e   4. d
2. c   5. a
3. b

Part III
1. d
2. b
3. c

Page 38
1. OK
2. positive
3. OK
4. OK
5. adjective
6. OK
7. attractive
8. negative
9. OK
10. executive
11. OK
12. sensitive
13. OK
14. OK
15. native

Page 39
1. motive
2. representatives
3. executive
4. relatives
5. competitive
6. negative
7. attractive
8. detective
9. effective
10. sensitive
11. adjective
12. active
13. talkative
14. positive
15. native

Riddle: Skunks. They'll give anyone a (s)cent.

Page 40
Part I
1. disposable
2. noticeable
3. believable
4. changeable
5. regrettable
6. admirable
7. replaceable
8. manageable
9. acceptable
10. controllable

Part II
1. d   6. g
2. j   7. e
3. f   8. c
4. a   9. b
5. i   10. h

Page 41
1. sentence; 5; absence
2. difference; 5; audience
3. influence; 8; conference
4. audience; 2; convenience
5. reference; 13; difference
6. evidence; 6; evidence
7. absence; 1; experience
8. experience; 7; influence
9. conference; 3; intelligence
10. occurrence; 10; occurrence
11. science; 14; patience
12. patience; 11; preference
13. preference; 12; reference
14. intelligence; 9; science
15. convenience; 4; sentence

Page 42

Page 43
Part I
1. physician
2. comedian
3. beautician
4. Canadians
5. magician

Answer Key (cont.)

6. politician
7. technician
8. vegetarian
9. musician
10. historian
11. Egyptian
12. librarian

Part II
Answers will vary.

Page 44
Part I
1. friendship
2. erupt
3. leadership
4. interrupt
5. citizenship
6. corrupt
7. sportsmanship
8. abruptly
9. scholarship
10. disrupted
11. hardship
12. bankrupt

Part II
Answers will vary.

Page 45
Part I
1. fictitious
2. nutritious
3. repetitious
4. spacious
5. cautious
6. ferocious
7. infectious
8. gracious

Part II
1. ambitious
2. luscious
3. repetitious
4. precious
5. infectious
6. delicious
7. cautious
8. nutritious
9. vicious
10. ferocious

Page 46
1.
  a. feathers   d. rock
  b. sugar   e. toast
  c. ice   f. mouse
2.
  a. coal   d. silk
  b. eel   e. bee

c. kitten   f. snow
3.
  a. Answers will vary.

Page 47
1.
  a. All the world is a stage.
  b. She was peaches and cream.
  c. Fred is a pig at the table.
  d. Headlines announcing the crime were screams.
  e. Life is a short summer, and man is a flower.
2. Answers will vary. Example: a. The clouds were gray all day long. The clouds were forecasts of the rain to come.

Page 56
  4,1,3,6,2,5

Page 57
1. a   3. c
2. a   4. b

Page 59
1. d   4. c
2. c   5. a
3. a   6. d

Page 60
1. c   3. b
2. c   4. a

Page 61
1. b   3. a
2. a   4. c

Page 62
1. c   3. b
2. b   4. c

Page 83
1. 168   9. 520
2. 357   10. 204
3. 88   11. 392
4. 48   12. 532
5. 384   13. 266
6. 567   14. 699
7. 336   15. 1,869
8. 175

Page 84
1. 44   15. 290
2. 273   16. 388
3. 276   17. 162
4. 295   18. 33
5. 104   19. 258
6. 51   20. 96
7. 252   21. 455
8. 291   22. 266
9. 44   23. 344
10. 284   24. 192
11. 84   25. 285
12. 78
13. 175
14. ~~225~~ **255**

Page 85
1. 350   11. 28,300
2. 650   12. 93,400
3. 380   13. 5,900
4. 940   14. 7,600
5. 990   15. 72,000
6. 770   16. 86,000
7. 520   17. 329,000
8. 420   18. 348,000
9. 34,600 19. 453,000
10. 55,900 20. 987,000

Page 87
1. 1,023   11. 2,805
2. 504   12. 2,673
3. 1,696   13. 2,516
4. 168   14. 1,755
5. 1,219   15. 4,816
6. 1,953   16. 2,072
7. 966   17. 2,444
8. 943   18. 3,219
9. 3,300   19. 5,742
10. 1,305 20. 2,548

Page 88
1. 3,000   15. 342
2. 855   16. 3,000
3. 4,125   17. 189
4. 504   18. 1,188
5. 342   19. 3,000
6. 1,800   20. 342
7. 4,125   21. 4,125
8. 504   22. 1,188
9. 3,000   23. 2,175
10. 10,350 24. 342
11. 4,836 25. 1,800
12. 99   26. 399
13. 99   27. 2,175
14. 1,800 28. 936
Answer: Sometimes rabbits just multiply.

Page 89
1. 832   14. 1,900 *3900*
2. 1,080   15. 3,350 *2200*
3. 700   16. 3,400 *1550*
4. 960   17. 3,900 *1200*
5. 922   18. 2,200 *2300*
6. 1,150   19. 1,550 *600*
7. 2,300   20. 1,200 *2050*
8. 1,755   21. 2,300 *189*
9. 4,200   22. 600   *288*
10. 2,900 23. 558
11. 1,900 24. 387
12. 3,350 ~~24. 387~~
13. 3,400 25. 504

Page 90
1. 600   7. 4,500
2. 5,400   8. 375
3. 775   9. 748
4. 1,540   10. 943
5. 3,312   11. 1,008
6. 2,784   12. 1,599

Page 91
1. 3,660   7. 2,896
2. 2,092   8. 3,590
3. 606   9. 1,414
4. 3,500   10. 1,905
5. 2,829   11. 1,910
6. 1,630

Answer: Clara Barton

Page 92
1. (84, 77, 70, 63, 56, 49, 42, 35, 28, 21, 14, 7)
2. 48, 44, 40, 36, 32, 28, 24, 20, 16, 12, 8, 4)
3. (24, 22, 20, 18, 16, 14, 12, 10, 8, 6, 4, 2)
4. (36, 33, 30, 27, 24, 21, 18, 15, 12, 9, 6, 3)
5. (144, 132, 120, 108, 96, 84, 72, 60, 48, 36, 24, 12)
6. (120, 110, 100, 90, 80, 70, 60, 50, 40, 30, 20, 10)
7. (72, 66, 60, 54, 48, 42, 36, 30, 24, 18, 12, 6)
8. Row 10

Page 93
1. 3   15. 11
2. 9   16. 12

Answer Key (cont.)

4. Square, 32
5. Trapezoid, 18
6. Triangle, 24

Page 133
1. 20 sq. units
2. 27 sq. units
3. 16 sq. units
4. 33 sq. units
5. 10 sq. units
6. 18 sq. units
7. 26 sq. units
8. 24 sq. units
9. 36 sq. units
10. 15 sq. units

Page 134
1. 64 ft.^{2}
2. 400 ft.^{2}
3. 225 m^2
4. 625 cm^2
5. 324 yd.^{2}
6. 121 cm^2
7. 3,844 ft.^{2}
8. 121 miles^2
9. 4.84 m^2
10. 1/4 ft.^{2}

Page 135
1. 70 in.^{2}
2. 72 cm^2
3. 180 m^2
4. 1,000 cm^2
5. 330 yd.^{2}
6. 700 mm^2
7. 3,150 ft.^{2}
8. 5,000 mm^2

Page 136
1. 48 yd.^{2}
2. 60 cm^2
3. 315 ft.^{2}
4. 72 cm^2
5. 595 m^2
6. 1,015 mm^2
7. 90 yd.^{2}
8. 1,720 cm^2
9. 137.5 in.^{2}
10. 156 ft.^{2}

Page 137
1. 63 cm^3
2. 1,000 ft.^{3}
3. 1,728 yd.^{3}
4. 343 mm^3
5. 729 ft.^{3}
6. 512 cm^3
7. 8,000 mm^3

8. 15,625 yd.^{3}
9. 125,000 cm^3
10. 1/8 yd.^{3}

Page 138
1. 8
2. 351.68
3. 40
4. 94.2
5. 113.04

Page 139
1–4. check diagrams
5. r = 7 ft.
   d = 14 ft.
   C = 44 ft.
6. r = 18 cm
   d = 36 cm
   C = 113 cm
7. r = 11 cm
   d = 22 cm
   C = 69 cm
8. r = 21 in.
   d = 42 in.
   C = 132 in.

Page 140
1. C = 18.84 in.
2. C = 21.98 cm
3. C = 15.7 cm
4. C = 37.68 yd.
5. C = 43.96 m
6. C = 62.8 in.

Page 141

Page 142
1. AC
2. ABD
3. AB
4. AD
5. AB
6. AC

Page 143
A New Bicycle

Page 144
Steal its Chair

Page 145

15 squares
26 triangles

Page 146
1. mall
2. school
3. bank
4. III
5. I
6. (3, -8)
7. library
8. (2, 3)
9. park
10. IV

Page 147
1. California
2. Minnesota/Maryland
3. Illinois/Pennsylvania
4. Michigan
5. 15
6. 20
7. 5th
8. 7th
9. 8th
10. 6th
11. 8th
12. 6th
13. 7th

Page 148
1. Races are run horizontally, not vertically.
2. Most plants grow vertically rather than horizontally.
3. buildings; vertical; snake: horizontal; baseball: horizontal; height: vertical; books: vertical stacks
4. Answers will vary.

Page 149
1. 35 years
2. 30 years
3. United States/1900
4. 47 years

5. 1750
6. 20th (1900-2000)
7. 2250 years
8. 2001
9. 1993
10. 1997/1998
11. 1994
12. 1992
13. 1994/1998-2001
14. 1992/1995/1996/1997
15. National League

Page 150
1. 150
2. 160
3. 160
4. 150
5. 160
6. 140
7. 180
8. 150
9. 150
10. 160
11. 160

Page 151
*(using the rounded numbers)
1. 1988
2. 140 mph
3. 1991
4. 180 mph
5. 180 - 140 = 40 mph
6. 160 + 140 + 180 = 480 ÷ 3 = 160 mph
7. 160 + 160 = 320 ÷ 2 = 160 mph

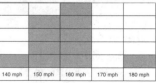

8. 160 mph
9. 140 mph, 180 mph
10. 170 mph

Page 152
1. 50
2. 10
3. 25
4. 45
5. soccer/basketball
6. swimming/bicycling
7. 45
8. 20

Answer Key (cont.)

9. 25
10. 2
11. 2
12. yes - 1
13. 2
14. 3
15. 8
16. 196

Page 153
1. 1,150
2. 450
3. 500
4. 550
5. 1,100
6. 300

Page 154
1. Checkers
2. Old Maid
3. 6
4. 6
5. 6
6. Solitaire/Twenty-One
7. 49
8. 23
9. 23 inches
10. 60 inches
11. bald eagle
12. sparrow hawk
13. 6 inches

Page 155
1. Art Supplies: $2.00
   Snacks: $3.00
   Clothes: $4.00
   Savings: $1.00
2. $4.00
3. $2.00 x 52 = $104.00
4. 7 weeks

Page 156
1. David Peterson
2. $5.80 - Kathryn Ross
3. Barbara Marshall
4. no
5. no
6. 614
7. $48.00

Page 157
1. a
2. a
3. b
4. c

Page 158
1. cross-staff
2. compass
3. lateen
4. rudder
5. astrolabe
6. carrack
7. ampoletta

Page 159
1. 90
2. 540
3. $100
4. $1,000
5. $10
6. 5,000 miles
7. 166.38
8. 55
9. 9
10. 24

Page 160
1. 3,500
2. 14
3. 250
4. 38
5. 415
6. 40
7. 62
8. 17
9. 90
10. 12
11. 250
12. 80

Page 161
Answers will vary.

Page 162
1. a   3. d
2. b   4. c

Page 163
Map 1
1. England
2. tobacco, rice, indigo
3. slaves
4. guns and cloth
Map 2
5. Africa (slave coast)
6. rum, iron
7. slaves
8. sugar and molasses
9. Atlantic Ocean
10. Europe, Africa, North
    America

Page 164
1. exported

2. exported
3. imported
4. exported
5. imported
6. exported
7. exported
8. exported

Page 165
wealthy
Native
cocoa
tomatoes
diseases
Smallpox
seventy-five
America
labor
tools
utensils
chickens

Page 167
Across:
1. gunpowder
5. Werowocomoco
7. diseases
10. Rebecca
11. Pocahontas
13. plantation
15. Thomas
17. Henrico
18. playful one

Down:
2. Powhatan
3. Jamestown
4. twenty-one
6. Opechancanough
8. John Smith
9. England
12. Samuel Argall
14. Thames
16. Lady Rolfe

Page 168
1. c
2. b
d. a
4. b

Page 169
1. Utah, Colorado,
   Arizona, and New
   Mexico touch the
   Navajo reservation.
2. The Navajo feel their
   land is sacred.

3. It is believed that the
   Navajo people
   originally came
   across the Bering
   Strail.
4. The Navajo
   are known for
   their weaving and
   silversmithing (or
   rugs and jewelry).

Page 171
1. d   4. c
2. a   5. b
3. a   6. d
7. Accept well-
   supported answers.

Page 172
1. *Arizona*-Hopi,
   Apache, and Navajo
2. *Colorado*-Arapaho,
   Cheyenne and Ute
3. *Idaho*-Nez Perce,
   Bannock, and
   Shoshone
4. *Kansas*-Cheyenne,
   Kansa, Kiowa
5. *Montana*-Flathead,
   Blackfoot, Gros
   Ventre, and Nez
   Perce
6. *Nebraska*-Ponca,
   Omaha, Pawnee,
   and Oto
7. *New Mexico*-Apache,
   Mescalero, Navajo,
   and Pueblo
8. *North Dakota*-
   Mandan, Hidatsa,
   and Yankatonai
9. *Oklahoma*-Kiowa
   Apache, Wichita
10. *South Dakota*-Lakota
    (Sioux), Arikara, and
    Yankatonai
11. *Texas*-Kiowa,
    Apache, Comanche,
    Mescalero (Apache),
    and Lipan
12. *Wyoming*-
    Cheyenne,
    Crow, and Shoshone

Page 173
New England Colonies
1. Connecticut

Answer Key (cont.)

2. Massachusetts
3. New Hampshire
4. Rhode Island

Middle Colonies
1. Delaware
2. New Jersey
3. New York
4. Pennsylvania

Southern Colonies
1. Georgia
2. Maryland
3. North Carolina
4. South Carolina
5. Virginia

Page 175
1. d   6. b
2. a   7. b
3. c   8. a
4. b   9. c
5. c   10. a

Page 177
1. d   6. d
2. a   7. c
3. c   8. c
4. d   9. a
5. b   10. c

Page 179
1. b
2. d
3. c
4. a
5. b
6. d
7. Accept reasonable answers.

Page 181
1. a
2. b
3. c
4. a
5. d
6. d
7. c
8. d
9. b
10. a

Page 183
1. Oregon Trail, California Trail, Mormon Trail, Santa Fe Trail, Old Spanish Trail, and the Gila River Trail
2. Independence,

Missouri
3. California and Oregon
4. Nauvoo, Illinois
5. Salt Lake City, Utah
6. Old Spanish Trail
7. Gila River Trail
8. Oregon Trail or Oregon-California Trail
9. Rocky Mountains and Sierra Nevada
10. Gila River Trail and Old Spanish Trail
11. California Trail
12. Oregon Trail
13. California Trail
14. Oregon Trail and Mormon Trail

Page 184
1. Arizona, California, Colorado, Nevada, New Mexico, Utah, and Wyoming
2. Idaho, Oregon, and Washington
3. Arkansas, Colorado, Iowa, Kansas, Louisiana, Minnesota, Missouri, Montana, Nebraska, New Mexico, North Dakota, Oklahoma, South Dakota, and Wyoming
4. Alabama, Florida, and Mississippi

Page 185
1. California, Nebraska, Nevada, Utah, and Wyoming
2. Cheyenne, North Platte, Ogden, Omaha, Promontory Point, Sacramento, and San Francisco
3. Arizona, California, Louisiana, New Mexico, and Texas
4. El Paso, Los Angeles, New Orleans, Tucson, and Yuma
5. Idaho, Minnesota,

Montana, North Dakota, Oregon, and Washington
6. Arizona, California, Colorado, Illinois, Kansas, Missouri, and New Mexico
7. Louisiana, Texas, and New Mexico

Page 186
1. soddy
2. corn dodgers
3. forty-niners
4. chips
5. emigrants
6. ague
7. rustlers
8. schooner

Page 187
1. a
2. c
3. d
4. b

Page 189
1. b   4. d
2. a   5. b
3. c   6. c

Page 191
1. d   4. c
2. b   5. a
3. c   6. d
7. Accept well-supported answers.

Page 192
1. It had unbelievable destructive power; it is awesome.
2. Secretary of War
3. He wanted to use the atomic bomb.
4. The Japanese ignored the warnings.
5. He believed it would save the lives of American soldiers.
6. Hiroshima and Nagasaki
7. Accept reasonable answers

Page 193
Accept reasonable answers.

Page 194
Fact 1: Colombia, rain
Fact 2: desert, driest, Andes Mountains, Chile
Fact 3: both, countries, continent, west coast, South America
Fact 4: dangerous, hurricanes, September

Page 195

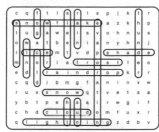

Page 197
1. d
2. b
3. a
4. c
5. d
6. a
7. Accept well-supported answers.

Page 199
1. a   4. b
2. c   5. b
3. d   6. d

Page 200
1. a
2. c
3. b
4. c

Page 201
1. blowing-bowing-owing, wing-win-in-I
2. torn, ad, do OR to, or, do
4. wind-wand-want-wart-warm (or any other acceptable solution)

Page 203
1. c
2. a
3. d
4. c
5. a
6. b

Answer Key (cont.)

7. Accept well-supported answers.

Page 204

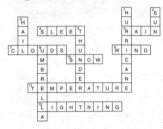

Page 205

1. mild
2. wind
3. hot
4. icy
5. season
6. sun
7. cold
8. heat
9. rain
10. thunder
11. cloud
12. tornado
13. clear
14. warm

Page 206

1. .6 or 60%
2. .5 or 50%
3. .6 or 60%
4. .9 or 90%
5. .67 or 67%
6. Example: 13 ÷ 22 = 59%

Page 207

Eureka 50%
Sacramento 59%
San Francisco 67%
Parkfield 90%
San Bernardino 60%
Los Angeles 60%

Page 208

Graphs may vary.
1. Parkfield, 90% probability
2. Eureka, 50% probability
3. California

Page 209

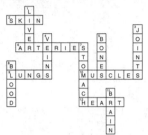

Page 211

1. a
2. a
3. b
4. c
5. c
6. c

Page 213

1. a
2. c
3. c
4. d
5. a
6. b
7. Accept well-supported answers.

Page 214

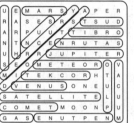

Page 215

2. urinary (H. kidneys)
3. nervous (F. spinal cord)
4. muscular (D. muscles)
5. endocrine (C. hormones
6. digestive (B. stomach)
7. circulatory (A. arteries
8. respiratory (G. lungs)

Page 216

1. touch
2. saliva
3. vegetable
4. blood
6. esophagus
7. exhale
8. digestive

Page 217

Green plants provide **food** for **plant**-eaters. Plant-**eaters** provide food for **meat**-eaters. Meat-eaters provide **waste** materials for the **decomposers**. Decomposers supply **chemicals** for **green** plants.

Page 219

1. b
2. c
3. b
4. d
5. c
6. a
7. Accept well-supported answers.

Page 220

Mercury, Venus, Earth, Mars, Jupiter, Saturn, Uranus, Neptune, Pluto
1. Mercury
2. Venus
3. Earth
4. Mars
5. Jupiter
6. Saturn
7. Uranus
8. Neptune
9. Pluto

Page 221

Page 222

A. 360
B. 321
C. 17
D. 39
E. 834
G. 338
H. 58
I. 3
L. 9
M. 121
N. 176
O. 18
P. 0
R. 22
S. 19
T. 13
U. 378
V. 300
1. star
2. orbit
3. comet
4. asteroids
5. satellites
6. revolution
7. meteoroid
8. eclipse

Page 223

1. satellites
2. Neptune
3. space
4. Milky Way
5. planets
6. meteorites
7. eclipse
8. Mercury
9. space station
10. Pluto
11. asteroids
12. moon
13. Venus
14. galaxy
15. earth
16. corona
17. shuttle
18. star
19. Apollo
20. Mir
21. astronauts

Page 225

1. c
2. a
3. b
4. c
5. a
6. d
7. Accept well-supported answers.

Page 227

1. d
2. c
3. b
4. a
5. b
6. c
7. Accept well-supported answers.

Page 229

1. c
2. b
3. a
4. d
5. c
6. b
7. Accept well-supported answers.

Page 230

1. b
2. c
3. a
4. c

Answer Key (cont.)

3. 5 17. 4
4. 5 18. 9
5. 4 19. 9
6. 12 20. 7
7. 6 21. 4
8. 3 22. 8
9. 12 23. 5
10. 7 24. 12
11. 10 25. 9
12. 6 26. 7
13. 9 27. 7
14. 7 28. 3

Page 94
1. 41 13. 79
2. 35 14. 49
3. 47 15. 59
4. 42 16. 108
5. 91 17. 49
6. 72 18. 157
7. 81 19. 69
8. 55 20. 99
9. 81 21. 63
10. 21 22. 49
11. 93 23. 97
12. 44 24. 65

Page 95
1. 206 R1 10. 228 R1
2. 49 R2 11. 268 R2
3. 43 R1 12. 91 R8
4. 119 R5 13. 162 R4
5. 165 R2 14. 79 R8
6. 73 R5 15. 132 R5
7. 25 R5 16. 475 R1
8. 52 R3 17. 102 R5
9. 19 R8 18. 90 R4

Page 96
1. 7 R20 9. 11 R13
2. 5 R24 10. 31 R11
3. 8 R14 11. 26 R5
4. 9 R21 12. 36 R23
5. 21 R2 13. 193 R4
6. 15 R9 14. 226 R15
7. 18 R9 15. 311 R13
8. 26 R19 16. 389 R4

Page 97
1. 161 12. 1,314
2. 443 13. 1,971
3. 484 14. 2,152
4. 600 15. 4,080
5. 4,442 16. 5
6. 5,318 17. 31
7. 17 18. 38
8. 112 19. 40
9. 193 20. 198

10. 200 21. 421
11. 425

Page 98
The optometrist fell into the lens grinder and made a spectacle of herself.

Page 99
1. (35 ÷ 5) x (27 ÷ 3) = 63
2. (32 ÷ 4) x (49 ÷ 7) = 56
3. (72 ÷ 9) x (24 ÷ 8) = 24
4. (56 ÷ 7) x (64 ÷ 8) = 64
5. (36 ÷ 6) x (35 ÷ 7) = 30

Page 100
1. 1/5 9. 3/10
2. 2/3 10. 5/7
3. 7/8 11. 1/8
4. 7/8 12. 4/5
5. 1/6 13. 5/12
6. 2/7 14. 2/9
7. 1/4 15. 8/11
8. 9/12 or 3/4

Page 101
1. 1/2 8. 1/3
2. 1/3 9. 1/4
3. 1/2 10. 1/9
4. 3/5 11. 1/4
5. 1/3 12. 2/9
6. 1/8 13. 1/2
7. 1/4 14. 1/6
   15. 1/8

Page 102
1. 3 1/2 6. 6 1/8
2. 8 1/3 7. 1 6/7
3. 5 2/3 8. 1 1/5
4. 3 1/3 9. 4 3/4
5. 5 8/9 10. 3 7/9

Page 103
1. < 7. >
2. < 8. >
3. > 9. <
4. < 10. <
5. < 11. >
6. < 12. >

Page 104
1. 2 1/6 16. 2 1/6

2. 1 1/3 17. 2 1/3
3. 1 ¾ 18. 1 4/5
4. 1 3/5 19. 1 ¼\
5. 2 2/9 20. 3/5
6. 8/9 21. 2 2/5
7. 1 7/11 22. 1/3
8. 1 23. 6
9. 11/12 24. 3/5
10. 1 7/11 25. 2 1/3
11. 2 26. 1 2/9
12. 1 7/8 27. 7/11
13. 4/7 28. 5/9
14. 5/6 29. 1 7/8
15. 1 11/12 30. 2 ¾

Page 105
1. .67 11. .11
2. .50 12. .17
3. .75 13. .83
4. .90 14. .30
5. .40 15. .20
6. .13 16. .50
7. .10 17. .43
8. .08 18. .25
9. .80 19. .60
10. .33 20. .55

Page 107
1. 0.345
2. 0.2111
3. 0.4563
4. 0.08
5. 0.6512
6. 0.098
7. 0.111
8. 0.7612
9. 0.005
10. 0.3018
11. 0.454
12. 0.2107
13. 17. 21.532
   3.9854
   1.6453
   0.6521
   0.0076
14. 54.942
   1.23
   0.96435
   0.02
   0.0023
15. 32.1
   4.8632
   4.86314
   0.7812
   0.77982
16. 0.0932
   0.02632

0.021001
0.013751
0.006321

Page 108
2. 1 ÷ 3 = .33; 33%
3. 2 ÷ 3 = 67; 67%
4. 1 ÷ 4 = .25; 25%
5. 3 ÷ 4 = .75; 75%
6. 1 ÷ 5 = .20; 20%
7. 2 ÷ 5 = .40; 40%
8. 3 ÷ 5 = .60; 60%
9. 4 ÷ 5 = .80; 80%
10. 1 ÷ 6 = .17; 17%
11. 5 ÷ 6 = .83; 83%
12. 1 ÷ 8 = .13; 13%
13. 5 ÷ 8 = .63; 63%
14. 7 ÷ 8 = .88; 88%
15. 1 ÷ 9 = .11; 11%

Page 109
1. 2
2. 8
3. 32
4. $.08,, $.09
5. $5.87
6. $225.88
7. $666.02
8. $9.32
9. $37.93
10. 4, 6
11. 2 1/2

Page 110
1. a. candy sale
   b. school store
   c. $400.00
   d. $250.00
   e. $50.00
2. $300.00, $90.00, $210.00
3. $26.45
4. 5 ½ miles
5. 80 miles

Page 111
1. 46/100; 0.46; 46%
2. 7/100; 0.07; 7%
3. 46/100; 0.46; 46%
4. 1/50; 0.02; 2%
5. 34/50; 0.68; 68%
6. 8/50; 0.16; 16%
7. carp
8. lin

Page 112
1. 1 quarter, 1 penny
2. 2 dimes, 2 pennies

Answer Key (cont.)

3. 1 quarter, 2 nickels
4. 3 dimes, 1 penny
5. 5 dimes, 1 penny
6. 3 quarters, 2 nickels
7. $1,356.00
8. $14.51
9. $31,978.00
10. $42.69
11. $6,803.00
12. $14,413.00
13. $85.45
14. $91.86
15. $9,099.00

Page 113
1. 4 dollars, 5 dimes, 10 nickels
2. 3 dollars, 2 quarters, 5 dimes
3. 9 dollars, 9 dimes, 10 pennies
4. 5 dollars, 1 quarter, 3 dimes, 6 nickels, 15 pennies
5. 3 dollars, 2 quarters, 4 dimes, 10 pennies
6. 14 dollars, 3 quarters, 2 dimes, 1 nickel
7. 20 dollars, 10 dimes
8. 12 dollars, 1 silver dollar
9. 14 dollars, 7 dimes, 5 nickels, 5 pennies
10. 4 dollars, 3 quarters, 25 pennies

Page 114
1. $3,076.15
2. $10.89
3. $2,265.34
4. $1,904.22
5. $1,107.44
6. $1,161.30
7. 13.69
8. 369

Page 115
9. $.01
10. $.02
11. $.05
12. $.04
13. $.04
14. $.02
15. $.03
16. $2.74

Page 116
1. $1,615.16 profit
2. She will save $.04.
3. Big Bill cheated him out of $10.00.
4. $14,000.00
5. $6,265.00
6. $6,275.60
7. 25% off $20 is $5. The drill costs $15. 30% off $22 is $6.60. The drill costs $15.40. Rick's offers the better savings.
8. $9,450

Page 117
1. a. 30% off
2. a. save $80.00
3. subtotal: $17.19; 15% top: $2.76

Page 118
1. $99.99
2. $2,237.75
3. $4.60
4. $30.12
5. $71.36
6. $17.37

Page 119
Answers will vary.

Page 120
1. $0.46
2. $5.20
3. $30
4. 14 super sundaes
5. $5.83
6. $29.80
7. 20 large sundaes
8. $4.87
9. $63
10. $0.90

Page 121
1. $4.24
2. $1.24
3. $8.51
4. $4.10
5. $7.23
6. $15.75
7. $67.50
8. $44.85
9. $4.94
10. $12.96

Page 122
1. $20.93
2. $16.01
3. $14.95
4. $29.25
5. $12.98
6. $4.10
7. $8.74
8. $6.01
9. $85.05
10. $17.95

Page 123
1. line
2. line segment
3. ray
4. line
5. perpendicular
6. intersecting
7. parallel
8. parallel

Page 124
1. right
2. acute
3. acute
4. acute
5. obtuse
6. acute
7. acute
8. straight
9. acute
10. right
11. obtuse
12. obtuse

Page 125
1. 90° right
2. 30° acute
3. 180° straight
4. 120° obtuse
5. 20° acute
6. 40° acute
7. 150° obtuse
8. 90° right
9. 170° obtuse
10. 60° acute
11. 35° acute
12. 180° straight

Page 126
1. equilateral
2. right
3. scalene/obtuse
4. isosceles/acute
5. right
6. equilateral
7. isosceles/obtuse
8. isosceles/obtuse
9. scalene/acute

Page 127
1. 30°
2. 70°
3. 60°
4. 50°
5. 50°
6. 60°
7. 30°
8. 90°
9. 60°
10. 10°
11. 20°
12. 20°

Page 128
1. square
2. hexagon
3. triangle
4. rhombus
5. rectangle
6. parallelogram
7. pentagon
8. trapezoid
9. octagon
10. parallelogram
11. isosceles triangle
12. trapezoid

Page 129
1. 32 ft.
2. 48 cm
3. 40 m
4. 28 in.
5. 48 ft.
6. 52 yd.
7. 44 cm
8. 84 mi.
9. 176 m
10. 308 mm
11. 564 ft.
12. 1,472 m

Page 130
1. 36 m
2. 42 ft.
3. 38 in.
4. 70 yd.
5. 56 ft.
6. 80 m
7. 70 cm
8. 256 mm
9. 234 ft.
10. 344 m.
11. 444 yd.
12. 408 in.

Page 131
1. 44 ft.
2. 51 m
3. 51 yd.
4. 58 cm
5. 28 cm
6. 230 m
7. 220 in.
8. 153 ft.

Page 132
1. Circle, 15.7
2. Parallelogram, 20
3. Rectangle, 20